THE MOST EXCELLENT BOOK OF COOKERY

The original title page of *The Most Excellent Book of Cookery* (Image courtesy of the Bibliothèque nationale de France).

THE MOST EXCELLENT BOOK OF COOKERY

Livre fort excellent de Cuysine
(1555)

edited and translated
by

TIMOTHY J. TOMASIK & KEN ALBALA

2014

First published in 2014 by Prospect Books,
Allaleigh House, Blackawton, Totnes, Devon TQ9 7DL.

The original French text was first published in Lyon in 1555.

© 2014, the translation and edition, Timothy J. Tomasik and Ken Albala.

The translators and editors assert their right to be identified as editors and translators of this work in accordance with the Copyright, Designs & Patents Act 1988.

No part of this publication may be reproduced, stored in a retrieval system, or transmitted in any form or by any means, electronic, mechanical, photocopying, recording or otherwise, without the prior permission of the copyright holders.

BRITISH LIBRARY CATALOGUING IN PUBLICATION DATA:
A catalogue entry of this book is available from the British Library.

Typeset by Tom Jaine.

ISBN 978-1-903018-96-5

Printed and bound by the Gutenberg Press, Malta.

TABLE OF CONTENTS

Introduction   7

How to use this book   19

Bibliography   29

The Most Excellent Book of Cookery   33
   Livre fort excellent de cuysine

French index   257

English index   271

INTRODUCTION

Renaissance French cuisine and cookbooks have gotten a bad rap. One explanation for the lack of attention to this cuisine is that it has been plagued by misconceptions, stereotypes and outright errors that have persisted with uncommon tenacity: spices were used to hide the taste of tainted meat; Catherine de' Medici single-handedly revolutionized French Renaissance cuisine by importing her Florentine cooks and introducing the fork; no new French cookbooks appeared during the Renaissance. Modern historians have gone to great lengths to dispel these and other myths; however their efforts have been impeded by the critical inertia of the culinary historiography of the nineteenth century.

One of the most pervasive and long-held myths about early modern cuisine is that all cookbooks printed in France in the sixteenth century were mere reprints of medieval texts or slavish continuations of medieval style and taste. This account finds its roots in Jérôme Pichon's introduction to his 1846 edition of the medieval household treatise and cookbook, the *Ménagier de Paris*. Pichon argues that the *Ménagier* borrows recipes from an earlier manuscript source that he found to be reprinted in the 1540s under the title *Le Grand Cuisinier de toute cuisine*, a later edition of the *Livre fort excellent de Cuysine*. Since this text is repeatedly reprinted under other titles throughout the sixteenth century, Pichon concludes that all sixteenth century cookbooks are reprints of medieval sources. Pichon's view is then ratified in Georges Vicaire's *Bibliographie gastronomique*

(1890). The latter's articles on the *Grand Cuisinier* suggest that this family of cookbooks is based entirely on medieval sources such as the *Ménagier*.[1]

The significance of this myth for culinary studies of sixteenth-century France can be glimpsed in an authoritative culinary dictionary, the 1938 *Larousse gastronomique*. After a preface by famed chef Auguste Escoffier, this culinary encyclopedia presents a bibliography of both ancient and modern culinary texts. The list begins with two medieval cookbooks, the *Viandier* and the *Ménagier de Paris*. The *Viandier* is dated 1370 with the *Ménagier* following in 1393. Astonishingly, the next item on the list is La Varenne's *Cuisinier francoys*, the first edition of which was published in 1651. The obvious implication here is that after the end of the fourteenth century, there is nothing new under the sun in French culinary matters for two and a half centuries.

From the late 1970s and early 1980s, scholarship begins to appear treating early modern French cuisine and culinary literature. Though the approaches in these works range from historical to sociological, two characteristics are shared by all. First, they forsake the anecdotal perspective inaugurated by early gastronomers of the nineteenth century such as Brillat-Savarin. In its place appears a rigorous attempt to study actual documents, whether in the form of cookbooks, dietetic texts, diaries and memoirs, or household accounting books. Second, their conclusions about early modern cuisine, particularly of the Renaissance, reiterate the claims made by Pichon and Vicaire more than a century earlier. For all of these scholars, the seventeenth century marks the beginning of truly French culinary literature and cuisine. Renaissance French cuisine is consistently represented as a static continuation of medieval conceptions of food and culinary practice.

1. See Jérôme Pichon's introduction to the *Ménagier de Paris* (1846), volume I, xxxiii–xxxv. In his commentary on editions of the *Livre fort excellent de Cuysine tresutille et proffitable*, Georges Vicaire indicates that this text 'date du XIVe siècle, M. Le B{on} Pichon l'a prouvé dans son introduction du *Ménagier de Paris* en constatant qu'un grand nombre de recettes du "Viandier" avaient été empruntées par l'auteur au *Livre fort excellent de Cuysine*. Or on sait que le *Ménagier* a été écrit entre 1392 et 1394' (1890, column 530).

Jean-François Revel's popular historical study *Festin en paroles* (1979, re-edited 1995) disputes a number of culinary clichés, particularly the overstated role of Catherine de' Medici in French culinary history. He disproves the Medici myth by claiming that French cuisine does not begin to evolve until the middle of the seventeenth century. Echoing the *Larousse gastronomique*, he asserts rather forcefully that between the fourteenth-century *Viandier* and the seventeenth-century *Cuisinier francois*, there appears in France '*aucun livre de cuisine qui soit à proprement parler un livre de cuisine*' [*no cookbook that is strictly speaking a cookbook*] (p. 146, emphasis in original). Revel's argument, though laudable for taking on the myth of the Medicis, does not exorcise the spirit of Pichon and Vicaire. Paradoxically, Revel affirms that the sign of gastronomic revolution is generally a proliferation of cookbooks. Because he attributes medieval origins to all Renaissance cookbooks, no 'new' cookbooks exist in this period and, by extension, no culinary innovation takes place. The heritage of Pichon and Vicaire thus masks the possibility of culinary evolution taking place in sixteenth-century France.

This mask remains to be doffed in one of the first modern inventories of sixteenth-century cookbooks. In 1979, the same year as Revel's study, a colloquium on Renaissance food was held at the Centre d'études supérieures de la Renaissance in Tours. The results of the colloquium were published in 1982 as *Pratiques et discours alimentaires à la Renaissance* under the direction of Jean-Claude Margolin and Robert Sauzet. The main themes of discussion involve medicine and dietetics, the sociology of table manners, and food symbolism. Seemingly out of place among these headings, Alain Girard's article ('Du manuscrit à l'imprimé: le livre de cuisine en Europe aux 15e et 16e siècles') nevertheless provides a welcome assessment of European cookbooks from the period. For France, the appendix to his article lists five different cookbooks. One is the printed edition of the medieval *Viandier* and the other four are various editions of the *Grand cuisinier* family of cookbooks, from which our edition springs. In spite of this textual proliferation, Girard maintains the conservative conclusions of Pichon and Vicaire. Regarding the proliferation of the *Grand cuisinier*

family of texts, Girard concludes with no discussion that they are 'plus neufs de titre que de contenu' [newer in title than in content] (p. 111). Girard thus acknowledges a proliferation of cookbooks in sixteenth-century France, but they are still seen as mere reprints of medieval sources.

The static nature of sixteenth-century cuisine continues to be promulgated in English-language studies from the early 1980s. Stephen Mennell's *All Manners of Food* (1985) presents a sociological approach to food studies inspired in large part by Norbert Elias's *Civilizing Process* (1939, English translation 1978). The limits to his approach are apparent in his assessment of the sources examined in order to make manifest these processes of change. Writing about sixteenth-century France, Mennell cites the conclusions of both Revel and Girard. Like them, he downplays the role of Italy in the evolution of Renaissance French cuisine. Echoing them as well as Pichon and Vicaire, Mennell writes: 'French cookery books of the sixteenth century…continued to be versions of medieval texts like Taillevent [the *Viandier*] and the *Grand cuisinier de toute cuisine*.' Moreover, he specifies that, 'Indisputable literary evidence of the emergence of a distinctively French style of cooking is not found until the publication in 1651 of La Varenne's *Le Cuisinier François*' (p. 71). Mennell's study thus continues to propagate myths about the conservative nature of sixteenth-century cookbooks and cuisine.

This trend in early modern French historiography carries on in one of the best-known studies of the period. Barbara Ketcham Wheaton's authoritative history of the French table, *Savoring the Past* (1983), appears two years before Mennell's, but in many ways typifies the trends sketched thus far. Indeed, Wheaton's work has become one of the standard references for French culinary history before the Revolution. In the closing paragraph to her chapter on the Middle Ages, Wheaton expresses a 'modern,' post-seventeenth century perspective on early modern cuisine. She writes:

> There is little that would be recognized as specifically French in this style of cooking, save some of the ingredients. The combinations were

> different, and most of the dishes familiar today were absent. The great array of stocks, other basic mixtures, and sauces that underlie modern French cuisine did not appear until much later. Most important, the organization of kitchen and staff that produced them had not yet developed. The slow growth of rational working methods began in the seventeenth century; the sixteenth century was, in most respects, a continuation of the medieval style of cooking. (p. 26)

Wheaton reads medieval and sixteenth-century cuisine through the filter of 'modern' cuisine. What we have come to expect in 'French cuisine' is thus seen as conspicuously absent in early modern cuisine. Moreover, her opening sentence presumes that something 'specifically French' could not have existed before the advent of what she considers 'modern' cuisine. Finally, if we accept her judgment that 'rational' cooking methods only begin to develop in the seventeenth century, we are forced to conclude that earlier cooking methods are somehow irrational. Like her immediate predecessors, Wheaton maintains that French cooking in the Renaissance was strictly conservative, staunchly clinging to medieval culinary practices. She concludes that the Renaissance is a 'stagnant, or at least a very static, period in the history of French cooking' (p. 30).

Beginning in the 1980s, and particularly in the early 1990s, historians begin to question the heritage of Pichon and Vicaire regarding the conservatism of early modern French cookery. Jean-Louis Flandrin and Philip and Mary Hyman are among the first historians to challenge the concept of sixteenth-century cuisine as a rehashing of medieval culinary norms. This new direction is initiated in the 1980s with the work of Flandrin, who began his study of food in conjunction with the *Annales* school of history.

Flandrin's approach differs somewhat from the empirical, nutrition-based study of the *Annales*. He makes a distinction between the physiological necessity of food (represented by the amount of food produced and sold) and the cultural aspect of food preparation (represented by culinary practices described in cookbooks). Culinary history thus moves from grain prices and account books to menus and

cookbooks. More importantly, in Flandrin's work sixteenth-century cookbooks are no longer considered a conservative rehash of medieval culinary literature.

In a pioneering article on the history of fats (1983), Flandrin argues that changes in cuisine and culinary literature cannot be fully explained by statistical studies of food consumption. Rather, these changes are equally subject to a history of taste. Though Flandrin remains committed to the kinds of statistical analyses employed by the *Annales* school, he trains his sights on cookbooks. His initial results demonstrate clearly that sixteenth-century cookbooks are far from stagnant. By means of statistical analysis, Flandrin traces a dramatic increase in references to butter in sixteenth-century cookbooks. His further work in the 1990s records a dramatic rise in sugar and green vegetables in these same sources. While sugar drops out of favour in the seventeenth century, green vegetables become even more popular. Such statistics suggest that significant transformation in culinary literature, and consequently of tastes, is beginning to manifest itself well before the 'revolutionary' shift in taste touted for the seventeenth century.

Taking a different tack to Flandrin's, and grounded in the history of the book and print culture, Philip and Mary Hyman corroborate his general assessment of sixteenth-century culinary innovation. In a series of groundbreaking articles in *Du manuscrit à la table* (1992), *L'Histoire de l'alimentation* (1996) and *Livres en bouche* (2001), the Hymans demonstrate that Renaissance French cookbooks manifest clear evidence of a developing culinary style. By comparing recipes in medieval and sixteenth-century cookbooks, they show that the latter contain primarily contemporary recipes and very few reprints of earlier ones. The Hymans offer a welcome challenge to the supposed conservatism of the *Livre fort excellent de Cuysine*, which serves as the basis for Pichon's conclusions about sixteenth-century cuisine. They indicate that this text is in fact the culmination of a long process of recycling and re-editing of recipes, which begins in the 1530s with the publication of a largely unknown cookbook published by Pierre Sergent. In fact, the Hymans are the only scholars to have analysed

INTRODUCTION

Pierre Sergent's rare *Petit traicté auquel verrez la maniere de faire cuisine et comment on doubt abiller toutes sortes de viandes*, which inaugurates a new generation of Renaissance cookbooks, among them the *Livre fort excellent de Cuysine*. Following this publication come a spate of new titles in the 1540s and beyond which recycle recipes from the *Petit traicté* all the while adding scores of new ones. The newly added recipes are shown to have no ties to medieval culinary collections. The Hymans' study of the Sergent cookbook family thus documents a profound divorce from medieval culinary practices and tastes in the cookbooks of Renaissance France.

The Hymans' work has cleared the path towards a larger reconsideration of sixteenth-century French cuisine based on the practical texts that describe it. Since their work has circulated primarily in French, the discoveries about Renaissance French cookbooks have not been fully assimilated by modern criticism and historiography. The myths established more than a century ago by Pichon and Vicaire continue to inform modern conceptions of sixteenth-century French cuisine and in fact continue to be published in historical accounts in both English and French. It is our hope that this modern edition and translation into English of the *Livre fort excellent de Cuysine* will open up this text to a wider audience, thereby making possible a more concerted effort to reconsider the cuisine of Renaissance France.

Textual History

We have chosen the *Livre fort excellent* as representative of the body of cookbooks published by Pierre Sergent from the 1540s onward primarily because it contains the greatest number of recipes, the fewest borrowed from earlier medieval cookbooks and because it became the basis for many successive editions, often under different titles. As a cookbook it also reflects the period of greatest mutual exchange between English, French and Italian cookbooks. We hope this translation will permanently lay to rest the persistent myth of Catherine de' Medici's formative influence on French cooking in this period, and will rather show a multi-directional borrowing of techniques, ingredients, and styles of service among cookbooks of the

mid-sixteenth century. The *Livre fort excellent de Cuysine* is indeed one edition of a large, interrelated group of cookbooks published by Pierre Sergent and his family. In order to justify our choice of this text, it is important to understand its status among the other editions.

Between 1536 and 1538, the Parisian printer Pierre Sergent published a *Petit traicté auquel verrez la maniere de faire cuisine*, the first sixteenth-century French cookbook entirely divorced from medieval culinary texts. Around 1539, following the success of this book, Sergent printed a new edition, expanded by two hundred recipes, the *Livre de cuisine tresutile & prouffitable*. This text is then reprinted in Lyon under the title *Le livre fort excellent de Cuysine* in 1542 and 1555. Between 1543 and 1547, Sergent issues yet a third member of the family, *La Fleur de toute cuysine*, combining recipes from his earlier editions with scores of new ones for an unprecedented grand total of 478 recipes. After Sergent's death in 1547, his son-in-law Jean Bonfons brings out yet another edition of *La Fleur de toute cuysine* under the title *Le Grand cuisinier de toute cuisine*, a title that became standard in numerous subsequent editions.[2] In total, twenty-seven editions of the Sergent family of cookbooks, from the *Petit traicté* to the *Grand cuisinier*, appeared between 1536 and 1620 (Hyman and Hyman 1992: pp. 66–68). The large number of editions, coupled with the remarkable recycling of recipes among them, bear witness to the literate public's appetite for cookery books around mid-century and beyond.

The first stage in the evolution of the Sergent family of cookbooks represents the passage from the first edition, the *Petit traicté*, to the second, the *Livre de cuisine*. The recipes confirm the affiliation of the two texts since the *Livre de cuisine* reproduces all but one of the recipes from the *Petit traicté* (Hyman and Hyman 2001: p. 57). However, the *Livre de cuisine* does offer two significant revisions. First, it adds 217

2. For the great majority of editions in this family of cookbooks, the dating is problematic because the title pages of the first editions do not provide clear dates. Philip and Mary Hyman, in conjunction with a number of curators from the Bibliothèque nationale de France, have tentatively offered the above dating in several of their studies of Renaissance cookbooks (1992, 1996, 2001).

new recipes to the collection. Second, it facilitates the reading of the cookbook by adding a table of contents that organizes all the recipes alphabetically and provides folio numbers where they appear. In all other respects, the *Livre de cuisine* shares format characteristics with the *Petit traicté*. The exact same text is then reprinted in Lyon under the title *Le livre fort excellent de Cuysine* in 1542 and 1555. The 1555 edition serves as the base text for our edition and translation.

The second stage in the evolution of this cookbook family is from the *Livre de cuisine / Livre fort excellent* to the *Fleur de toute cuysine / Grand Cuisinier*. The base text of the *Fleur*, and thus all later editions of the *Grand cuisinier de toute cuisine*, is 302 recipes taken from the 305 recipes of the *Livre de cuisine / Livre fort excellent*. To this are added 109 recipes taken from the medieval *Ménagier de Paris*, sixteen recipes from the French translation of a dietetic treatise by the Italian humanist Platina, and fifty-one recipes from an unidentified, presumably medieval source. Given the clear affiliation among members of the Sergent family of cookbooks, the recipes taken from the medieval *Ménagier* led Pichon and Vicaire to assume that sixteenth-century cookbooks were mere reprints of medieval sources. Unfortunately, they did not take into account the bulk of the other recipes that have in fact no medieval antecedents. The present edition offers a cookbook that signals the status of French cuisine around the mid-sixteenth century.

Transcription and Translation

Our primary objective in transcribing and translating the present text is to accurately represent and render the original text so that the recipes could be used to actually reproduce dishes and meals from this period. To that end, we have also included a supplementary text on how to use this cookbook. In terms of translation, this text presents a number of challenges, but we tried to limit our interventions and changes to the text except where the original truly inhibits readability. For example, whereas the recipes are often a long string of what we would consider run-on sentences, we have chosen in many places to impose full stops to clarify the different steps in a recipe's preparation.

Our choice of words in the translation has been guided by our wish to be comprehensible to the modern reader. We have tried to avoid archaic and obsolete English vocabulary, choosing what we think are modern yet equivalent terms.

Among the many challenges to transcribing and translating this text, the most daunting stems from the numerous printer's mistakes. Throughout the text can be found missing words or parts of recipes, transposed letters or phrases, and mismatched titles and recipe texts. Some of these difficulties have been mitigated by consulting the most immediate predecessor – the *Livre de cuisine* – or by looking at later editions, such as the *Grand cuisinier de toute cuisine*. Sometimes these offer a slightly different spelling that would elucidate a given word in our source text. Just as often, the same difficulty would be present in all three sources, necessitating additional reflection and the creation of an explanatory note. Generally, in undertaking the transcription of the French, the original spelling has been retained with occasional corrections inserted in square brackets. However, all abbreviations have been expanded and absent apostrophes have been inserted. The letter 'u' used as a 'v' has been replaced with 'v' throughout; likewise for instances of 'i' and 'j'.

Another challenge for translation is the varying style of the work. Clearly, this text is a compilation from different sources and so in some recipes the language is particularly sparse and laconic, while in others instructions are spelled out in careful detail. Translation tends to flatten out some of these stylistic differences, but clearly this cookbook is rendered from multiple sources and multiple voices.

In terms of culinary vocabulary, Cotgrave's 1611 *Dictionarie of the French and English Tongues* was a precious resource that helped us elucidate a number of perplexing words or phrases. In the course of our work of translation, we discovered that Cotgrave had consulted one or more editions of this cookbook family. In fact, in the translation of certain terms, he clearly transcribed a translated version of a recipe word for word from the *Livre fort excellent de Cuysine* or one of the other editions of this cookbook family. Even with the help of Cotgrave's familiarity with this text and its language, some terms

and foodstuffs simply no longer exist in any recognizable currency in modern English vocabulary. As with other problematic points in the text, we have endeavoured to explain these terms in context by way of explanatory footnotes.

In closing, we would like to thank Philip and Mary Hyman for their assistance in deciphering some of the more perplexing passages and phrases in this rich culinary text. Tom Jaine's detailed editorial queries and steadfast patience allowed us to further elucidate problematic translations and negotiate occasional divergences between American and English vocabulary. Any errors or infelicities that remain are strictly our own.

Cuysine.　　　　Fueillet.vj.

¶ Perdrix aulx choulx.

¶ Jté pour faire pdrix aulx choulx/venes choulx & les faictes fort pbouillir puis les haches menu puis les mettes en bō bouillon de beuf auec de bō lart pour donner goust/puis ayes du popure et en bouteras en lesdictz choulx/mais garde quilz ne soyent trop espices/ce faict ayes tes pdrix ou bi, et en lieu de perdrix & les feras rostir et larderas de cloud de giroffle/puis quāt feront quasi cuyctes les bouteras en tes choulx & quilz soyent de bon sel.

¶ Perdrix a la tonollette.
¶ Pour faire perdrix a la tōnollete/prenes perdrix et les faictes rostir puis les tires et les boutes en ung pot/ce faict pnes du pain blāc hasle bi? roup sās bru̅sler et se mettes trēper en bō vin vermeil/puis quant sera trempe le passeras par lestamine auec ung bouillon de beuf ung petit de vinaigre et bouteras tout en ung pot auec les perdrix ung petit doignon souffrit en sain de lart pour espices canelle cloud muguette, & menues espices ung petit de sucre/et gouttes de sel & nouslyes a y bouter vne poignee de Raisins de Karesme.

¶ Capilotaste.

c iij

HOW TO USE THIS BOOK
RENAISSANCE COOKING TECHNIQUES

As a cookbook, this work was not meant to sit on a bookshelf to be admired. It appeared in an era when relatively cheap, rather poorly produced books, designed to be used much like 'how to' books today, began to issue from presses across Europe. It was marketed to a literate audience obviously, but without the elegance or flourishes of language so typical of this period. Rather it was written in a homespun vernacular, intended for those who wished to impress dinner guests, decidedly intended for the cook or perhaps banquet manager, an official in a wealthy household, though not necessarily noble. Perhaps the target was a well-to-do middle-class family whose station in life demanded that they entertain guests with some panache, both to show off their wealth and the skills of a professional chef whose services they could retain. The sometimes brusque shorthand prose assumes some familiarity with the kitchen and this was certainly not intended for beginners, but also not for seasoned chefs who already knew all the tricks of the trade. The title page claims that the work has been corrected and augmented by the 'grant Escuyer de Cuysine du Roy', or King's Head Chef, suggesting that, at least in the publisher's mind, this might satisfy the socially conscious aspirations of rising householders. We have no idea whether this is true, although the different usage of terminology may suggest that there were two hands at work on this manuscript. Whoever wrote it, and whatever may have been borrowed from other sources, this is emphatically a book to be used in the kitchen.

The book remains eminently practical today and this edition is intended to make these bygone recipes accessible to modern cooks. There are few ingredients – either prohibitively expensive, rare or disgusting – that might dissuade readers from trying to cook these recipes. Yet before embarking on such a venture it is crucial to consider exactly why one might want to cook them. There are two fundamental approaches to historic cookery. One, which arguably has its merits, is to borrow recipes, techniques and flavour combinations for use in modern cookery. In some respects, this cookbook can be used much as cooks use any cookbook or food magazine, gleaning from it new ideas. Often the cuisine described in this book sounds as if it comes from some far-off exotic place, and indeed it does. There is not much that will be familiar here, and if someone wants to try a Renaissance spice combination, or perhaps use breadcrumbs as a thickener, verjuice to add a little piquancy, or test one of the really unusual cooking techniques, why not? Sugar was used in profusion in many savoury dishes, in ways that have disappeared entirely from our modern repertoire and this certainly has the power to amuse and titillate modern palates. It is something like a modern painter referencing a historic motif or adopting an old technique. Borrowing is perfectly fine, just don't claim that you are serving something from the Renaissance.

The other approach is far more valuable. Stick to the recipe as closely as possible. Substitute no ingredients. Take no short cuts. Do your best to use heat sources and equipment that were used in the past. Understandably this is not always possible, but the closer you can follow the author's directions, the more you will learn about the past – and that is the ultimate goal of reading and using old cookbooks. If ingredients are beyond your means or too difficult to find, there are plenty here that use inexpensive cuts and, thankfully, the spices called for throughout this book are pretty affordable today.

What follows here are practical directions for cooking with this book. That is not to say that it can't be read for purely academic or linguistic purposes, or merely for personal entertainment, but so much more is to be gained by cooking these recipes well and sharing

them with others, that we implore you to give it a shot. We also guarantee that the flavour combinations you encounter here will surprise and delight you, as you may find when trying a foreign cuisine or some fantastic modernist concoction. Directly tasting food from the past is no different from appreciating a 500-year-old building or listening to classical music on period instruments. Of course our aesthetic appreciation is tempered by our modern palates. We have no concrete idea what this food actually tasted like in the past. In some cases the species used in cooking have changed dramatically. Our pigs are leaner, our vegetables have been hybridized and selected for size, and countless details of our kitchens are so completely different that anything approaching authenticity might seem impossible. None of these are insurmountable problems and the majority of these recipes are so simple and forthright that doing it correctly is eminently feasible.

Fire

The largest hurdle you will encounter is the source of heat which, until a few centuries ago, was exclusively burning wood and hot coals drawn from the hearth. Although it takes a little practice, learning to manage fire is not very difficult and in some respects offers infinitely greater variation in temperature than modern appliances. The author here roasts food beside a fire, places pots or even a ceramic dish directly on hot coals, or puts a vessel near the fire to keep warm. That is to say, a roaring fire, apart from being a waste of fuel, is not the only way to cook. Perhaps the technique that has changed the least is grilling, though again this would have been over wooden coals rather than briquettes and, of course, not gas.

A regular fireplace is thus the most appropriate place to set up your Renaissance kitchen, though admittedly they are almost always in the living room nowadays, far from the cutting boards. Cooking on the floor of the hearth, as one often sees in historic houses in the United States and elsewhere, is one possibility. But professional kitchens in the past usually had a raised stone or brick platform at waist height with a hood above to draw the smoke upward. One would simply remove hot coals from the hearth or even make a small fire directly

on the top of the platform and then arrange pots on top of the coals. In many ways it makes much more sense than a stovetop which you can only face from one direction. The Renaissance platform was often free-standing so you could approach it from many sides, or at least three if it abutted the wall. Happily this platform has no effect on the taste of the food; it just keeps you from bending down or kneeling while cooking. It also keeps the hem of your clothes out of the fire.

Another viable option for those without a hearth is to cook outdoors. Many cookbooks illustrated outdoor cooking, and for households that travelled this was sometimes a practical necessity. It also seems to have been a conscious choice, for example, when roasting a large animal or when a lot of smoke might fill the kitchen. Sometimes Renaissance kitchens would have open courtyards as well, partly for dirty jobs and washing dishes, but also sometimes for cooking. All you really need is a small pit, or a flat surface encircled with bricks or rocks. Anyone who has done campfire cooking is already familiar with the basic techniques.

Whether in a hearth or fire-pit, start by making a fire with hardwood logs. You will rarely cook directly above a roaring fire, which would burn most foods. The exception is a boiling pot of water. It seems our author intends the cook to always have a pot of stock or bouillon simmering away since it is used in many recipes. A cauldron of water would also be necessary for blanching. Otherwise, most cooking is done on a spit beside the fire or in a pot set on hot coals drawn from the fire after the flame has subsided.

Equipment

It is advisable to keep a separate set of pots and pans for cooking with fire. Not that your expensive stainless steel set won't work in this context, but they will get sooty. Cast-iron is the material of choice for modern campfire cooking, and the techniques for making it actually date from the fifteenth and sixteenth centuries, but it was mostly used for artillery rather than cookware. Not until the eighteenth century did cast-iron pots become a common household commodity. Moreover, the acidic ingredients that go into so much

Renaissance cooking will give food an off colour and make it taste metallic if prepared in cast-iron. Wealthy kitchens would have used tin-lined copper. This is not only very expensive and difficult to clean, but the tin wears off and needs to be replaced with a lot of use. For more humble households, pottery was the way to go and remains the material of choice for this period. It would have been earthenware and the author often specifies to use an earthenware pot in these recipes. The reason is that the material stays warm but does not conduct heat with intense hotspots in the way a steel pan does on a gas flame. Quick searing in a pan or sautéeing is really a modern technique. Here the clay casserole or round bottomed pot, often with legs, what in English was called a pipkin, is ideal. These are set on top of a bed of hot coals and the heat gently circulates within the vessel. Many of these recipes simply will not work well without clay pots. Keep in mind you cannot use stoneware or porcelain on an open flame; it will crack. However, you can bake in them.

An iron pan is still useful for frying, as is a large metal pot for boiling. In the past such cauldrons would have been made of hammered sections of copper or other material riveted together. Today any big old pot you don't mind getting covered in soot will work fine. Although you can balance a big pot over three bricks or set it on a large tripod with flame beneath, most 'spiders' and trivets were made for small pots. Large pots are better suspended from chains supported by either a trammel – a kind of swinging arm attached to the inside wall of the fireplace or by another chain mechanism from above. Sometimes a simple iron bar hung with ratchets for raising or lowering the pots sufficed. Modern fireplaces are usually too small for the latter to work effectively. Remember the standard Renaissance hearth was about shoulder height and sometimes six or eight feet long. Outdoors, boiling a large pot of water is a little easier. Three sturdy metal poles set up like a teepee over the fire with the pot suspended from them will work well. Otherwise the three-brick method will do. For food that is stewed for hours you can also dig a pit, make a fire in it and when it burns down to coals, place the pot directly inside. It is just more difficult to adjust for temperature this way.

Roaring fires are meant almost exclusively for roasting food, which is never situated above the fire, but always next to it. For this you need a proper turnspit. There were mechanical versions in the past that could be driven by a clock mechanism or a spit jack powered by the rising hot air in the chimney, which turned a kind of fan, which then turned the spit. A hand-cranked wrought iron spit was most typical, but obviously demands a great deal of time and patience. The spit itself should be slightly flat to prevent the food from loosening and turning, or have tines that keep the meat in place. There are also mechanisms that skewer and affix the food in place. Our author also makes a number of what we would call kebabs, small pieces of meat threaded on a skewer, which were also cooked beside the fire rather than on a grill.

Typically to hold the spits and skewers there would be a set of andirons on either side of the fire. These are not meant to hold logs – the fire is made on the floor of the hearth. Rather they include upright bars like an A-Frame that would have a number of notched grooves so you could set several spits or skewers before the fire. The logic of the inward angle of the bars is so that each skewer is proximate to the flame, which wouldn't happen if it were vertical. Outside, a spit could be mounted either above hot coals or on supports set beside a fire.

Beneath the spit you should also set a roasting pan, usually rectangular in shape rather than round. This is not only to collect drippings, but often food will be cooked directly in the pan with the hot fat.

Wrought iron grills were simply a set of bars in a frame with a handle. You simply shovelled out some hot coals into a bed and placed the grill on top. These devices could be very large, as well as small hand-held versions for quickly grilling small pieces of meat.

The hearth might also contain an oven set into one of the walls. A fire would be made directly inside and then, after it was very hot, the coals would be raked out. Our author does cook a number of dishes in an oven, but by this time professional bakers made bread for most families, although in a small village there might be a communal oven in which individuals baked once a week or so. If you have a wood-fired oven of course feel free to use it when called for here, but

HOW TO USE THIS BOOK

a modern oven will be an adequate substitute for the kind of recipes included in this book – pies especially.

The author also sometimes calls for sausages to be hung in the chimney, far from the fire. This is exactly what it sounds like, a way to slowly smoke food for preservation and flavour. It means going on the roof and hanging the food down the flue. A modern smoker is perhaps a little less adventurous but should not lead to a serious sacrifice of flavour.

Apart from a retinue of sturdy kitchen knives, wooden spoons and serving vessels, not much else is necessary in terms of equipment. All of these are relatively unchanged and modern versions are sufficient. But there are two items without which no sixteenth-century kitchen could function: the mortar and the sieve. Mortars were not the dainty little ceramic or wooden versions one sees today for crushing spices or making pesto. They were huge, usually thick bronze vessels intended to hold a large quantity of ingredients. The pestle was often the size of a baseball bat, though also bronze. Pounding spices, almonds, or even vegetables or meat, is an essential part of this cuisine, and a smooth texture is a goal in a large proportion of the recipes here. Asian grocery stores are the best place to find large mortars today and they are not invariably expensive. Be sure to choose one with a smooth interior designed for pounding, rather than a coarse or ridged surface, which is more for grinding ingredients into a coarse paste. A food processor will not yield the texture achieved by pounding.

The sieve is probably the most difficult tool to replicate in the modern kitchen. They were usually a wooden hoop strung tightly with horsehair through which liquids could be strained out of solids or, more typically, a cooked food would be 'passed' through by means of a wooden spoon or small wooden wedge rubbed over the interior surface to force the food through the hairs. Sieves of this nature can still be found and in French are called a *tamis*. Nowadays, they are almost always strung with metal mesh and there are also inexpensive plastic versions. A very fine-meshed bowl-shaped strainer makes an adequate substitute, as does a cone shaped 'China hat' sieve, although it takes considerably more effort to pass food through these. We have

found the food mill (the *moulin-légumes*) to be the best substitute as it does purée food well. This has a perforated disk at the bottom of the bowl and a crank that forces a wedge in a circular motion to press the food through. For all practical purposes it achieves the same effect as an early-modern sieve, leaving seeds or larger bits of food behind. Again a food processor will not work if the intention is to separate out part of the ingredients to form a purée. Our author usually takes a cooked food and adds a liquid to facilitate the sieving process.

Ingredients

Few ingredients in this cookbook will be impossible to find. A number will have to be hunted and, at least in the US, are illegal to sell. There, game birds especially, and venison, you will need to shoot yourself or receive from a friend who hunts, although there are some farms that raise domestic deer, and wild or feral boar is beginning to come on the market in the US in places which are plagued by too great a feral population. In Britain and Europe you can find game in good butchers, although larks and smaller birds will be either very difficult or illegal to obtain. Renaissance cooks were clearly much interested in game, for which both cooking methods and flavourings are quite different from those used with domestic species. Happily, there are many recipes for domesticated animals as well. The capon, a castrated rooster, is probably the most called-for fowl and they can be specially ordered from a good butcher (although the caponization may nowadays be chemical, not surgical, if indeed they are caponized at all, rather than a large, quick-growing hybrid). But there are also recipes for chicken and pullets – young chickens or poussins, which is what you will find in markets today. When hen is called for, a boiling fowl or mature roaster is preferred. Beef, pork and lamb should present no problem; kid is a little harder to find. Some species of fish can only be found in European waters though any species recognizable to an American by name should work fine in these recipes. Porpoise is not something we can try nowadays.

As for vegetables, New World species appear nowhere here. Tomatoes, peppers and squash were just beginning to appear in

Europe – and some were adopted quite quickly – as were beans in the Phaseolus genus and even turkeys. But there is no evidence of any being used in this cookbook. One generation later, that would change, although some ingredients, like tomatoes, don't appear in a cookbook for another century and a half. In a few cases, a New World species simply adopted the name of an old world vegetable, as seems to be the case with *courge*, which is a gourd here rather than squash or pumpkin. Some newly fashionable vegetables – artichokes in particular – appear in the menus but not in the recipes. Otherwise the varieties called for will be very familiar: onions, cabbage, turnips, parsnips. Herbs make their way into most of the recipes. Fresh herbs are recommended here, especially since the author sometimes changes a recipe for the winter when fresh herbs are not available. Some, however, are fine to use dried. A few, like hyssop, are a little rare – certainly for a casual shopper, although they are easily grown for yourself. Some of these less common herbs may also taste both strong and unfamiliar. Hop shoots will be hard to find, as will samphire in the US. Among the fruits, medlars will be impossible to find unless you have your own tree. They must ripen to the point of being rotten, a process called bletting, and thus are practically never for sale commercially.

Verjuice is required in a large proportion of the recipes, seemingly regardless of season. This is the juice of unripe grapes which, if freshly squeezed, leaves a window of about a month in which they will yield juice but are not yet ripe. We think the must (crushed whole grapes) was actually fermented and then strained, which acted as a preservative and thus could be used year round. Verjuice is now available commercially. Some contemporary recipes exist that put salt in the verjuice to better preserve it; others cook it down to a syrup with the consistency of honey. Our author doesn't distinguish between these, so it is probably safe to assume he means liquid verjuice. Other grape products include vinegar, used throughout the book, and several forms of wine: *vin vermeil* which is red, young and tart, but also imported sweet wines like malvasia and spiced wine like hippocras. Sourness is a nearly universal flavour that will be surprising here, especially when whole fruits are used such as gooseberries or unripe grapes.

Spices are the other essential ingredient in the Renaissance kitchen and they too are almost universal. Our author kept on hand a series of spice mixes or powders, which would keep for several weeks, but also used individual spices whole and ground. He offers recipes for the mixtures, and only a few ingredients will be difficult to find: grains of paradise (*Aframomum melegueta*) and long pepper, though through the Internet you can find nearly anything nowadays. Ginger is easy to find, as is galangal, in Asian groceries, though in the past they would have been used in dried form.

Our author also loves pies and they come in several different forms. Sometimes the crusts were meant to be eaten, especially in tarts, but pastry could also serve as a kind of coffer into which whole cooked food was place and kept for several days. These are made of a thick pastry of rye, and often a gravy or vinegar is poured into a hole in the top to prevent spoilage.

Techniques and Measurements

Some of the techniques used here will seem perplexing, especially twice-cooking. That is, a food is first blanched and then roasted, or something is first poached and then pounded, sieved and cooked again with spices. The rule is to always follow the author's directions. Although sometimes we can fault the typesetter for a missing line, or a garbled word here or there , or an occasional absolutely baffling passage, when the directions can be understood, the recipes really do work. Please do not be tempted to skip steps or follow a similar modern method, which defeats the whole point of learning about the past.

Lastly, our author is very unusual about offering measurements and they are often in ounces and pounds. We will not even try to sort out whether the Troy pound was exactly the same then or how much a cup or spoon might have been. There are no measurements so exact here that they will make or break a recipe and actually the ones we might expect to be precise (as for baked goods) are not at all. Following as closely as you can will yield excellent results and for more difficult techniques, the footnotes will offer an explanation.

BIBLIOGRAPHY

Adamson, Melitta Weiss, *Regional Cuisines of Medieval Europe.* New York: Routledge, 2002.

Albala, Ken, *The Banquet: Dining in the Great Courts of Late Renaissance Europe.* Urbana: University of Illinois Press, 2007.

Albala, Ken, ed., *A Cultural History of Food in the Renaissance.* London: Berg, 2012.

A Proper Newe Book of Cookery. London: John Kynge, 1555.

Austin, Thomas, ed., *Two Fifteenth Century Cookery-Books.* London: Oxford University Press for the Early English Text Society, 2000.

Belon, Pierre, *L'Histoire de la nature des oyseaux: avec leurs descriptions, & naïfs portraicts retirez du naturel.* Paris, 1555.

——, *La Nature et diversité des poissons.* Paris, 1555.

——, *L'Histoire de la nature des oyseaux.* Ed. Philippe Glardon. Genève, 1997.

Bitting, Katherine Golden, *Gastronomic Bibliography.* Mansfield Centre, CT: Martino Publishing, 2004 (1st edition, 1939).

Brears, Peter, *Cooking and Dining in Medieval England.* Totnes: Prospect, 2008.

Bruyérin-Champier, Jean, *De re cibaria.* Lyon, 1560.

——, *L'Alimentation de tous les peuples et de tous les temps jusqu'au XVIe siècle,* Sigurd Amundsen, trans. Paris, 1998.

Cotgrave, Randle, *A Dictionarie of the French and English Tongues.* London, Adam Islip, 1611.

Dalby, Andrew, *Dangerous Tastes.* Berkeley: University of California Press, 2002.

Elias, Norbert, *The Civilizing Process*. Oxford, Basil Blackwell, 1978.
Fitzpatrick, Joan, ed., *Renaissance Food from Rabelais to Shakespeare*. Farnham, Surrey: Ashgate, 2010.
Flandrin, Jean-Louis, *Arranging the Meal*, Julie E. Johnson with Sylvie and Antonio Roder, trans. Berkeley: Univ. of California Press, 2007.
———, 'Différences et différenciation des goûts: Réflexions sur quelques exemples européens entre le 14e et le 18e siècle', in *Oxford Symposium Proceedings* (1981): 191–207.
———, 'La diversité des goûts et des pratiques alimentaires en Europe du 16e au 18e siècle', *Revue d'histoire moderne et contemporaine* 30 (1983): 66–83.
———, 'Le goût et la nécessité: Sur l'usage des graisses dans les cuisines d'Europe occidentale (XIV–XVIIIe siècles)', *Annales E.S.C.* 38, 2 (1983): 369–401.
———, and Carole Lambert, *Fêtes gourmandes au Moyen Age*. Paris: Imprimerie Nationale, 1988.
———, and Massimo Montanari, eds., *Histoire de l'alimentation*. Paris, 1996.
La Fleur de tout cuysine, c. 1543–1547. Paris, [Pierre Sergent].
Floyd, Janet and Laurel Forster, *The Recipe Reader: Narratives, Contexts, Traditions*. Aldershot: Ashgate, 2003.
Freedman, Paul, *Out of the East: Spices and the Medieval Imagination*. New Haven: Yale Univerity Press, 2008.
Girard, Alain R., 'Du manuscrit à l'imprimé: le livre de cuisine en Europe aux 15e et 16e siècles', in *Pratiques et discours alimentaires à la Renaissance,* Jean Claude Margolin and Robert Sauzet, eds., pp. 107–117.
Godefroy, Frédéric, *Dictionnaire de l'ancienne langue française et de tous ses dialectes du IXe au XVe siècles*. Paris, F. Vieweg, 1881–1902.
Hieatt, Constance, and Sharon Butler, eds., *Curye on Inglysch*. London: Oxford University Press for the Early English Text Society, 1985.
———, Brenda Hosington and Sharon Butler. *Pleyn Delit*. Toronto: University of Toronto Press, 1996.
Henisch, Bridget Anne, *Fast and Feast*. State College: Pennsylvania State College Press, 1976.

———, *The Medieval Cook*. Woodbridge: Boydell Press, 2009.

Huguet, Edmond, *Dictionnaire de la langue française du seizième siècle*. Paris, Didier, 1925–1967.

Hyman, Philip, and Mary Hyman, 'Les livres de cuisine et le commerce des recettes en France aux XVe et XVIe siècles', in *Du manuscrit à la table*, Carole Lambert, ed., pp. 59–68.

———, 'Imprimer la cuisine: les livres de cuisine en France entre le XVe et le XIXe siècle', in *Histoire de l'alimentation*, Jean-Louis Flandrin and Massimo Montanari, eds., pp. 643–655.

———, 'Les livres de cuisine imprimés en France: Du règne de Charles VIII à la fin de l'Ancien régime', in *Livres en bouche: Cinq siècles d'art culinaire français*, pp. 55–75.

Jeanneret, Michael, *A Feast of Words*. Chicago: Chicago University Press, 1991.

Keay, John, *The Spice Route: A History*. Berkeley: University of California Press, 2006.

Lambert, Carole, ed., *Du manuscrit à la table*. Montreal: Les Presses de l'Université de Montréal, 1992.

Laurioux, Bruno, *Manger au Moyen Âge*. Paris: Hachette, 2002.

Livre de Cuysine, c. 1539–1540. Paris: [Pierre Sergent].

Livre fort excellent de Cuysine, 1542, 1555. Lyon, Olivier Arnoullet. Available online at http://gallica.bnf.fr/ark:/12148/btv1b8626163t.r=Livre+fort+excellent+de+cuysine.langEN (accessed 10 January 2014). The Bibliothèque Nationale catalogue entry reads in part as follows: *Livre fort excellent de cuysine....*; Date d'édition : 1555; Type : monographie imprimée; Langue : Français moyen; Format: In-8°, car. goth., sign. A-K, fig. gr. sur bois au titre.

Livres en bouche: Cinque siècles d'art culinaire français. Paris: Bibliothèque nationale de France/Hermann, 2001.

Margolin, Jean Claude and Robert Sauzet, eds., *Pratiques et discours alimentaires à la Renaissance: actes du Colloque de Tours de mars 1979*. Paris: Maisonneuve et Larose, 1982.

Mennell, Stephen. *All Manners of Food: Eating and Taste in England and France from the Middle Ages to the Present*. Oxford and New York: B. Blackwell, 1985.

Messisbugo, Christoforo di, *Banchetti*. Ferrara: Buglhat and Hucher, 1549.

Milham, Mary Ella, ed., *Platina, on Right Pleasure and Good Health: A Critical Edition and Translation of De honesta voluptate et valetudine.* Tempe, Ariz.: Medieval & Renaissance Texts & Studies, 1998.

Montagné, Prosper, *Larousse gastronomique*. Paris: Larousse, 1938.

Montanari, Massimo, *The Culture of Food,* Carl Ipsen, trans. Oxford: Blackwell, 1994.

Notaker, Henry, *Printed Cookbooks of Europe 1470–1700*. New Castle, DE: Oak Knoll Press, 2010.

Petit traicte, c. 1536–1538. Paris: [Pierre Sergent].

Pichon, Jérôme, ed., *Le Ménagier de Paris: Traité de morale et d'économie domestique composé vers 1393… par un bourgeois parisien.* Paris: Société des bibliophiles français, 1846.

Platina, *De honesta voluptate et valetudine*. Venice: Laurentius de Aquila and Sibyllinus Umber, 1475.

Revel, Jean-Francois, *Un festin en paroles: histoire littéraire de la sensibilité gastronomique de l'antiquité à nos jours*. Paris: Pauvert, 1979.

Rondelet, Guillaume, *L'Histoire entière des poissons*. Lyon: Mace Bonhomme, 1558.

Santanach, Joan, ed., *The Book of Sent Soví: Medieval Recipes from Catalonia*, trans. Robin Vogelzang. Barcelona: Barcino Tamesis, 2008.

Scully, Terence, *The Art of Cookery in the Middle Ages*. Woodbridge: Boydell, 1995.

——, ed., *Viandier of Taillevent*. Ottawa: University of Ottawa Press, 1988.

van Winter, Johanna Maria, *Spices and Comfits: Collected Papers on Medieval Food*. Totnes: Prospect Books, 2007.

Vicaire, Georges, *Bibliographie gastronomique*. Paris: Roquette et fils, 1890.

Wheaton, Barbara Ketcham, *Savoring the Past: The French Kitchen and Table from 1300 to 1789*. New York: Simon and Schuster, 1983.

ℭ Livre fort excellent de

Cuysine tresutille & profitable contenant en soy la maniere d'abiller toutes viandes. Avec la maniere de servir es banquetz & festins. Le tout veu & corrige oultre la premiere impression par le grant Escuyer de Cuysine du Roy.

ℭ On les vend a Lyon au pres de nostre dame de Confort chez Olivier Arnoullet.*

The most excellent book of

cookery, very useful and profitable, containing within the methods for dressing all foods, along with methods for serving banquets and feasts. All of it reviewed and revised beyond the first edition by the King's head Cook.

Sold in Lyon near Notre Dame de Confort at Olivier Arnoullet's.

---

* The conventions followed in this transcription have been explained on pages 15–16 of the Introduction.

LIVRE FORT EXCELLENT DE CUYSINE

[fol. a ii] La Table.
⊂ S'ensuyt la table de ce present livre
Intitule Le livre de Cuysine.

⊂ Et premierement.

A

⊂ Anguilles bouillies	fueillet.xv.
Anguilles rostyes	fueillet.xvi.
Anguilles en potaige*	eodem
Anguilles en paste	eodem.
Alozes	fueillet.xlvii.
Alozes a la castille	eodem
Aulx blancz	fueillet.l.
Abremont du laict	fueillet.xix.
Alouette	fueillet.xxxvii.&.liiij.
Amandes confictes	fueillet.lxiij.
Abricotz confictz	eodem
Andouilles de foye de veau.	fueillet.lxvij.

B

⊂ Brouet† georget.	fueillet.xxvij.
Aultre brouet	eodem
Bouldins§	fueillet.xxxj.
Bouldins blancz	fueillet.xxxj.
Aultres bouldins	eodem

* The modern French derivation from *potaige*, *potage*, we now take to mean 'soup', but this was not the case in the Middle Ages or the early modern period. 'Soup', in any event, derives from 'sops' or pieces of bread soaked in broth. Pottage was the standard medieval stewed meat or vegetable, often with a broth, thickened or not.
† We have left the word *brouet* untranslated. In the Middle Ages, the usual English terms were 'brewet' or 'brewis' (defined as a broth or liquor in which meat and vegetables are cooked, sometimes thickened with bread or meal), from which the word 'brose' derives. We feel this archaic word will convey little to the modern reader.
§ Although the straightforward translation of *bouldin* is 'pudding', we have sometimes used the word 'sausage', as in American usage pudding conveys a different meaning; however 'white pudding' and 'blood pudding' are well-enough known.

THE MOST EXCELLENT BOOK OF COOKERY

Table of Contents
The following is a table of contents of this book entitled The Cookbook

And firstly:

A

Boiled eels	fol. xv
Roasted eels	fol. xvi
Eels in pottage	the same
Eel pie	the same
Shad	fol. xlvii
Shad *à la castille*	the same
White garlic	fol. l
Abremont of milk	fol. xix
Larks	fols. xxxvii & liiij
Preserved green almonds	fol. lxiij
Preserved apricots	the same
Andouille of calf's liver	fol. lxvij

B

Brouet georget	fol. xxvij
Another *brouet*	the same
Sausages	fol. xxxj
White sausages	fol. xxxj
Other sausages	the same

Becquet a la saulce d'angleterre   fueillet.viij.
Brochet pour ung bancquet   fueille.viij.
Brocheton rosty   fueillet.xiiij.
Brochet a l'estuvee   eodem
Brochet frit   fueillet.xv.
Brochet boully   fueillet.xxxix.
Beurre frais frit   fueillet.xxiij.
Beurre d'amandes en Karesme.   fueillet.lxiiij.
Becasses   fueillet.lij.
Blanc menger   eodem.
Blanc menger de chapon   fueillet.lvij.
Brideaulx a veaulx   eodem
Brochet larde   fueillet.lxv.

C

¶ Chapon boully   fueillet.i.
Idem   fueillet.i.
Chapon rosty   fueillet.ij.
Idem   fueillet.ij.
Chapon barde   fueillet.lxv.
Chapon en paste   fueillet.liij.
Chapon au brouet d'allemaigne.   fu.lxiiij.
Chapons a la canelle   fueillet.lxix.
Couldres   fueillet.xx.
Cocombres   fueillet.xx.xliiij.
Choulx en potaige   fueillet.xxi.
Choulx d'une aultre sorte   fueillet.xxij.
[fol. a iii] Choulx cabufz   fueillet.lxilj.
Cretonnee de poys nouveaulx   fueillet.xxvj.
Cyves de liepvre   eodem
Carbonnades pour souppe   fueillet.xxxij.
Cocombres contrefaictes   fueillet.xxxiij.
Cochons   fueillet.xxxiiij.
Champignons   fueillet.xxxvi.
Cerises confictes   fueillet.xxxvij.

Pike in English sauce	fol. viij
Pike for a banquet	fol. viij
Roasted pickerel	fol. xiiij
Stewed pike	the same
Fried pike	fol. xv
Boiled pike	fol. xxxix
Fresh butter fried	fol. xxiij
Almond butter for Lent	fol. lxiiij
Woodcock	fol. lij
Blancmange	the same
Blancmange of capon	fol. lvij
Calf's bridles	the same
Larded pike	fol. lxv

C

Boiled capon	fol. i
The same	fol. i
Roast capon	fol. ij
The same	fol. ij
Larded capon	fol. lxv
Capon pie	fol. liij
Capon in German broth	fol. lxiiij
Capon with cinnamon	fol. lxix
Gourds	fol. xx
Cucumbers	fol. xx.xliiij
Cabbage in pottage	fol. xxi
Cabbage of another kind	fol. xxij
Cabbage heads	fol. lxilj
Cretonnée of new peas	fol. xxvj
Civet of hare	the same
Carbonade for sops	fol. xxxij
Counterfeit cucumbers	fol. xxxiij
Pigs	fol. xxxiiij
Mushrooms	fol. xxxvi
Preserved cherries	fol. xxxvij

Cresson	fueillet.xxvij.
Chauldeau	fueillet.xxxviij.
Chauldume pour le cerveau	fueillet.xlij.
croste de paste de papier	fueillet.xlvj.
connins	fueillet.xlix.
chevreaulx	fueillet.liij.
canardz concasses	fueillet.liiij.
cresme bastarde	fueillet.x.
Cresme fritte.	eodem
capilotaste	fueillet.xj.
carpes a l'estuvee	fueillet.xiij.
carpes rostyes	eodem
carpes pour ung becquet	fueillet.viij.
carpes boullies	fueillet.xiiij.
carpes en paste en pot	eodem
carpes aulx bignetz	eodem
Carpes braves [*recte* bremes]	fueillet.lvij.
coings en paste	eodem
Cevelat	fueillet.lxix.
cresme houssue	fueillet.lxvij.
cresme de poys nouveaulx	eodem
cresme d'amandes nouvelles	fueillet.lxviij
Cresme de noix nouvelles	fueillet.vij.&.lxvij
crespes frites en poelle	fueillet.lxviij.

D

⸿ Dodine	fueillet.lv.&.lxiiij.
Dodine rouge.	fuellet.lxiiij.
Dariolles pour l'este.	fueillet.l.vij.

E

Esturgeon rosty	fueillet.vij.
Esturgeon en paste	eodem
Esturgeon boully	fueillet.xviij.
Entree de table grasses	fueillet.xxix.

Cress	fol. xxvij
Caudle	fol. xxxviij
Chowder for the brain	fol. xlij
Crust for pastry made of paper	fol. xlvj
Rabbits	fol. xlix
Kid	fol. liij
Crushed ducks	fol. liiij
Counterfeit cream	fol. x
Fried cream	the same
Capirotada	fol. xj
Stewed carp	fol. xiij
Roast carp	the same
Carp for a pike	fol. viij
Boiled carp	fol. xiiij
A potted pie of carp	the same
Carp fritters	the same
Carp *braves* [*recte* bream]	fol. lvij
Quince pie	the same
Cervelat sausage	fol. lxix
Fuzzy cream	fol. lxvij
Cream of new peas	the same
Cream of new almonds	fol. lxviij
Cream of new walnuts	fols. vij & lxvij
Crepes fried in a pan	fol. lxviij

D

Dodine sauce	fols. lv & lxiiij
Red dodine sauce	fol. lxiij
Dariole pastries for summer	fol. lvij

E

Roast sturgeon	fol. vij
Sturgeon pie	the same
Boiled sturgeon	fol. xviij
Rich first courses	fol. xxix

Entrees de table de trippes fueillet.xxx.
Eufz a l'andouille. fueillet.xxxix.
Eufz poches au beurre en plat eodem
Eufz de plusieurs couleurs eodem
Eufz cuyctz sans feu eodem
Eufz durs cuictz en l'eaue eodem
Eufz en paste en pot fueillet.xlj.
Eufz perdus fueillet.lxiiij.
Escrevisses fueillet.xvi.&.xl.
Estuvee noire fueillet.xlij.
[fol. a iiij] Espinars fueillet.xlij.xliij.

F

¶ Friteaulx de fleur de suc fueillet.xxiij.
Fricassees fueillet.xxxj.
Friteaulx fueillet.xxxvij.
Febves* fueillet.xl.
Fritures de mer fueillet.xlvij.
Fromentee fueillet.ix.
Froyde saulce fueillet.xij.
Fromentee de venayson fueillet.lxviij.
Fromentee de chevreau eodem

G

Galemaffree fueillet.xxxiij.
Galentine fueillet.xiij.
Gellee† de poyres fueillet.iij.
Gelee a l'ypocras eodem
Gardons fueillet.xvi.

---

* We have translated *febves* throughout as 'fava beans'. English readers know them more commonly as broad beans.

† We have translated the French *gellee/gelee* as 'jelly' throughout, although in some cases 'aspic' might be the preferred term. In America, jelly may be the equivalent of the English jam, but in this text it is taken to be a sweet or savoury liquid that is set by some gelatinous agent.

THE MOST EXCELLENT BOOK OF COOKERY

Tripe first courses — fol. xxx
Andouille of eggs — fol. xxxix
Eggs poached in butter in a plate — the same
Eggs of many colours — the same
Eggs cooked without fire — the same
Hard-boiled eggs cooked in water — the same
A potted pie of eggs — fol. xlj
Lost eggs — fol. lxiiij
Crayfish — fols. xvi & xl
Black stew — fol. xlij
Spinach — fols. xlij & xliij

F

Elderflower fritters — fol. xxiij
Fricassees — fol. xxxij
Fritters — fol. xxxvij
Fava beans — fol. xl
Fritters of seafood — fol. xlvij
Frumenty — fol. ix
Cold sauce — fol. xij
Frumenty of venison — fol. lxviij
Frumenty of kid — the same

G

Gallimaufry — fol. xxxiij
Galantine — fol. xiij
Pear jelly — fol. iij
Mulled wine jelly — the same
Loach — fol. xvi

Goujons   eodem
Greneault   fueillet.xj.
Gigot de mouton a l'estuvee.   fueillet.lxiiij.

H

❧ Hastereauex   fueillet.xxxij.
Haricot de foye de veau   fueillet.xxxvij.
Huytres en l'escaille   fueillet.xviij.
Huytres a l'estuvee   eodem
Huytres frites   fueillet.xviij.
Huyctres au cyve   fueillet.xli.
Hastelees d'esturgeon   fueillet.vij.
Hastellees de plyes   fueillet.viij.
Hochepot de pigeons   fueillet.xij.
Hochepot de possins   eodem
Hure de sanglier   fueillet.lvij.

J

Jaspe de laict   fueillet.xxiiij.
Jambons   fueillet.xxxij

L

❧ Laict cretonne   fueillet.xxvj.
Lamproye de chair   fueillet.iiij.
Lamproyes   fueillet.l.&.lvij.
Lievre   fueillet.lv.
Lievre   eodem
Lardeaulx de venaison   fueillet.vj.
Laict d'amandes   fueillet.xij.
Loches
Limatz d'allemaigne   fueillet.lxvij.
Luganes.   fueillet.lxix.

M

Mesles en cresme   fueillet.xxxvj.
Mesles d'autre sorte   fueillet.xliij.

Gudgeon — the same
Monkfish — fol. xj
Stewed leg of mutton — fol. lxiiij

H

Hastereaux — fol. xxxij
Haricot of calf's liver — fol. xxxvij
Oysters in the shell — fol. xviij
Stewed oysters — the same
Fried oysters — fol. xviij
Civet of oysters — fol. xli
Kebabs of sturgeon — fol. vij
Kebabs of plaice — fol. viij
Hodge-podge of pigeon — fol. xij
Hodge-podge of chicken — the same
Boar's head — fol. lvij

J

Milk jasper — fol. xxiiij
Ham — fol. xxxij

L

Milk *cretonné* — fol. xxvj
Meat lamprey — fol. iiij
Lampreys — fols. l & lvij
Hare — fol. lv
Hare — the same
Larded venison — fol. vj
Almond milk — fol. xij
Loach
German snails — fol. lxvij
Lucanica sausages — fol. lxix

M

Medlars in cream — fol. xxxvj
Medlars of another sort — fol. xliij

Marrons	fueillet.xliij.
Mouton rosty	fueillet.xlv.
[fol. a v] Moust de raisins	fueillet.l.
Mullet	fueillet.xvi.
Marsouin rosty	eodem
Marsouin en potaige	eodem.

N

☞ Naveaulx de venayson	fueillet.xx.
Neige contrefaicte	fueillet.xlvij.
Neige de gelee.	fueillet.v.

O

☞ Oyseaulx de riviere en potaige	fueillet.vj.
Orgemunde	fueillet.xj.
Oublyes farcees	fueillet.iiij.
Oyseaulx de riviere a la dodine	fueillet.xlv.
Oygnons	fueillet.xxxvj.

P

☞ Paste de coste de blettes	fueillet.xxix.
Poree broyee	eodem
Poireaulx	fueillet.xx.&.xliij.
poys de Lundy	fueillet.xx.
paste en pot mouton	eodem
paste en pot de gigot de mouton rosty au [ou] longe de veau rostye froide	fueillet.xxi.
Paste de gigot	fueillet.lxvj.
Pommes	fueillet.xv.
Pastes en pot de langue de beuf	fueillet.xxxiij.
paste de veau	fueillet.xxiij.
potaige blanc de chapons ou de poulles.	fuel.xxiiij.
potaige vert	eodem
potaige rouge	eodem
potaige violet	fueillet.xxv.

Chestnuts	fol. xliij
Roasted mutton	fol. xlv
Grape sauce	fol. l
Mullet	fol. xvi
Roasted porpoise	the same
Porpoise in a pottage	the same

N

Venison with turnips	fol. xx
Counterfeit snow	fol. xlvij
Snow of jelly.	fol. v

O

River fowl pottage	fol. vj
French barley	fol. xj
Stuffed wafers	fol. iiij
River fowl in dodine sauce	fol. xlv
Onions	fol. xxxvj

P

Chard pie	fol. xxix
Puréed leeks	the same
Leeks	fols. xx & xliij
Monday peas	fol. xx
Mutton potted pie	the same
A potted pie of roast leg of mutton or cold roast loin of veal	fol. xxi
Leg of mutton pie	fol. lxvi
Apples	fol. xv
Potted pies of ox tongue	fol. xxxiij
Veal pie	fol. xxiij
White pottage of capons or hens	fol. xxiiij
Green pottage	the same
Red pottage	the same
Violet pottage	fol. xxv

Pommes de veaulx ou de ventre de Chevreaulx	fueillet eodem
potaige de ventre de veaulx/ou de chevreaulx	fueillet eodem
potaige cretonne	fueillet.xxvj.
perdrix motee	fueillet.i.
pomme de coing	fueillet.iij.
pastes nourris	eodem
potaige de courge	fueillet.v.
potaige de piedz de mouton	eodem
pastes de carpes et d'anguilles	fueillet.viij.
paste en pot	fueillet.x.
paste en pot de veau	eodem
perdrix aulx choulx	fueillet.xj.
pigeons confictz	fueillet.xij.
pour faire pouldre de duc	fueillet.xxviij.
pour faire eaue d'amande	eodem
pour faire hastereaulx de foye de veau	fuel.xxix.
pour faire saulce a foye de veau ou d'aultres	fueillet eodem
[fol. a vj] Pour faire cuyre foye de Cerf beuf ou chevreaulx.	fueillet.xxix.
Pour faire foye de veau de mouton Chevreaulx.	fueillet.xxviij.
paste de veau ou de mouton a la Saulce Chaulde.	fueillet.xxx.
Aultres pastes a la saulce chaulde.	fueillet.lij.
piedz de mouton pour le gouster	fueillet.xxxj.
paste en pot de trippes	fueillet.xxxviij.
potaiges	eodem
poix nouveaulx	fueillet.xij.
poix a la saulgrenee	Eodem
poissons a saulce sanglant	fueillet.xliij.
perdrix a la tonnellette	fueillet.xj.
Pan revestu	fueillet.xlv.
Pans d'aultre sorte	eodem
Paste au gigot de mouton	eodem
pour mettre la main en eaue boullante.	fueillet.xlvj.
pastes a troys	fueillet.eodem.
paste d'alebran	fueillet.liiij.
poullailles a la saulce robert	eodem

Apples made from calves' or kids' stomachs	fol. the same
Calves' or kids' stomach pottage	fol. the same
Cretonné pottage	fol. xxvj
Partridge on a hill	fol. i
Quince pie	fol. iij
Nourishing pies	the same
Gourd soup	fol. v
Pottage of sheep's trotters	the same
Carp and eel pies	fol. viij
Potted pie	fol. x
Veal potted pie	the same
Partridge with cabbage	fol. xj
Pigeons confit	fol. xij
To make Duke's powder	fol. xxviij
To make almond milk	the same
To make calf's liver kebabs	fol. xxix
To make calf's liver sauce or others	fol. the same
How to cook stag, beef, or kid's liver	fol. xxix
For making veal, mutton or kid's liver	fol. xxviij
Veal or mutton pie with hot sauce	fol. xxx
Other pies with hot sauce	fol. lij
Sheep's trotters for a snack	fol. xxxj
Potted pie of tripe	fol. xxxviij
Pottages	the same
New peas	fol. xij
Pease pottage	the same
Fish in a bloody sauce	fol. xliij
Partridge *à la tonnelette*	fol. xj
Peacocks in their feathers	fol. xlv
Peacocks of another kind	the same
Mutton leg pâté	the same
To put your hand in boiling water	fol. xlvj
Triple pies	fol. the same
Teal pie	fol. liiij
Chicken in sauce Robert	the same

Paste de veau   eodem
paste de mouton   eodem
pinsons   fueillet.liij.
pigeons rames   fueillet.liij.
Pasteaulx   eodem
Perche boullye   fueillet.xv.
Perche fritte   fueillet.xv.
Perche en paste   eodem
papillons de pommes de capendu   fueillet.lxiiij.
potaige lavatif   fueillet.lxv.
potaige digestif.   fueillet.lxvj.

R

❧ Raymoulles de blanc de chapon   fueillet.lxviij.
Rys   fueillet.xi.
Rys de couleur   eodem
Rouget   fueillet.lvj.
Rosty sanglant   fueillet.xvj.

S

❧ Soupes a la capilorde   fueillet.xxj.
Sanglier   fueillet.xxvj.
Saulcisses de gigot de mouton   fueillet.xxx.
Saulcisses de lombardie   fueillet.xxxij.
Saulcisses de Boulongne   fueillet.xxxij.
Saulce d'enfer   fueillet.xxxiij.
Saulcyrion an may   fueillet.xxxvj.
Saulce barbe robert   fueillet.xij.
Saulce noire   fueillet.xlix.
Saulce pour beuf rosty   eodem
[fol. a vij] Saulce madame   eodem
Saulce d'aulx au lait   eodem
Saulce vert   eodem &.l.
Saulce de venayson   fueillet.li.
Solles en paste   fueillet.lvij.

Veal pie	the same
Mutton pie	the same
Chaffinch	fol. liij
Wood pigeon	fol. liij
Little pies	the same
Boiled perch	fol. xv
Fried perch	fol. xv
Perch pie	the same
Butterflies of short start apples	fol. lxiiij
Cleansing pottage	fol. lxv
Digestive pottage	fol. lxvj

R

Raymo[u]lles of capon breast	fol. lxviij
Rice	fol. xi
Coloured rice	the same
Red mullet	fol. lvj
Bloody roast	fol. xvj

S

Sops *à la capirotada*	fol. xxj
Boar	fol. xxvj
Sausages of leg of mutton	fol. xxx
Lombard sausages	fol. xxxij
Bologna sausages	fol. xxxij
Hell sauce	fol. xxxiij
Button mushrooms in May	fol. xxxvj
Robert's beard sauce	fol. xij
Black sauce	fol. xlix
Sauce for roast beef	the same
Sauce madame	the same
Garlic sauce with milk	the same
Green sauce	the same & l
Venison sauce	fol. li
Sole pie	fol. lvij

Saulce d'alemine [cameline]	fueillet.lij.
Saulce jacopine	fueillet.j.
Saulce de trahyson	fueillet.ij.
Soustrees	fueillet.ij.
Soupe aux aulx	fueillet.ix.
Soupe vermeil	eodem
Saulmon frais rosty	fueillet.xvij.
Saulmon boully	eodem
Saulmon en paste	fueillet.xvij.
Seiches frittes	fueillet.xviij.
Saulce realle	fueillet.lxiij.
Saulce [*recte* Saulcisses] de blanc chapon.	fueillet.lxix.

T

Tortue de lombardie	fueillet.iij.
Tartes a mouelle de beuf	fueillet.iiij.
Tartellette de cresme	eodem
Taillis d'angleterre	fueillet.v.
Tortue en poelle	fueillet.vj.
Truicte fricte	fueillet neuf.
Truictes boullues	fueillet.xvj.
Turbot	fueillet.xviij.&.lvj.
Tartes rouges	fueillet.lxiij.
Trippes	fueillet.xliiij.
Tenches	fueillet.xlviij.
Tartes jacopine	fueillet.lviij.
Tartes d'espinars	fueillet.lxix.

V

Venayson contrefaicte en potaige	fueillet.xxvij.
Venayson de sanglier	fueillet.x.
Vives boullue	fueillet.xvij.

¶ Finis

[Cameline] sauce	fol. lij
Jacobin sauce	fol. j
Treason sauce	fol. ij
Rendered fat	fol. ij
Garlic soup	fol. ix
Red soup	the same
Roasted fresh salmon	fol. xvij
Boiled salmon	the same
Salmon pie	fol. xvij
Fried cuttlefish	fol. xviij
Royal sauce	fol. lxiij
[Sausages] of capon breast	fol. lxix

T

Lombard tart	fol. iij
Beef marrow tart	fol. iiij
Cream tartlets	the same
English slices	fol. v
Tart in a pan	fol. vj
Fried trout	fol. nine
Boiled trout	fol. xvi
Turbot	fols. xviij & lvj
Red tarts	fol. lxiij
Tripe	fol. xliiij
Tench	fol. xlvij
Jacobin tarts	fol. lviij
Spinach tarts	fol. lxix

V

Counterfeit venison pottage	fol. xxvij
Boar venison	fol. x
Boiled weever	fol. xvij

End

⁋ Fontaine d'eaue dedans ung bassin ou plat sur une table.

⁋ Prenes ung beau rondeau de boys ataches ung cercle a l'entour faict a carreaulx & un baston Carre d'ung pied & demi ou de trois de hault attache audict Rondeau par le meillieu du bor[d] avec ung trenchoir ledict par le millieu que feres entrer dedans ledict baston par le hault bout ung pied & sera la arreste attache sur ung petit pommeau faict par dessus ledict trenchoir & que ledict trenchoyr soit faconne pour assieger troys fiolles ou bouteilles de fer blanc que atacheres & feres en facon de pommeaulx par dessus et dores lesdictz pommeaulx & sercle & y mettres les escus*[fol. a viii]*sons qu'il vous plaira audict pommeau & soyent lesdictz Rondeaulx couvers de violette et fleur par dessus la doreure laquelle sera doree de vert & le sercle de faulne & y aura plusieurs pertuys pour planter voz fleurs en facon de jardin avec Romarin peignes ledict arbre avec la couleur convenable & ung pertuys que ferez au dessus dudict arbre pour planter ce que vouldres & fault avoir tuyau de leton plye par le millieu qui yra jusques au cul de la fiolle & qui sera plus dehors que dedans de demy doy & feres serpens & lesardes ils ne seront pas si grans de la moytie que j'ay dict devant lesditz tuyaulx emplyes les troys bouteille l'une d'eau l'aultre d'eau rose la tierce de leton de vin ou ce que vouldres/ & quant ce viendra a servir succez avec la bouche lesditz tuyaulx pour faire distiller & en celuy d'eaue ardant mettre le feu et distilleront et degouteront dedans les tasses.

⁋ Finis.

Water Fountain in a Basin or Plate on the Table[1]

Take a nice flat, round board of wood and attach planks in a circle around it. Attach a foot and a half to three-foot long square post to the bottom of the round board. Take a trencher, said trencher having a hole in the middle, and pass it over the other end of the post, securing it a foot down from the top by means of a pommel. Make sure the trencher can hold three tin vials or flasks that you will fashion to appear like they have pommels on top. Gild these pommels and the round board and add some ornamental shields if you like. Cover the round board with violets and other flowers after having painted over the gilding with green and tawny colours. Make some holes in order to plant flowers as in a garden and include rosemary fashioned like a tree and painted with an appropriate colour. Add some holes above this tree in which to plant what you like. You'll need some tin pipes bent in the middle so that they reach within a half an inch of the bottom of the flasks. Add some serpents and lizards about half as big as said pipes to cover them up. Fill the three flasks, one with water, one with rosewater, and the third with wine or whatever you wish. When it's time to serve, suck on the end of the pipes to begin siphoning and light the one containing alcohol and they will siphon and pour into cups.

The End

---

1. This water fountain could conceivably be used for hand-washing given that two of the liquids used are water and rosewater. However, it is much more likely that this fountain serves a purely decorative purpose. Much detail about how to decorate it is provided. One of the liquids designed to flow is alcohol that is supposed to be set on fire. Furthermore, though the liquids are designed to flow from vials via a siphoning process, it is not clear how this flow would be circular since the liquids flow from the vials into cups placed in the basin. One might imagine a servant periodically refilling the vials from the cups.

[fol. 1r] ⁋ S'ensuyt l'ordonnance de cuysine.

⁋ Chapon boully.
Premierement pour ung Chapon boully, fault prendre de la marjolaine & broyer en ung mortier, & en saulce de Marjolaine, du Romarin et passer parmy une estamine ave[c] moyeulx d'oeufx et mye de pain blanc et pour boullon prenez du laict & du verjus et passez cela parmy une estamine & le mettez bouillir en ung pot ou telle sur les charbons & le remuez bien qu'il ne brusle & y mettez grant foison de sucre et de gingembre pour les espices et le gectez sur le chapon comme feriez blanc menger & mettez dessus de la belle dragee et en faulte de dragee grant foyson de sucre.

⁋ Item, aultre maniere de chapon boully.
⁋ Prenez des essees et moulles & le mettez cuyre avec & quant il est prest de cuyt vous recoucherez le boullon & mettez toute la cortisse dedans ayez du romarin & toutes bonnes herbes comme saulge, ysope, persil, & marjolaine hachee bien deslyee avecques du laict et metez dedans le pot avecque le chapon. Prenez du verjus ou du vin blanc, pour les espices, du gingembre & cloudz de giroffle entiers et les laissez estuver a court boullon. *[fol. 1v]* Et en deffault de chappon prenez des poussins pour toutes les deulx saulces aussi bien Pour l'une que pour l'aultre.

Hereafter follows the Ordinance of Cooking.

Boiled capon

First off, for boiled capon take some marjoram and grind it in a mortar. To make a marjoram sauce, add some rosemary and put it through a sieve along with some egg yolks and white breadcrumbs. For the broth take some milk and verjuice and put it through a sieve, then let it boil in a pot or earthenware dish over the coals. Stir it well so that it doesn't burn. Add a copious amount of sugar and ginger for spices. Pour it over the capon as you would do for a blancmange [2] and add some *dragée* candies [3] on top. In the absence of *dragées*, a copious amount of sugar will do.

Item, another version of boiled capon

Take some wings, pound them and put them on to cook together. When they're almost done add back some broth and put in the whole skin. [4] Take some rosemary and some other good herbs such as sage, hyssop, parsley, and marjoram chopped finely and thinned out with some milk. Put it in the pot with the capon. Add some verjuice or white wine and for spices some ginger and whole clove, and let it simmer. In the absence of capon, use young chicken for both sauces. It works as well for one as for the other.

---

2. Recipes for a *blancmanger* can be found in the earliest French medieval cookbooks and appear in other cookbooks all across Europe through the seventeenth century and beyond. Though each recipe contains slight variations, the vast majority of them are for a white mixture of ground cooked poultry and almond, which is served either as a sauce or as an accompaniment to other foods.
3. The French *dragée* is a sort of candied sugar similar to the candied almonds traditionally served at weddings or baptisms. Cotgrave's entry on this word reflects the medicinal use of sugar and sweets in the cuisine of the period. Given that sugar is often sprinkled on many dishes in this collection, the use of *dragées* here suggests a more specialized or fanciful dish.
4. The word *cortisse* in the French is somewhat problematic because no such word appears in standard dictionaries. Either it is a printer's mistake or it is related to the Spanish word *corteza*, which refers to the rind, bark, or skin. We surmise that the cook is to make an initial broth with the wings and skin of the capon. This broth is then added to another pot containing the rest of the capon.

€ Souppe jacopine.

€ Item pour une souppe jacopine sur les perdrix, poussins, ou pigeons, vous prendrez du vin Vermeil, de la canelle, & le passer parmy l'estamine & le mettez boullir avec la moesle de beuf affinee: mettez des cloudz de giroffle tous entiers dedans grant foison de sucre assavoir de comanges coupez de romarin bien deslye & le mettez bouillir avec.

€ Pour une aultre souppe jacopine.

€ Vous prendrez des perdrix, poussins, ou pigeons comme cy devant et prenez du bon fromaige pour faire bouillon prenez de la gresse de chappon ou de bouillon de beuf et du vin blanc & en faire vostre boullon. Et aussi le faictes bouillir en ung plat avec lesdictes perdrix, poussins, ou pigeons, le formaige par dessus & des rostyes dessoubz & le mettez bouillir sur les charbons. Et au dresser, mettez y grant foison de sucre dessus mesle avec canelle.

€ Perdrix motee.

€ Pour perdrix motee, prenez des perdrix et les ros*[fol. 2r]*tissez, et prenez le c[r]esme du raisin & le broyez et cassez. Et le passez par une estamine avec du pain hasle trempe en boullon de beuf ou en vin vermeil passe par ladicte estamine avec des espices. Comme canelle. Et avec ung peu de moustarde. Et le tout mettez bouillir en ung pot avec grant foyson de sucre. Et gardez qu'il ne brusle. Et au servir, mettez dessus lesdictes perdrix, chapons, ou poussins de la dragee par dessus.

Jacobin Soup

Item, for a Jacobin soup with partridge, young chicken, or pigeon, take some red wine, some cinnamon and put it through a sieve. Put it on to boil with some refined beef marrow. Add some whole cloves and a copious amount of sugar, that from Le Comminges,[5] chop some rosemary very finely, and set it all to boil together.

For another Jacobin Soup

Take some partridge, young chicken, or pigeon as above and some good cheese. To make the broth, take some capon fat, beef broth, and some white wine and make your broth from them. Set it to boil in a dish with the aforementioned partridge, chicken or pigeon on a bed of grilled bread with cheese added on top. Let it boil over the coals. And for garnish, add a copious amount of sugar on top mixed with cinnamon.

Partridge on a Hill[6]

For partridges on a hill, take some partridges and roast them. Take some of the best grapes [7] and grind and crush them. Pass them through a sieve with some toasted bread soaked in beef broth or in red wine passed through the aforementioned sieve with spices such as cinnamon and a little bit of mustard. Set all of it to boil in a pot with a copious amount of sugar. Make sure that it does not burn. For service, sprinkle some candy on top of the said partridges, capons, or young chicken.

---

5. *Comanges* seems to be a place name. According to Philip and Mary Hyman, it may refer to Le Comminges, an area near the Garonne river at the base of the Pyrenees. This is clearly not a sugar-producing region so it is not obvious why sugar from there is to be preferred to any other.

6. Cotgrave glosses *moté* and *motté* as versions of *motet* which refers to a musical line in a song or poem. However, he also glosses *motté* in a separate entry as 'set, or (usually) sitting, on a clod, or sodd.' A related word, *mottelet*, is defined as a 'little clod, lumpe, sodd, or turfe of earth.' These words are of course all related to 'motte', which can be a clump of earth or a small hill.

7. The original text reads '*le cesme du raisin*' though the 1576 *Grand Cuisinier* corrects this with '*le cresme du raisin.*' Cotgrave glosses the masculine form of *cresme* as the baptismal ointment. No culinary context is mentioned. Rather than a particular part of the grape, the 'cream' here perhaps reflects the quality of said grapes.

❡ Saulce de trahyson.
❡ Pour faire saulce de trahyson, prenez des perdrix, pour l'escort, vous frirez de l'ongnon avec du sain ou du lard fondu. Et passez parmy une estamine avec du pain hasle trempe du boullon de beuf, vin vermeil, & vinaigre canelle. En lieu d'espices mostarde et menues espices et grant foyson de sucre.

❡ Soustree.
❡ Pour faire soustree vous prendrez du lard & le mettez boullir pour le pressurer vous prendrez houstelard & y mettez tant que elle soyt forte pour le pressurer. Et pour les espice de gingimbre avec grant foyson de sucre & cella demourra blanc.
❡ Pour une aultre soustree vous y mettrez dedans de la marjolaine de semence de fenoil & vous broyerez des hosblutz & mettez du saffran gingembre & sucre par les *[fol. 2v]* espices & passez parmy l'estamine et puis le mettez en ung plat.
❡Pour une aultre soustree vermeil prenez du vin vermeil et ung peu de vin aigre & le mettez boullir en ung pot & y mettez du hosblutz* pour le pressurer pour les espices de la canelle poyvre cloudz de girofle grant foyson de sucre quant il a boully passez parmy l'estamine et le jectez en moulle ou en plat.

---

* The printer has written *hosblutz* here, but we think he meant to write *houstelard*, cloth, or there are some words that have been omitted.

Treason sauce

To make treason sauce, take some partridges and for an accompaniment, fry some onions in fat or rendered lard. Pass them through a sieve with toasted bread soaked in beef broth, red wine, cinnamon and vinegar. In place of the spices, you can use mustard and fine spices[8] and a copious amount of sugar.

Rendered fat[9]

To make rendered fat, take some pork fat and set it to boil. In order to squeeze out the liquid, take a cloth[10] and put in as much as it is capable of holding without breaking. And for spices, some ginger and copious amounts of sugar. It should remain white.

For another rendered fat recipe, add some marjoram, fennel seed. Grind up some hop shoots[11] and add some saffron, ginger, and sugar for spices and put it through a sieve and then place it in a dish.

For red rendered fat, take some red wine and a bit of vinegar and set it to boil in a pot. Put it in a cloth to squeeze out the liquid. For spices, some cinnamon, pepper, clove, and a copious amount of sugar. When it comes to a boil, put it through a sieve and then pour it into a mould or a dish.

---

8. The '*menues espices*' here refer to a mixture of common spices (ginger, cinnamon, pepper, nutmeg, clove, grains of paradise) that began to be used in late medieval and early Renaissance cookbook references as a shorthand for the traditional long list of medieval spices. The make-up of the group of spices labelled *menues* or *grosses* varied according to time and place.

9. The title of this recipe, *Soustree*, is an unfamiliar word in French, possibly linked etymologically to the verb *soustraire* (to take away). All variations of this recipe use pig fat that is cooked and then squeezed in a cloth, presumably to purefy the melted lard, which is subsequently flavoured with various spices.

10. The *houstelard* here is used in a number of subsequent recipes. The word or its variations do not appear in Cotgrave, but similar words (*houseau* or *housée*) refer to cloths of various kinds. Given its use in this context, we can assume that it is something akin to cheesecloth.

11. The *hosblutz* here show up in a number of subsequent recipes in various spellings. We assume that this is a variant or simply incorrect spelling of *houbelon*, or hops. Given the culinary use here, we suspect it actually refers to hop shoots.

Chapon rosty.

❡ Prenez ung chapon ou poussin rosti prenez des amandes sans peler & les lavez & broyez en ung mortier prenez du vin vermeil, puis le passez avec ung peu de mye de pain blanc prenez pour les espices canelle ou gingembre duquel vouldrez des deulx & prenez grant foyson de sucre et le mettez bouillir en ung beau pot & au servir mettez sur ledict chapon ou poussin foison de dragee dessus.

Chapon rosty.

❡ Pour ung chapon rosty a l'orenge vermeille prenez du vin vermeil. Et du bouillon de beuf qui soit gras & prenez po[u]r les espices canelle et ung peu de menue espices grant foison de sucre pelez voz orenges et les coupez par rouelles mettez les bouillir avec ung petit de Romarin & le mettez avec. Et ne le laissez gueres *[fol. 3r]* bouillir, et a servir mettez y du sucre par dessus.

Pomme de coing.

❡ Pour faire pomme de coing en potaige, prenez du vin vermeil & du meilleur boullon de beuf gras que vous pourrez trouver & le mettez par quartiers et le mettez bouillir en ung pot & laissez confire tant qu'il vous semblera qu'elle sera assez cuytte, prenez pour les espices canelle, & cloud de girofle. Pareillement pour poires et a cuyre grant foison de sucre, et quant vous aurez de veau et mouelle de beuf vous le mettrez dessus, et aussi des rostyes de pain dessoubz.

Gelees de poires.

❡ Pour faire gellee de poires, vous les mettrez cuire en vin et en sucre en canelle entiere, en cloud de giroffle, & quant les poires seront cuittes vous les tirerez dehors et vous mettrez apres vostre houselat pour le faire prendre. Et passez vostre gelee & jectez dessus les poires en vostre plat foison de sucre seme par dessus.

Roast capon

Take a roast capon or young chicken. Take some unpeeled almonds and wash them then grind them in a mortar. Take some red wine and then put it through a sieve with a few white breadcrumbs. For spices, add some cinnamon or ginger, whichever of the two you prefer, and a copious amount of sugar. Set it to boil in a nice pot and when serving put on top of said capon or chicken a copious amount of candied sugar.

Roast capon

For red roasted capon *à l'orange*, take some red wine and some beef broth that has some fat in it. For spices, take some cinnamon and a bit of fine spice and a copious amount of sugar. Peel your oranges and slice them into rounds. Set them to boil with a little rosemary and add them to the rest. Let it just come to the boil. When serving, add some sugar on top.

Quince

To make quinces in a pottage, take some red wine and the best fatty beef broth that you can find. Cut the quinces into quarters and set them to boil in the pot. Let them steep until it seems that they are sufficiently cooked. For spices, take some cinnamon and clove. Pears can be prepared the same way and while cooking add a copious amount of sugar. When you have some veal and beef marrow, put that on top with toasted bread underneath.

Pear jelly

To make a jelly of pears, put them on to cook in wine with sugar, whole cinnamon, and clove. When the pears are cooked, take them out of the liquid and add to your cloth so it will firm up.[12] Sieve your jelly and add it on top of the pears in your dish with a copious amount of sugar sprinkled on top.

---

12. As was the case for the preceding 'rendered fat' recipes, this recipe and the one following it call for the use of a cloth through which to strain liquids from cooked fruit and/or spices. Since both recipes are 'jellies', it is unclear how they would set in the absence of any gelatin or like ingredient.

❡ Gelee a l'ypocras.*
❡ Pour faire gellee a l'ypocras prenez du vin blanc & mettez pour les espices de la canelle entiere des cloudz de giroffle entiers du houseblas pour la pressurer, & si vous le voulez avoir blanc si le faictes ainsi et y met*[fol. 3v]*tez grant foyson de sucre. Et semblablement pourrez faire vermeil & prenez ung peu de saffran et tourneson.

❡ Tortue de lombardie.
❡ Pour faire une tortue de Lombardie a la poille prenez de la marjolaine et la broyez en ung mortier. Et ung fromaige tout nouveau faict mettez y dessus moyeulx d'oeufz et ung peu de cresme pour le faire prendre et les broiez bien fort ensemble en ung mortier, puis prenez une poille de fer et l'engressez bien de beurre et quant elle sera bien engressee jectez le beurre hors & puis ayez de la belle farine & la semez tresbien en vostre poille, & alors jectez en icelle poille vostre faict, & le mettez sur cendres chauldes. Et couvrez bien icelle poille d'une aultre ou d'ung bassin & mettez du feu par dessus & gardez qu'elle ne brusle. Puis les laverez par les costez de beurre, affin qu'elle ne tienne a la poille, puis quant elle sera cuicte mettez les en ung plat seme de belle eaue rose et grant foyson de sucre dessus.

❡ Pastez nourris.
❡ Pour faire pastez nourriz prenez des raisins de corains & les lavez tresbien. Puis les elisez et quant ilz seront eslitz vous les mettres en petitz paste le plus petit et le plus chault que vous pourrez mettre des amandes desliees hachez avec petit de canelle, et des *[fol. 4r]* cloudz de giroffle entiers et grant foyson de sucre bouillez avec. Et puis le frisez en sain de porc ou en beurre confict & a frire gardez de les fondre. Et puis quant vous les vouldrez servir boutez y de l'ypocras dedans & le sucrez tresbien.

---

*   We have here translated *ypocras* as 'mulled wine' as being a readily understandable modern equivalent of hippocras. In the Middle Ages, it was the spiced wine made by steeping the wine with sugar and spices, then filtering it through a cloth bag – the Hippocratic sleeve developed by the ancient Greek physician of that name for filtering water – that aided digestion and was served at the end of a meal.

Mulled wine jelly

To make a jelly of mulled wine, take some white wine and add for spices some whole cinnamon and cloves and use a cloth to squeeze out the moisture. If you want it to be white, make it so and add a copious amount of sugar. Likewise, you can make it red by adding a little saffron and turnsole.[13]

Lombard tart

To make a Lombard tart in a pan, take some marjoram and grind it in a mortar. Take a freshly made cheese, some egg yolks and a bit of cream to thicken it up and grind them well in a mortar. Then take an iron pan and grease it well with butter. When it is well greased, remove the excess butter, take some fine flour and sprinkle it all over the pan. Then add your mixture to this pan and put it over hot coals. Cover this pan with another or with a bowl and put some coals on top. Make sure it doesn't burn. Baste the sides of the tart with butter so that it doesn't stick to the pan. When it's cooked, place it on a dish and sprinkle it with rosewater and a copious amount of sugar.

Nourishing pies [14]

To make nourishing pies, take some currants and wash them well. Cull through them and when they have been culled, put them inside small pastries, the smallest and hottest you can. Add some skinned and chopped almonds to them with some cinnamon, whole cloves, and boil it with copious amounts of sugar. Then fry them in lard or melted butter. When frying, make sure that they don't fall apart. When you are ready to serve, pour some hippocras on them and sugar it well.

---

13.   Turnsole or tournesol is defined by the *SOED* as 'a violet-blue or purple substance obtained from the plant *Chrozophora tinctoria*,' also known as dyer's croton, a spurge grown in the Mediterranean region. Orchil lichen (*Roccella tinctoria*) is also used in dye-making to produce the same blue or purple colour. When turnsole is mixed with an acid, in this case white wine, it turns red.

14.   Scully's critical edition of the *Viandier* manuscripts translates a similarly named dish as 'Norse Pies' (p. 303), but it is not clear why this English cognate is appropriate. We have chosen a more literal translation.

⁌ Tartre a moelle de beuf.
⁌ Pour faire tartre a moelle de beuf vous pourbouillirez vostre moelle de beuf et le mettez en ung plat et mettez chascune piece a part ainsi que vous vouldrez faire voz tartres. Et les faictes de la grandeur d'ung poulce ou de ung doy puis dismellez grant foison de sucre avec ung peu de canelle, & semez tout par dessus, et puis les mettez en voz feuilles et en ferez vos tartelettes. Puis les frisez en sain de porc ou en beurre, et gardez de les enffondrer. Et a servir foison de sucre par dessus.

⁌ Tartelettes de cresme.
⁌ Pour tartelettes de cresme bastarde. Laissez les refroidir avant que les faciez, et les faictes petites ainsi que celles de moelle de beuf. Et les frisez comme lesdictes de mouelle de beuf. Et mettez au servir du sucre. Et gardez de les effondrer comme dict est devant.

⁌ Oublyes farcees.
[fol. 4v] ⁌Pour faire oublyes farcees vous prendrez du cerfueil & le pourbouillez & le hachez bien deslye. Et quant est bien hache vous le broyrez avec du succre, puis le frisez en beurre ou en sain de porc. Et y metez ung peu de sel. Et puis vous prendrez voz oublyes quant ilz seront frictes. Et mettez dessus beurre d'une part et d'aultre succre. Et moillez ung peu le bort affin de les attacher l'ung contre l'autre puis frises en beurre ou sain de porc a servir succrez les bien. Et pareillement vous pourrez faire tartelettes faictes de paste bien succrees au servir.

⁌ Lamproye de chair.
⁌ Pour faire lamproye de chair vous cuyrez de la teste de veau & chappons, cuysez les fort qu'ilz soyent bien cuictz puis tirez la chair de dehors. Et quant aures tire la chair mettes de la chair de chapon et de la teste de veau tout ensemble. Puis prenes pour les espices de

Beef marrow tart

To make beef marrow tart, parboil your beef marrow and then put it in a dish. Separate it into pieces according to how many tarts you are making. Make them into pieces about as big as a thumb or a finger. Then mix together a copious amount of sugar with a bit of cinnamon and sprinkle it over the marrow. Put the marrow into your pastry and make them into tartlets. Then fry them in lard or butter and make sure they don't fall apart. When serving, add a copious amount of sugar on top.

Custard tartlets [15]

For counterfeit custard tarts. Allow them to cool before you make them and make them as small as the beef marrow ones. Fry them like said beef marrow ones. And add sugar when serving. And keep them from falling apart as mentioned above.

Stuffed wafers [16]

To make stuffed wafers, take some chervil, parboil it, and chop it finely. When it is chopped well, grind it up with some sugar and then fry it in lard or butter. Add a little salt. Take your wafers, once they've been fried, and put butter on one side and sugar on the other. Moisten the sides so that they will stick together and then fry them in butter or lard. When serving, sugar them well. Likewise, you can make tartlets with pastry dough, which are sprinkled with sugar upon serving.

Meat lamprey

To make lamprey out of meat, cook some calf's head and capons. Cook them until they are well done and then remove the meat from the bones. When you have removed all the meat, mix it all together.

---

15. The title mentions only 'custard tarts' but the first line specifies that they are made from 'bastard' or counterfeit custard. Unfortunately, all the details about making the actual custard are left out; but see the recipe on pp. 80–81.
16. Though this recipe begins by making a mixture of fried chervil and sugar, it never explains what to do with this mixture. Given the recipe title, we can surmise that the wafers are somehow topped, layered or stuffed with this mixture.

la pouldre de canelle Du succre poyvre cloudz de giroffle. Et assaulce de sel & mettes tout ensemble ayez la taye de veau & l'enveloppes dedans & faictes la langue en facon de lamproye ou d'une anguille. Et la mettez cuyre dedans une tille en ung four puis faictes une saulce de lamproye de pain halle trempe en vin avec ung peu de vinaigre. Et passes la canelle & pain parmy l'estamine, ung peu de moustarde grant foyson de sucre & laisser le tout bouillir. Et au servir jectez ladi*[fol. 5r]*cte saulce dessus vostre lamproye. Et le succrez tresbien.

⁋ Taillis d'angleterre.
⁋ Pour faire taillis D'angleterre vous jecterez de la gelee blanche & vermeille & couleur d'embre pour faire du vert prenes la fueille de persil et broyes en ung mortier prenes le jus et puis elle sera verte. Pour la grise prenes de la gelee qui est dict ung peu de couleur d'ambre prenes de la canelle & le passes avec vostre gelee parmy l'estamine et elle sera grise & quant la vouldres jecter laisses la refroidir tant que le feu sera dehors, puis quant la vouldres jecter mesles la tresbien & si vous la laisses esclarcir l'aultre sera plus grise.

⁋ Noire gelee.
⁋ Pour faire noire gellee, prenes une chandelle de cire & la mettes contre vostre plat & la flambe fera noire vous prendres vostre blanche gelee & la jecteres dedans & la mesleres tresbien ensemble et elle demourra noire puis fauldra faire ung moulle pour la jecter et a chascune foys que la jecteres il fault qu'elle soit prinse.

⁋ Potaige de courge.
⁋ Item pour faire potaige de courge prendres des cogourdes & les pourbouilles et quant elles seront fort *[fol. 5v]* bouilles si les haches tresbien et les broyes en ung mortier, puis les passes avec du beurre frais et laict pour le boullon & ayes des moyeulx d'oeufz quant il sera

For spices, add some powder, cinnamon, sugar, pepper, and clove. Season with salt and mix everything together. Wrap it all in a calf's caul fat and then fashion a tongue so that it looks like a lamprey or an eel. Let it cook in the oven placed on a tile.[17] Then make a lamprey sauce with toasted bread soaked in wine with a bit of vinegar. Strain some cinnamon and bread through a sieve along with a little mustard and an abundance of sugar and then bring it all to a boil. When serving, pour this sauce over the lamprey and sprinkle with sugar.

English slices

To make English slices, throw in some white jelly as well as red and amber coloured ones. To make green jelly, take some parsley leaf and grind it up in a mortar. Add the juice and the jelly will be green. For grey-coloured jelly, take some amber coloured jelly and add some cinnamon before putting it through a sieve, which will turn it grey. When you want to turn it out, let it cool away from the heat. When you want to turn it out, mix it well and if you then let it settle, it will be even greyer.

Black jelly

To make black jelly take a wax candle and hold it up to your dish which the flame will make black. Take your clear jelly and pour it into this dish and mix it around thoroughly so that it becomes black. Then you need a mould to pour it into. When you turn it out, it needs to have set.

Gourd soup

To make gourd soup, take some bottle gourds[18] and parboil them. When they are sufficiently cooked, chop them up well and grind them in a mortar. Then put them through a sieve with fresh butter and milk in place of broth. Add some egg yolks when it comes to a

---

17. The French here indicates that the caul-wrapped stuffing should be cooked '*dedans une tille en ung four.*' The 1576 *Grand Cuisinier* reads '*dessus une tuile en un four.*' The tile in question is presumably a sort of earthenware dish.
18. Cotgrave glosses '*cougourde*' as a 'bottle gourd.'

boully & les frises dedans comme vous feries pour cresme fritte. Ayes du fin fourmaige & le mettes fondre avec & troublez & mouilles tout ensemble & y mettes ung peu de Gingembre. Ung peu de saffran, grant foison de sucre

⁋ Item pour avoir bonne gelee avec des espices vous y mettres avec d'espices cerfueil.

⁋ Potaige de piedz de mouton.
⁋ Pour faire potaige de piedz de mouton fendes les a moytie puis les mettes en une belle poelle de terre prenes du boullon de beuf qui soit gras, prenes du verjus & du vin blanc prenes pour les espices poyvre & gingembre et cloud de giroffle entiers et du saffran ung peu de Romarin haches bien deslye et le mettes estuver sur beaulx charbons tant que ilz baignent ung peu a court bouillon.

⁋ De piedz de mouton en aultre maniere.
⁋ Pour avoir une aultre maniere de piedz. Prenes du vin vermeil & du boullon de beuf qui soit gras ung peu de vinaigre prenes pour les espices de la canelle noix de muscade & romarin hachez bien deslye prenes *[fol. 6r]* des oranges pelees et tout cela frises ensemble tant qu'il vienne a court boullon et y mettes grant foyson de sucre.

⁋ Lardeaulx de venaison.
⁋ Pour faire lardeaulx de venayson ou par faulte de venaison prenes du beuf & le couppez par pieces aussi grant que quatre doigz carre & le lardez chascun de trois ou de quatre lardons mettez le cuyre en beau boullon de beuf, prenes du vin vermeil & le mettes cuyre avec, et du vinaigre. Et le mettez cuire a court boullon pour les espices canelle menue espice noix de muscade et le assavoures de sel. Aussi pour une aultre prenes du boullon de beuf de verjus gingembre pour les espices fenoil vert & laissez venir a court boullon.

⁋ Oyseau de riviere en potaige.
⁋ Pour ung oyseau de riuiere en potaige, prenes vostre oyseau par quartiers ou entier ainsi qu'il vous plaira mettre, prenez du boullon

boil and cook them as you would for a fried cream dish. Add some fine cheese and allow it to melt. Stir it all together and add liquid if necessary before putting in a bit of ginger. Add some saffron as well, with an abundance of sugar.

To make a good jelly with spices, add some chervil.[19]

Sheep's trotter pottage

To make pottage with sheep's trotters, split them in half and then put them in an earthenware pot. Add some beef broth that is fatty, some verjuice, and some white wine. For spices, add some pepper, ginger, whole clove, saffron, a bit of finely chopped rosemary. Let it stew over nice coals until it comes to a simmer.

Sheep's trotters in another way

To make another kind of trotter: add some red wine, fatty beef broth, and a bit of vinegar. For spices, add cinnamon, nutmeg, and finely chopped rosemary. Add some peeled oranges and cook it all together until it comes to a simmer. Add a copious amount of sugar.

Venison slices[20]

To make venison slices (in the absence of venison, use beef), cut the meat into four-inch square pieces and lard each piece with three or four lardons. Let it cook in a nice beef broth and add some red wine and vinegar. Let it simmer. For spices, add cinnamon, fine spice, nutmeg and season with salt. For another version, use beef broth, verjuice and ginger for spice, with green fennel and let it come to a simmer.

Waterfowl pottage

To make waterfowl in a pottage, use the bird in quarters or whole as you wish. Add some fatty beef broth and allow it to cook in a pot

---

19. This separate paragraph appears misplaced. It would fit more suitably with the preceding recipes for various jellies.
20. Godefroy glosses a *'lardel'* as a *'morceau de lard, morceau de chair.'* In this context, the small bits of meat are venison.

de beuf qui soit gras mettes le cuyre en ung pot et du verjus ou du vin blanc prenez pour les espices poyvre beau et gingembre & poyvre entier & chapplez du lard bien deslye et le mettez boullir avec saulge & ysope largement fait venir a court boullon.

[fol. 6v] ❡ Tortue de lombardie en aultre maniere.
❡ Pour une tortue de lombardi, prenez de la mouelle de beuf fort boully & puis le haches bien deslye pour les espices de la canelle et grant foison de succre hachez avec la mye de pain & moieux d'eufz & hachez tout ensemble, puis fondes du beurre ou du sain de porc en une poelle mettes ung peu vostre paste dedans la poille sur charbons et puis le descendes aulcuneffois qu'elle ne tienne a la poille, & si elle tient aulcunement si l'engresses d'ung peu de beurre. Et la servez toute chaulde & a le servir mettes du succre dessus.

❡ Tortue en poille d'une aultre sorte.
❡ Pour faire encore une tortue en poille prenes du pain blanc & le couppes par petis doigz puis les frises en beurre en une petite poille de fer. Et quant il sera cuyt vous aures des oeufz frais et les passez par dessus vostre dict pain vous le laisseres sur les dictz charbons la poille a quoy vous les cuyses la feres toute rouge sur le feu et puis vous le mettrez sur la Poille affin qu'elle se chauffe aussi bien dessus que dessoubz. Et quant il est cuict vous le mettres en ung plat et prenez de vostre gresse de vive & la gectes arriere dedans la poille et puis la chauffes [b]ien chault faictes bouillir vinaigre & cloudz de giroffle de l'eaue rose ensemble jectes dessus voz oeufz & a les servir vous *[fol. 7r]* y mettrez beaucop de sucre dessus.

❡ Esturgeon rosty.
❡ Pour esturgeon rosty il le fault fort bouillir, & quant il est fort bouilly il le fault bien nettoyer, & puis embrocher en une broche & rotisser & larder de cloud de giroffle au rostir arroser de beurre et vinaigre, puis faictes saulces dessus de sa gresse du vinaigre et menues espices & de la canelle, bien sucree, mettes y du romarin hache bien

with some verjuice or white wine. For spices, add some nice pepper, ginger, and whole peppercorns. Add some finely chopped salted pork fat and let it come to a boil with sage and hyssop. Simmer.

Lombard tart, in another way [21]

For a Lombard tart, take some beef marrow that has been boiled and chop it up finely. For spices, add some cinnamon and an abundance of sugar chopped up with breadcrumbs and egg yolks and everything chopped up together. Then, melt some butter or lard in a pan. Put a little of your dough in the pan over the coals, but take it off occasionally so that it does not stick. If it starts to stick at all, grease it with a bit of butter. Serve it hot with some sugar sprinkled over it.

Tart in a pan in another way

To make another kind of tart in a pan, take some white bread and cut it into strips then fry them in butter in a small iron pan. When it's fried, pour some fresh strained eggs over the bread. Leave them over the coals and then place another pan over the fire until it is red hot. Place the second pan over the first so that it can be heated from both above and below. When it's cooked, place it on a dish. Take your hot grease and put it back on the pan. Heat up and then boil some vinegar, clove, and rosewater together. Pour this over your eggs and when serving add a lot of sugar on top.

Roast sturgeon

For roast sturgeon, you have to first boil it vigorously. When it's boiled enough, it needs to be cleaned well. Then put it on a spit and roast it spiked with cloves. While roasting, baste with butter and vinegar. Then make a sauce for it from its own fat with some vinegar, fine spices, and cinnamon added. Add some sugar and finely chopped

---

21. See the previous recipe for *Tortue de lombardie* on pp. 62–63, above.

deslie et laisses bien confire au boullir. Et & si vous le voulez faire lyer prenes du pain hasle au dresser mettez du sucre.

⁌ Esturgeon en paste.
⁌ Pour faire petis pastes d'esturgeon vous le cuires en bon bouillon, & quant il sera cuyt vous le nestoires & le chappleres bien menu comme chair de pastes vous cueillires la gresse de vostre bouillon d'esturgeon et vous prendres des moyeulx d'oeufz avec ung peu de saffran & des espices du gingembre poyvre cloud de giroffle et puis les mettes ensemble, avec gresse de bouillon. Et s[i] elle n'est asses grasse si mectes ung peu de beurre, puis faictes des petis pastes comme pastes de veau.

⁌ Hastellees d'esturgeon.
⁌ Pour faire hastellees d'esturgeon vous coupperez *[fol. 7v]* comme vous feries du veau. Et prendres du commain & de la marjolaine. Et les mesles dedans voz hastellees & puis incontinent l'embrochez en une broche & au rostir arrouser de beurre & vinaigre & menues espices & a les envelopper n'oublies a mettre du sel, & quant vous les vouldrez servir sec si jectes hardiment vostre gresse par dessus.
⁌ Pour faire sur lesdictes hastellees saulce comme sur l'esturgeon rosty comme cy devant est dict.

⁌ Hastellees d'esturgeon en aultre maniere.
⁌ Pour faire hastellee d'esturgeon en aultre maniere. Vous prendres vostre esturgeo[n] & le couppes pour faire vos hastellees puis les rolles & les mettez en une belle toille a la mesure que vous les coulles prenes du verjus & et du vin blanc & en faictes vostre boullon, pour

rosemary and let it steep until it boils. And if you want to thicken it, add some toasted bread and when serving add some sugar.

Sturgeon in a pie

To make little sturgeon pies, cook it [the sturgeon] in a good broth and when it is cooked, clean it and chop it up finely like mince. Collect the fat from the sturgeon broth and mix it up together with some egg yolks, a bit of saffron, and for spices ginger, pepper, and clove. If there is not enough fat, add a little butter then make little pies like veal pies.

Kebabs of sturgeon [22]

To make kebabs of sturgeon, slice it up as you would veal. Take some cumin and marjoram and mix them with your kebabs. Immediately put them on a spit and during roasting, baste them with butter, vinegar, and fine spices. When basting them all over, don't forget to add some salt. And when you want to serve them dry, pour your fat over them generously.

To make a sauce for said kebabs, use the one from the roast sturgeon recipe above.

Kebabs of sturgeon in another way

To make kebabs of sturgeon in another way, take your sturgeon and fillet it to make your kebabs. Then roll up the fillets and put them in a nice earthenware dish as you roll them.[23] Take some verjuice and

---

22. Cotgrave defines *hastelettes* as 'little splints.' Godefroy writes of *hastelet* as a diminutive of '*haste*', which is defined as a '*viande rôtie*' (roast meat). Hastelets, in French and archaic English, are small spits, sometimes in English called broaches and often as haslets (now referring to a meatloaf of pig's offal). The term survives in kitchen French and English as *attelet*, nowadays an ornamental small skewer. In the language of international cookery today, they would be best described as kebabs. Clearly, the sturgeon is cut into small pieces, skewered and spit-roasted over an open flame

23. Given that this recipe is a variant on the earlier sturgeon haslet recipe, we would expect them to be skewered and roasted over an open flame. However, the instruction here is for the fillets to be rolled up and placed in a '*toille*' (a tile or earthenware dish). There are no further instructions on how to cook the rolled-up fillets. Perhaps the dish is just to hold them until they are later skewered and roasted. Or perhaps they are to be cooked in this dish, in which case they are not traditional haslets.

les espices gingembre. Et cloud de giroffle cuyses avec du verd fenoil faictes les gras de bon beurre frays boutes y ung peu de saffran & du sel & au servir mettes du vert fenoil dessus comme vous feriez en l'esturgeon bouilly.

☙ Hastellees de plyes.
☙ Pour faire hastellees de plyes coupes le et comme dit est cy dessus mettes les cuyre en boullon de verjus & du vin, prenes pour les espices gingembre, cloud de *[fol. 8r]* giroffle entier, ung peu de pomme d'orenge mettez y grant foyson de sucre romarin hache, & ayes du beurre frais et le laissez boullir a court bouillon.

☙ Pastez de carpes & d'anguilles.
☙ Pour faire de petis pastes de carpes et d'anguilles prenez voz carpes et anguilles et mettez boullir ensemble, & puis quant elles seront cuyttes ostes les herestes dehors et les chaples bien deslye, pour les espices vous prendres du gingembre & saffran & mettez des ongnons avec puis en faictes voz petis pastes et gardes a frire que vous ne brusles voz ongnons & en pouves faire en Karesme comme en aultre temps.

☙ Becquet a saulce d'angleterre.
☙ Pour faire ung becquet a saulce d'angleterre. Presnes vostre becquet fendu & le mettes en une poesle de terre, prenes du beau vin vermeil, et vinaigre et de la cervoyse ayes grant foison de romarin & le mettes cuire avec prenes bon beurre, canelle pour les espices et noix muguette, et le estuves bien sur les charbons a court bouillon.

☙ Carpes & plye pour ung becquet.
☙ Pour une carpe fresche pour ung becquet, pareillement pour une plye, prenes des oygnons, & les fri*[fol. 8v]*ses, ayes de la mye de pain blanc, & le frises tresbien, & apres jettes les oignons avec le beurre boully avec la mye de pain ensemble prenes de la canelle ung peu d'espice ung petit de sucre, de la semence de fenoil, puis frises vostre poisson & si vous le voules encores rostir sur le Gril vous le poves

white wine and make your broth. For spices, ginger and clove cooked with green fennel. Add some fat by way of good fresh butter. Throw in a bit of saffron and salt. When serving, put some green fennel on top as you would for boiled sturgeon.

Kebabs of plaice

To make kebabs of plaice, fillet them and as is mentioned above cook them in a broth of verjuice and wine. For spices, add ginger, whole clove, and a bit of orange. Add an abundance of sugar, some chopped rosemary, and fresh butter. Let it come to a simmer.

Carp and eel pies

To make little carp and eel pies, take your carp and eels and let them boil together. When they are cooked, remove all the bones and chop the flesh finely. For spices, add some ginger and saffron along with some onions. Then make your little pies and when frying, make sure not to burn your onions. They can be made during Lent or any other time.

Pike in English sauce

To make pike in English sauce, take your pike slit down the middle and put in an earthenware pan. Add some nice red wine, vinegar, and beer. Add an abundance of rosemary and allow it to cook together. Then add some good butter and both cinnamon and nutmeg for spices. Stew it well over the coals at a simmer.

Carp and plaice in place of pike

To make fresh carp in place of pike and likewise with plaice, take some onions and fry them up with some white breadcrumbs. Fry it well. Afterwards, add the onions and breadcrumbs to some melted butter. Add some cinnamon, a bit of spice, a bit of sugar, and some fennel seeds. Then fry your fish and if you still want to roast it on the grill, you can roast it.[24] If you want to serve it dry, go ahead. To

---

24. The relationship between the onion/breadcrumb mixture and the fish is not specified by the author. We might assume that the fish is to be coated in this mixture before frying. Or perhaps it is meant to top the fish after the latter has been fried.

rostir, si vous le voules servir tout sec si le serves, & pour le mettre en saulce vous le mettres en une toille et feres le boullon de vin vermeil & du vinaigre, pour espices canelle noix muguette & sucre, et le faictes boullir a court boullon et du beurre dedans.

⁌ Brochet pour ung becquet.
⁌ Et pareillement pour le brochet vous le mettres en vin blanc ou en verjus, & prendres pour les espices poyvre gingembre. Et cloud de giroffle, et du beurre saffran sucre, & le laisses confire a court boullon.

⁌ Becquet en aultre maniere.
⁌ Pour ung becquet ou une plye vous prendres des bonnes herbes, comme du persil fueille de ysope. Romarin Marjolaine moyeulx d'oeufz & broyes tout ensemble & du gingembre & mettes du beurre dedans avec vostre farce, puis farcises vostre bequcet ou plye. Et mettes boullir en une belle Toille en vin Blanc ou en verjus mettes y poivre les espices pouldre de gin*[fol. 9r]*gembre cloud & Saffran mettes du persil bouillir avec hachee bien deslie avec du beurre frais & mettes bouillir ensemble & les faictes estuver a court boullon.

⁌ Truicte fritte.
⁌ Pour une truicte frite en pagelle de fer prenes des pinguelles et des amandes et ung peu d'amidon. Et broyes en ung mortier prenes de l'eaue rose et desmelles a grant foyson de farce. Et le broyes bien & le mettes en la poelle des oublyes dessoubz au feu. Et puis mettes cuyre en farce de Sucre puis le mettes cuyre en fort feu avec la poelle aulcuneffoys qu'elle ne breusle au four & serves les froides ou aultrement.

serve it in a sauce, put it in an earthenware dish and make a broth of red wine and vinegar. For spices, add cinnamon, nutmeg, and sugar and bring it to simmer with some butter in it.

A LARGE PIKE FOR A SMALL PIKE [25]

Likewise for a pike, put it in some white wine or verjuice. For spices, add pepper and ginger. Put in also some clove, butter, and saffron and let it steep at a simmer.

PIKE IN ANOTHER WAY

For a pike or a plaice, take some nice herbs such as parsley, hyssop leaves, rosemary, and marjoram and grind them together with some egg yolks and ginger. Add some butter to this stuffing and then stuff your pike or plaice. Set it to boil in a nice earthenware dish with white wine or verjuice. Add some pepper, powdered ginger, clove, and saffron. Put in some finely chopped parsley to boil with it along with some fresh butter and let it boil together and stew at a simmer.

FRIED TROUT

For trout fried in an iron pan, take some pine nuts and almonds and a bit of starch and grind it up in a mortar. Add some rosewater and mix it up into an abundance of stuffing. Grind it up well and put it over some wafers in the pan on the fire. Allow it to cook in the stuffing with some sugar and put it over a hot fire, but take it off the fire occasionally to prevent it from burning on the stove.[26] Serve cold or otherwise.

25.   It is unclear whether the difference between these two fish is one of species or size. According to Rondelet (*L'Histoire entière des poissons*, 1558, seconde partie, p. 136), these are both names for the same fish: 'd'aucuns est nommé Bequet, ou Bechet, à cause du bec long... Plusieurs en France l'appellent Brocheton quand il est bien petit, Lanceron quand il est un peu plus grand, quand il est bien fort grand comme de trois pieds ou plus, Brochet.' [For some, it is called *bequet* or *bechet* because of its long nose...Many in France call it a *brocheton* when it is small, a *lanceron* when it's slightly larger, and *brochet* when it's really large such as three feet long or more.]
26.   There is perhaps a missing word in this recipe (*retirée*?) to indicate that the pan has to be pulled off the fire occasionally to avoid burning. It is also unclear how the stuffing figures in this recipe. Perhaps the fish is cooked on top of it or the stuffing is placed inside the fish before it is fried in the pan.

⁌ Souppe aux aulx.

⁌ Pour une souppe aux aulx, prenes du vin blanc et mettes de la moesle de beuf dedans qui ayt este fort boully et des beaulx aulx avec prenes des aulx et les pilles & les mettes bouillir avec, prenes une perdrix ou deulx rosties et les mettes par quartiers parmy pour les espices gingembre & cloud de giroffle grant foyson de sucre Romarin hache bien deslye et laisser bien boullir ensemble. Et a dresser des belles rostyes, & les mettes au fond du plat mettes a servir de canelle bien peu ou du Gingembre.

[fol. 9v] ⁌ Soupe vermeil.

⁌ Pour une souppe vermeil prenes du vin vermeil & du vinaigre de la canelle & le passes parmy une estamine prenes vostre moelle de beuf comme il a este dit par cy devant, et mettes boullir et la tenes tousjours grasse mettes des cloudz de giroffle entiers autour du plat perdrix esquatelees pigeons ou poussins mettes du romarin avec pigeons ou poussins mettez du romarin avec hache bien deslye, & semes grant foison de sucre dessus a le servir.

⁌ Fromentee.

⁌ Pour faire fromentee prenes votre fromentee & le faictes cuyre de longue main a petit feu jusques a ce qu'elle soit creve & bien cuict ce faict auras laict de vache & passeras ledict forment avec ledict laict & quant sera passe le boutteras sur les charbons en ung pot loing de la flambe, & quant commencera a boullir tu boutteras dedans sucre et ung peu de pouldre de gingembre ensemble du saffran battu & gousteras de sel puis quant verras qu'elle sera cuyte et bien assaisonnee a ton goust tu prendras des moyeufz d'oeulx selon la quantite que tu verras que tu auras de formentee & les pas[seras] par l'estamine ensemble ung petit de laict de Vache et le jecteras dedans ton froment pour la trousser et la plus troussee est la plus belle et meilleure & garde quant jecteras les oeufz dedans *[fol. 10r]* qu'elle ne soit trop chaulde. Car elle feroit tourner les oeufz & brusler.

Garlic soup

To make garlic soup, take some white wine and add some beef marrow that has been blanched. Take some nice garlic, grind it up, and add it to cook with the wine and marrow. Add one or two roast partridges, cut into quarters. For spices, add ginger, clove, an abundance of sugar, and finely chopped rosemary. Let it all boil together. When serving, place some nice slices of toasted bread in the bottom of the dish and sprinkle just a bit of cinnamon or ginger over the soup.

Red soup

To make red soup, take some red wine, vinegar, and cinnamon and put them through a sieve. Take your beef marrow as mentioned above and put it on to boil, retaining all of the fat. Add some clove. Put some quartered partridges, pigeons, or young chicken around the plate along with some finely chopped rosemary.[27] Sprinkle an abundance of sugar over the top when serving.

Frumenty

To make frumenty, take your whole-wheat berries and allow them to cook slowly over a low heat until they burst and are well done. At this point, add some cow's milk and strain the said frumenty with said milk and when it is strained, put it over the coals in a pot far from the flames. When it starts to boil, add some sugar along with some powdered ginger and ground saffron. Salt to taste. When you see that it's cooked and well seasoned to your taste, take enough egg yolks for the amount of frumenty that you are making and strain them with some cow's milk. Add this to your frumenty to thicken it. The thickest is the nicest and best. Make sure that it's not too hot when you add the eggs for they will curdle and burn.

---

27. The repetition present in the original French has been eliminated from the translation for clarity.

❧ Cresme bastarde.

❧ Pour faire cresme bastarde la feras en ceste facon Prens du vin blanc & le boute sur le feu en une terine avec une livre de bon beurre frais. Puis quant il commen[c]era a boullir tu auras mye de pain blanc esmye bien deslye que tu bouteras dedans. Et quant tu verras qu'elle se lyera tu jecteras du sucre dedans a foyson & ung petit de saffran batu. Et non gueres. Ce faict tu auras moyeulx d'oeufz passez par l'estamine avec ung petit de vin blanc que tu jecteras dedans ta poelle. Et quant verras qu'elle sera asses troussee ostes la du feu & la boute en plat sucre par dessus.

❧ Cresme fritte.

❧ Pour faire cresme fritte la feras en ceste maniere: prens bonne cresme & la boutte sur le feu avec bon beurre frais quant commencera a bouillir ayes mye de pain blanc que gecteras dedans pour la trousser & force de sucre. Ce faict ayes moyeulx d'oeufz passes par l'estamine avec laict de vache & les bouttes en ladicte poelle puis quant verres qu'elle sera asses cuycte et troussee la serviras en platz & bouteres sucre par dessus.

[fol.10v] ❧ Paste en pot.

❧ Pour faire paste en pot le feras en ceste facon tu prendras ung gigot de mouton avec de gresse de beuf et le faictz hacher bien deslye ce faict le bouteras en ung pot avec bon boullon pour espices, canelle muscade cloud de giroffle gingembre & menues espices et gouttes de sel n'oublyes a boutter force de Chastaignes en la sayson.

❧ Paste en pot de veau.

❧ Pour faire paste en pot de veau, le feras comme celuy dessus nomme. Sinon que tu y bouteras du saffran & force moyeulx d'oeufz durs lardes de beaulx cloudz de girofle.

❧ Pour venayson de sanglier.

❧ Pour faire Venaison de sanglier aux navveaulx tu bouteras ta venaison en belle piece larde de deux doigz puis la feras bouillir en

Counterfeit cream

To make counterfeit cream, you'll make it this way. Take some white wine and put it over the fire in a terrine with a pound of fresh butter. When it begins to boil, put in some finely crumbled white breadcrumbs. When you see it start to thicken, throw in a good bit of sugar and a little ground saffron. But not too much. Then take some strained egg yolks and a little white wine and add them to the pan. When you see that it's thickened enough, take it off the fire and put it in a dish with some sugar on top.

Fried cream

Make fried cream in the following way: Take some good cream and put it over the fire with some good fresh butter. When it starts to boil, add some white breadcrumbs to thicken it along with a good deal of sugar. With this done, add some strained egg yolks and cow's milk to the pan. When you see that it's sufficiently cooked and thickened, serve it in dishes and throw some sugar on top.

Potted pie

To make a potted pie, do as follows. Take a leg of mutton and some beef fat and chop them up finely. Then put it all in a pot with some good broth. For spices, add cinnamon, nutmeg, clove, ginger and fine spices and salt to taste. Don't forget to add a lot of chestnuts when they are in season.

Veal potted pie

To make veal potted pie, make it as above. Except that you will add saffron and a lot of hard-boiled egg yolks studded with nice cloves.

For boar venison

To make boar venison with turnips, take a two-inch larded piece of venison and bring it to boil with some good broth. Then add some

bon bouillon, ce faict tu bouteras des nouveaulx dedens tu auras du pain bis brusle & le feras tremper en vin et passer par l'estamine avec boullon de ladicte venaison et la bouter en ton pot, pour espices muscade menue espice et canelle, n'oublie avoir de l'oignon cuytz en bon boullon et passer par une estamine & bouter en ton pot et goustes de sel.

[fol.11r] ℭ Perdrix aulx choulx.
ℭ Item pour faire perdrix aulx choulx, prenes choulx & les faictes fort parboullir puis les haches menu puis les mettes en bon bouillon de beuf avec de bon lart pour donner goust, puis ayes du poyvre et en bouteras en lesdictz choulx, mais garde qu'ilz ne soyent trop espices, ce faict ayes tes perdrix ou bizet[z] en lieu de perdrix & les feras rostir et larderas de cloud de giroffle, puis quant seront quasi cuyctes les bouteras en tes choulx & qu'ilz soyent de bon sel.

ℭ Perdrix a la tonollette.
ℭ Pour faire perdrix a la tonnollete, prenes perdrix et les faictes rostir puis les tires et les boutes en ung pot, ce faict prenes du pain blanc hasle bien roux sans brusler et le mettes tremper en bon vin vermeil, puis quant sera trempe le passeras par l'estamine avec ung boullon de beuf ung petit de vinaigre et bouteras tout en ung pot avec les perdrix ung petit d'oignon souffrit en sain de lart pour espices canelle cloud muguette, & menues espices ung petit de sucre, et goustes de sel & n'oublyes a y boutter une poignee de Raisins de Karesme.

ℭ Capilotaste.
[fol. 11v] ℭ Item pour une capilotaste, prenes une perdrix et la haches menu. Haches vostre pain en souppes faictes ung lict de soupe en

turnips to it. Take some burnt coarse bread and soak it in wine. Then put it through a sieve with the broth of said venison and add it all to the pot. For spices, add nutmeg, fine spice, and cinnamon. Don't forget to add onion cooked in good broth and put through a sieve before adding back to the pot. Salt to taste.

Partridges with cabbage

To make partridges with cabbage, take cabbage and blanch it thoroughly then chop it finely. Then add it to a good beef broth with some nice salted pork fat to give it flavour. Then take some pepper and add it to said cabbage, but make sure it is not too spicy. Then take your partridges, or rock pigeons [28] in place of partridges, and roast them studded with cloves. When they are almost cooked, add them to the cabbage and salt them accordingly.

Partridges À LA TONNOLETTE

To make partridges *à la tonnolette*, take partridges and have them roasted, then take them off the fire and put them in a pot. Then take some darkly toasted white bread and soak it in some nice red wine. After it soaks, put it through a sieve with some beef broth and a bit of vinegar. Add it all to the pot with the partridges along with some onions fried in lard. For spices, add cinnamon, clove, nutmeg, fine spices, and a bit of sugar. Salt to taste and don't forget to add a handful of raisins.

Capirotada [29]

To make a *capirotada*, take a partridge and chop it up finely. Slice your bread into sops and put a layer of them in your dish to top with

---

28. Cotgrave glosses the *bizet* as 'A kind of small stockdove, or Queest, resembling a partridge, but much worse meat.' Belon (1555) refers to the *biset* as the Greek *Pelias* or Latin *Livia* (311–312). According to Avibase, the online world bird database, the *Columba livia* is the common rock pigeon (http://avibase.bsc-eoc.org/species.jsp?avibaseid=BBA263C235B15B88).

29. Huguet glosses *capirotade* as 'Menus morceaux de viande, hachis de viande en ragoût' [Small bits of meat, a stew of chopped meat]. This dictionary then cites the *LFE*, referring to the recipe '*soupe a la capilotade*.' Cotgrave translates it as 'A Capirotadoe; or, stued meat, compounded of Veale, Capon, Chicken, or Partridge, minced, spiced, and layered upon severall beds of cheese.'

vostre plat ung lict de vostre perdrix hachee & faictes de lict en lict tant que vostre plat en soit plein. Ce faict ayes de bon boullon de beuf auquel aura boully cinq ou six gosses d'aulx puis jecteras ton boullon en ton plat et le feras ung petit estuver sur le feu, aulcuns y bouttent du fourmaige gras.

❧ Ris.
❧ Pour faire ris prenes du ris & le laves bel et nect & faictes seicher, puis bouter en ung pot avecques bon boullon de beuf & le cuyres a petit feu de longne main ce faict y boutes ung petit de fromaige fin et ung petit de saffran battu & goste qu'il soit de bon sel.
❧ Au jour maigre le feras au laict d'amandres ou de vache.

❧Orge munde.
❧ Pour faire orge munde faictes cuyre orge jusques a ce qu'elle soit toute crevee: ce faict ayes des amandres pellees & broyez au mortier destrempees de belle eaue clere & boullue puis feras passer tondict orge & amandres ensemble par une estamine, et boutteras en ung beau pot net et le feras boullir devant le feu loing *[fol. 12r]* de la fumee, & n'oublyes a y bouter de sel raisonnablement et du Sucre. Et le remues fort qui ne preigne au pot.

❧ Laict d'amandes.
❧ Pour faire laict d'amandes ayes de belle amandes qui ayent este trempees ung jour et une nuict qu'elles se puissent plumer sans chauffer, ce faict broyez les au mortier avecques la mye de pain blanc rostis & le destrempe de belle eaue boullue. Ce faict passes par l'estamine & boutes en ung pot & faictes boullir & le salez & y bouttes du sucre.

❧ Cresmes d'amandes.
❧ Pour faire cresme d'amandes la feres en ceste facon Ayes livre et demye D'amandes trempees jour et nuict entier tellement qu'elles se puissent plumer sans chauffer puis les broyes en ung mortier et les

a layer of chopped partridge. Continue making layers of sops and partridge until the dish is full. Then take some beef broth in which you boiled five or six garlic cloves. Pour this broth into your dish and allow it to stew a bit over the fire. Some cooks add rich cheese.

Rice

To make rice, take it, wash it thoroughly, and dry it. Then put it in a pot with nice beef broth and cook it over low heat for a long time. Then add a bit of fine cheese and a bit of ground saffron and taste it to make sure it has enough salt.

On fast days, you can make it with almond or cow's milk.

French barley[30]

To make French barley, cook the barley until it has burst open. Then take some peeled almonds and grind them in a mortar and moisten them with some clear boiled water. Then put your barley and almonds through a sieve together and then into a nice clean pot. Leave it to boil in front of the fire, far from the smoke. Don't forget to add a reasonable amount of salt and sugar. Stir it well so that it doesn't stick to the bottom of the pot.

Almond milk

To make almond milk, start with some nice almonds that have soaked for a day and a night so that they can be peeled without heating them up. Once this is done, grind them in a mortar with toasted white breadcrumbs and moisten them with nice boiled water. Then put them through a sieve and into a pot. Bring it to a boil, and add salt and sugar.

Almond cream

Make almond cream in the following way. Take a pound and a half of almonds soaked for an entire day and night so that they can be peeled without heating them up. Then grind them in a mortar and

---

30. Cotgrave refers to *orge mondé* as either 'naked barlie' or 'French barlie' because it is a type of barley whose husk falls off on its own.

destrempes de vin blanc, puis les passes en une estamine et qu'elles soyent bien espesses puis les b[o]uttes sur le feu en une terrine & le faictes bouillir en le remuant qu'elle ne brusle & y bouttes du sucre & gouste de sel.

ℭItem pour faire hochepot de pigeons ayes des pigeons & les bouttez en ung pot en bon bouilon et du lart hache par lesches cloud de Giroffle Gingembre & muguette ung petit de saffran pour donner couleur, *[fol.12v]* & les faictes cuyre a court boullon, puis quant seron quasi cuyctz boutes y du verjus de grain & ung fillet de vinaigre & goustes de sel.

ℭ Pigeons confitz.

ℭ Item pour faire pigeons confitz. Prenez pigeons et les faictes bien rostir puis les boutes en ung pot. Ce faict ayes du pain blanc qui soit rosty bien roux sur le gril & le faictes tremper en bon vin vermeil et le passer par l'[e]stamine & boutes en ton pot pruneaulx qui ayent paravant boully ung boullon en eaue dattes et raisins de Karesme pour espices. Canelle batue muguette. Cloud et Gingembre et sucre & gouster de sel & gardes qu'il ne brusle. N'oublie aussi bouter ung fillet de vinaigre.

ℭ Hochepot de poussins.

ℭ Hochepot de poussi[n]s se faict comme celuy de pigeons excepte qu'il fault bouter les possins par quartiers & les larder de chascun ung lardon.

ℭ Froide saulce.

ℭ Pour faire froide saulce, prenes poussins foye et gisiers de poussins et faictes tout boullir ensemble et ung petit de lard pour donner goust puis quant seront cuictz tires les et les laisses froidir, ce faict ayes du

moisten them with white wine. Then put them through a sieve and make sure they are really thick. Then put them on the fire in a terrine and bring them to a boil while stirring so that it doesn't burn. Add some sugar and salt to taste.

To make a hodge-podge of pigeons,[31] take some pigeons and put them in a pot with some nice broth and some salted pork fat cut into slices. Add some clove, ginger, nutmeg, and a bit of saffron to give it some colour. Let it cook at a simmer. When it's almost done, add some new verjuice and a splash of vinegar.[32] Salt to taste.

Pigeon confit

To make pigeon confit, take some pigeons and roast them well then place them in a pot. Next, take some white bread that has been toasted dark on the grill, soak it in some nice red wine, and then put it through a sieve. Add to the pot some prunes that have been previously boiled for a bit in water, some dates, and some currants. For spices, add ground cinnamon, nutmeg, clove, ginger, and sugar. Salt to taste and make sure it doesn't burn. Don't forget to also add a splash of vinegar.

Hodge-podge of young chicken [33]

Chicken hodge-podge is made like that for pigeon except that you need to add the chicken quartered, with each quarter larded with one lardon.

Cold sauce

To make cold sauce, take some young chicken and some chicken livers and gizzards and boil them altogether with some salted pork fat to give them flavour. Then, when they are cooked, remove them and

---

31. This recipe is added with no space after the previous one, to which it seems entirely unrelated. Though there is a paragraph marker, there is no formal title for the recipe.
32. In his entry for *grain* Cotgrave cites a French proverb, '*Vin de grain est plus doux que n'est pas Vin de presse,*' which he then translates as 'The first wine is better than the second expression.'
33. Cotgrave refers to a *hochepot* as 'A hotch-pot, or Gallimaufrey, a confused mingle-mangle of divers things iumbled, or put together.'

[fol. 13r] pain blanc trempe en verjus et vinaigre puis ayes bled vert, marjolaine persil et ung petit de Saulge passes ton pain et verdure par l'estamine, et pour espices gingembre blanc & goustes de sel ce faict dresses en plat et ayes des oeufz durs par moytie que serutrez [servirez]* parmy vostre saulce.

⁌ Gallentine.
⁌ Pour faire gallentine, prenes anguilles ou lamproye. Aulx anguilles fendez les du long et ostes l'arete qui est du long et les couppes en deulx ou en troys et les renversez et lyes ensemble que cela soit rond comme une grosse andouille & le faictes bouillir a meille[ur] vin vermeil que vous pourres trouer ensemble quelque fueille de laurier, puis quant sera cuict descendez le du feu ayez pain brun & le trenches par trenches et le faictes hasler s[u]r le gril qu'il soit bien roulx sans brusler & bouttes tremper dedans le boullon ou aura boully vostre anguille puis quant sera trempe le passeres par lestamine le plus espes que faire se pourra, puis quant sera passe la boutterez dedans une poelle d'arain sur le feu, ou le feras fort boullir, et pour les espices menues espices de canelle. Gingembre muscade. Graine de paradis & galingal. Et fault que la muscade excede toutes les aultres espices, & n'oublies ung fillet de vinaigre et gouttes de sel le remuant fort qu'elle ne brusle *[fol. 13v]* puis quant elle aura assez bouily & qu'elle sera descendue du feu laisses la froidir & la passes derechief par l'estamine & la mettes en ung beau gardemenger et se garde douze ou quinze jours.

⁌ Carpes a l'estuvee.
⁌ Pour faire carpes a l'estuvee prenes carpes mises par troncons dedans une poelle ou Chaulderon ung petit de vin & de puree de poys verj[us] & vinaigre cloud menues espices et gingembre goustes de sel et de bon beurre frais avec une couple d'oignons.

⁌ Carpes rostyes.
⁌ Carpe rostie sur le gril tu escailleras tes carpes et les bouteras sur le

---

*   The text reads *serutrez* which seems to be a typographical mistake for *servirez*. The 1576 *Grand cuisinier* reads *serviras*.

let them cool. Next, take some white bread soaked in verjuice and vinegar, some new wheat, marjoram, parsley, and a bit of sage and put the bread and greens through a sieve. For spices, add white ginger and salt to taste. Then serve on a dish and take some hard-boiled eggs to serve with your sauce.

Galantine

To make a galantine, take some eels or lamprey. Split the eels lengthwise and remove the backbone. Cut them into two or three pieces, turn them over and tie them together so that they look round like a fat sausage. Bring them to a boil in the best red wine you can find along with some bay leaves. When it's cooked, take it off the fire. Take some dark bread, cut it into slices, and toast it over the grill until it's dark but not burned. Soak it in the broth used to cook your eel. When it's soaked, put it through a sieve but keep it as thick as possible. When it's strained, put it in a brass pan over the fire and boil it vigorously. For spices add fine spices, cinnamon, ginger, nutmeg, grains of paradise, and galingale. The nutmeg should dominate. Don't forget a splash of vinegar and some salt to taste, stirring it often so that it doesn't burn. When it's done and taken off the fire, let it cool and then strain it again. Place it in a nice pantry and it will keep for twelve to fifteen days.[34]

Stewed carp

To make stewed carp, take carp cut into steaks and put them in a pan or cauldron. Add a bit of wine, some puréed peas, verjuice, vinegar, clove, fine spice, ginger, and salt to taste. Add some nice fresh butter and a couple of onions.

Roast carp

For carp roasted on the grill, scale your carp and put them on the

---

34. Though it is not explicitly stated in the recipe, we can presume that the boiled bread/spice mixture and the fish should be put together before the dish is cooled and stored.

gril et les feras tresbien rostir, ce faict auras ung petit de pain hasle sur le gril trempe en vin vermeil et vinaigre & passeras par l'estamine asses cler, & ce fait le feras bouillir sur le feu, pour espice cloud, muscades et gingembre sucre & des raisins de Karesme et goustes de sel.

⁋ Carpes boullies.
⁋ Aultrement peult faire lesdictes carpes boullir en vin et eaue verjus vinaigre, et sel ung petit saulge, et ysope et se doibt menger a la saulce vert ou persil, et vinaigre.

[fol. 14r] ⁋ Paste en pot de carpes.
⁋ Tu en peulx aussi faire paste en pot. Escorcher la dicte carpe prendre toute la chair & la haches avec ung oignon puis la bouttes en ung pot avec ung petit de puree de pois beurre frais. Clodz Muscades, gingembre & goustes de sel. Aulcuns y boutent de Chastaignes paravant brasilles & pellees & mises dedans tondit paste en pot.

⁋ Carpes aulx bignetz.
⁋ Tu peulx aussi prendre les testes desdictes carpes & leur faire ung boullon & les laisser froidir, puis prendre des oeufz & les battre fort avec ung petit de pouldre blanche & de saffran & de sel menu & tremper les testes de carpes dedans, & les frire a beau beurre et semblera que ce soyent bignetz. Tu le peulx succrer si tu veulx.

⁋ Brocheton rosty.
⁋ Pour habiller ung Brocheton le feras rostir sur le gril & l'inciseras puis l'arrouseras de beurre avec quelque fueille de saulge ce faict auras de l'ongnon que friras en bon beurre frais puis quant sera frit auras du verjus de la moustarde & ung fillet de vinaigre, de la pouldre blanche & gouster de sel & faictes tout bouillir ensemble et jectes sur vostre brocheton.

grill. Roast them well. Then take a bit of bread toasted on the grill and moisten it in red wine and vinegar before putting it through a fine sieve. Next, put it on to boil over the fire. For spices, add clove, nutmeg, ginger, sugar and raisins. Salt to taste.

Boiled carp

Otherwise, you can prepare said carp by boiling them in wine, water, verjuice, and vinegar. Add salt, a bit of sage, and hyssop. It should be eaten with green sauce or with parsley and vinegar.

A potted pie of carp

You can also make a potted pie with it. Skin said carp, remove all the flesh and chop it up with an onion. Then put it in a pan with a bit of puréed peas and fresh butter. Add clove, nutmeg, ginger, and salt to taste. Some add chestnuts that have been roasted [35] and peeled to said potted pie.

Carp fritters [36]

You can also take the heads of said carp and make a broth of them before allowing them to cool. Then take some eggs and whip them well with a bit of white powder, saffron, and fine salt. Soak the carp heads in this mixture. Then fry them in nice butter and it will seem as if they are fritters. You can sprinkle sugar on them if you wish.

Roast pickerel

To prepare pickerel, roast it on the grill. Score it and then brush butter on it with some sage leaves. Then fry some onion in nice fresh butter. When it's fried, add some verjuice, mustard, a splash of vinegar, and some white powder. Salt to taste, bring to a boil together, and then pour it over your pickerel.

35. Cotgrave glosses the verb *brasiller* as 'To rost, broyle, or boyle on quick coals, or hot embers.'
36. Cotgrave glosses *bignetz* as 'Little round loaves, or lumps made of fine meale, oyle, or butter, and reasons; bunnes, Lenten loaves; also flat fritters made like small pancakes.' Given the absence of flour in this recipe, the carp heads would not be true fritters, but simply glazed with an egg mixture and fried.

[fol. 14v] Aultrement faictes rostir vos brochetons comme dessus est dict, prenes du beurre frais & le faictes fondre en la poelle tant qu'il commence a devenir roux, puis ayes du persil hache & le jecteres en la poelle Du verjus de grain en la saison pouldre blanche ung petit de saffran destrempe en verjus vieil et goustes de sel & faictes tout boullir ensemble et jectes sur vostre brocheton.

ℂ Brochet boully.
ℂ Le gros brochet se veult habiller en ceste facon, prenes ung gros brochet & le fendes par quartiers & le baconner de sel par l'espace de troys heures. Ce faict le faictes boullir en bon vin Blanc verjus ung petit de vinaigre & sel ce faict le boutes en Beurre et moustarde.
ℂ Aultrement le faire bouillir comme dessus est dit & menger a la saulce verte & ne veult estre fort salle.

ℂ Brochet a l'estuvee.
ℂ Aultrement prenes ung brochet gros ou moyen fendu par quartiers ou coupe par troncons puis boutez en ung chaulderon du verjus du beurre frais cloud muguette batue gingembre ung petit de romarin et persil, et sauge & gostes de sel et n'oublyez a y bouter une orenge ou deulx coupes par rouelles selon la quantite que appresteres dudict brochet.

[fol. 15r] ℂ Brochet frit.
ℂ Aultrement prens ton brochet fendu par quartiers puis le friras en beurre affine apres le tireras & bouteras dessus du verjus vieil et du jus de l'orange ou du citron.

ℂ Perche boullie.
ℂ Pour habiller une perche ou plusieurs faictes les bouillir en eaue sel verjus vinaigre & la boutes au persil & vinaigre.

Otherwise, roast the pickerel as above, then take some fresh butter, melt it in a pan, and cook it until it starts to brown. Then throw in some chopped parsley, some new verjuice in season, white powder, and a bit of saffron steeped in old verjuice. Salt to taste, bring it all to a boil, and pour over your pickerel.

Boiled pike

A large pike should be prepared in the following way. Take a large pike and split it into quarters. Cure it in salt for about three hours.[37] Then boil it in good white wine, verjuice, a little vinegar and salt. Then add some butter and mustard.

Otherwise, boil it as above and eat it with green sauce. It should not be over salted.

Stewed pike

Otherwise, take a large or medium-sized pike and split it into quarters or slice it into steaks. Then place it in a cauldron with some verjuice, fresh butter, clove, ground nutmeg, ginger, a bit of rosemary, parsley, and sage. Salt to taste. Don't forget to add an orange or two cut into slices according to the amount of said pike that you are preparing.

Fried pike

Otherwise, take pike split into quarters and fry it in clarified butter.[38] Afterwards, remove it and sprinkle on some old verjuice and the juice of either orange or citron.

Boiled perch

To prepare one perch or several, boil them in water with salt, verjuice, vinegar, and add some parsley and vinegar.[39]

---

37. La Curne defines the verb *baconner* as 'to salt,' but adds a further description that suggests it is more like brining: 'C'est-à-dire saler en mettant dans un baquet d'eau salée' [That is, to salt by placing in a bucket of salted water]. It is unclear from this recipe whether the fish is to be coated in salt or soaked in salted water before boiling.
38. Cotgrave gives one translation of *affiné* as 'purified'. We might assume that it refers here to a kind of clarified butter.
39. It is unclear why vinegar shows up twice in this recipe unless the fish is to be boiled in vinegar and then removed and garnished with the parsley and vinegar.

❧ Aultrement prenes amandes pellez broyez au mortier destrempes de ung petit de vin blanc et ung fillet de verjus vieil et passer tout par l'estamine. Puis bouter en ung petit pot avec ung petit de Gingembre blanc en pouldre du sucre par raison & gouster de sel.

❧ Perche fritte.
❧ Tu la pourras peller & fariner & frire en bon beurre ung petit de verjus vieil dessus avec jus d'orenge.
❧ Aultrement est bonne en paste pelee paravant et mise au chaudune.

❧ Perche en paste.
❧ La bresme se veult habiller en ceste facon prenez une bresme escaillee cavee & incisee mise sur le gril ung petit de feu nect dessoubz qu'elle ne prengne au Gril, et *[fol. 15v]* l'arrouser souvent de beurre fondu, puis quant sera cuycte prenes beurre frais & le faictes fondre en la poelle quant commencera a roustir ayes persil hache verjus de grain pouldre blanche ung petit de saffran batu destrempe de verjus vieil gouster de sel et faictes tout bouillir ensemble & jectes sur vostre bresme.

❧ Bresme.
❧ Aultrement quant ladicte bresme sera cuicte rostie ou bouillie ayes des moieulx passes par l'estamine avecques du verjus du beurre, fondu du verjus desgruin [des grain] du persil hache, & faictes tout boullir ensemble et goustez de sel & jectes sur vostre bresme. Tu la peux aussi menger au persil et au vinaigre ou en paste et elle est tresbonne.

Otherwise, take some peeled almonds, grind them in a mortar, and moisten them with a bit of white wine and a splash of old verjuice. Put it through a sieve. Then put it into a little pot with a bit of ground white ginger, a reasonable amount of sugar, and salt to taste.[40]

Fried perch

You can skin it, flour it, and fry it in good butter. Sprinkle over a bit of old verjuice and orange juice.

Otherwise, it's good in a pie, skinned beforehand and put in a *chaudumé*.[41]

Perch pie

Bream should be prepared in the following way.[42] Take a gutted and scaled bream that has been scored and place it over the grill with a brisk fire below so that it doesn't stick to the grill. Baste it often with melted butter. When it's cooked, take some fresh butter and melt it in a pan. When it starts to brown, add chopped parsley, new verjuice, white powder, and a bit of ground saffron. Moisten with some old verjuice, salt to taste, and bring it all to a boil before pouring over your bream.

Bream

Otherwise, when said bream is cooked, whether roasted or boiled, take some egg yolks and put them through a sieve along with some verjuice, melted butter, new verjuice, and chopped parsley. Boil it all together and salt to taste before pouring it over your bream. You can also eat it with parsley and vinegar or in a pie and it's very good.

---

40. This recipe is separated from the previous one, but it has no title. This could be another garnish for the boiled perch.
41. Godefroy refers to *chaudumé* as a 'sorte de sauce' [a kind of sauce] (referring to Taillevent's *Viandier*) and then to *chaudumee* as a 'plat de poisson accommodés à la sauce appelée chaudumé' [a fish dish garnished with the sauce called *chaudumé*] (referring to the *Ménagier de Paris*).
42. The title reads *Perche en paste*, but the recipe itself refers to *bresme*. Since the actual recipe does not seem to be for a pâté or a pie, it may be that this recipe title simply does not correspond to the recipe at all.

⁋ Anguilles boullies.
⁋ Les anguilles se veullent apprester en ceste maniere. Tu escorcheras ladicte anguille et la feras en troncons et feras bouillir, puis quant sera boullie en vin vinaigre verjus, eaue & sel la tireras et la feras de rechef rostir sur le gril tu auras ung petit de verjus vinaigre & beurre & feras tout boullir ensemble & jecteras sur ton anguille ung petit de sel.

⁋ Anguilles rosties.
[fol. 16r] ⁋ Aultrement tu feras rostir ladicte anguille en la broche ou sur le gril puis auras ung petit de pain hasle sur le gril que feras tremper en vin vermeil ung filet de vinaigre et feras tout passer par l'estamine assez chault puis le boutteras en la leschefrite qui sera dessoubz ton anguille ung petit de beurre muscades canelle. Menue espice, & cloud et gouster de sel & ferez tout boullir ensemble.

⁋ Anguilles en potaige.
⁋ Aultrement peulx faire potaige de ladtcte anguille, prenes l'anguille mise par troncons & la faictz ung petit frire en beurre jusques qu'elle soit ung petit rossette: ce faict la bouteras en ung pot, puis auras de pain hasle sur le gril lequel feras tremper en puree de poys puis quant sera trempe le passeras par l'estamine avec ung petit de vin vermeil, verjus & un fillet de vinaigre & bouteras tout on ton pot ou est la dessusdicte anguille, et feras tout bouillir ensemble, et pour espices muscades batues, cloud, menue espice & saffran ce faict tu auras des ongnons paravant boullis & cuictz en eaue et puree de poys que tu passeras par l'estamine et bouteras en ton pot & gousteras de sel.

⁋ Anguille en paste.
⁋ Les anguilles se peuvent parellement bouter en *[fol. 16v]* paste & ilz sont bonnes.
⁋ Loches & goujons requierent estre frites bien roussettes en bon beurre, du verjus dessus et du jus de l'orenge.
⁋ Se tu veulx farcir lesdictes loches ou goujons prens du laict de vache & le boute en ung bacin ung petit de persil hache menu & marjolaine, des moyeulx d'oeufz durs haches menu ung petit de pouldre blanche

Boiled eel

Eel should be prepared in the following way. Skin said eel, slice it into steaks, and boil it. When it has boiled in wine, vinegar, verjuice, water, and salt, remove it and roast it on the grill again. Boil a bit of verjuice, vinegar, and butter together and pour it over your eel with a bit of salt.

Roast eel

Otherwise, you can roast said eel on a spit or on the grill. Then take a bit of bread toasted over the grill that you will then soak in red wine and a splash of vinegar. Put it all through a sieve while still rather warm. Then pour it into the dripping pan that is below your eel with a bit of butter, nutmeg, cinnamon, fine spice, and clove. Salt to taste and let it all boil together.

Eel pottage

Otherwise you can make a pottage of said eel. Take the eel sliced into steaks and fry it lightly in butter until is just begins to turn golden brown. Then put it in a pot. Take some bread toasted on the grill and soaked in puréed peas. When it is soaked, put it through a sieve with a bit of red wine, verjuice, and a splash of vinegar. Pour this mixture into your pot with the aforementioned eel and boil together. For spices, add ground nutmeg, clove, fine spice, and saffron. Then take some onions boiled and cooked in water ahead of time and some puréed peas and put them through a sieve. Pour it into your pot and salt to taste.

Eel pie

Eel can be prepared in a pie and they are good.

Loach and gudgeon need to be fried until just golden brown in good butter with verjuice and orange juice sprinkled on top.

If you want to stuff said loach and gudgeon, take some cow's milk and put it in a basin. Add a bit of finely chopped parsley, rosemary, chopped hard-boiled egg yolks, a bit of white powder, and a bit of

puis ung petit de sel blanc, et ce fait prens tes loches et goujons et les jecte dedans toutes vives, & elles se farciront de elles mesmes.

⁌ Escrevisses.
⁌ Les escrevisses se veullent boullir en vinaigre et verjus et sel largement plus que aultre poisson.
⁌ Gardons & vendoyses se doibvent rostir sur le gril et mis au beurre & verjus. Aulcuns les veullent frire et escailler premierement du verjus & de l'orenge et du sel menu.

⁌ Truicte boullye.
⁌ La truicte se veult boullir en vin verjus vinaigre & sel puis cuyses avec persil et vinaigre. Aulcuns les font rostir sur le gril lardes de clod de giroffle puis feras la saulce en ceste facon du vin vermeil sucre canelle gingembre & vinaigre & goustez de sel: puis faire *[fol. 17r]* [t]out bouillir ensemble, puis gecter ladicte saulce sur [l]a truicte, aultrement sont bonnes en paste.

⁌ Saulmon frais rosty.
⁌ Le saulmon frais se veutt habiller en ceste facon larde de cloudz de giroffle & faire cuire en une poelle devant le feu avecques du beurre frais & pareille saulce comme a la truicte. Aultrement faire cuire ledict saulmon avec carpes et brochetz, puis quant sera cuyt prendre toute la gresse qui est dessus le chaulderon ung fillet de vinaigre & verjus pouldre blanche avec du persil hache, & faictes tout cuire ensemble puis jectes sur vostre saulmon avec le jus de une orenge.

⁌ Saulmon boully.
⁌ Le saulmon sale faictes le bouillir en grant eaue puis quant sera cuyt tires le dehors du chaulderon puis aye[s] de l'ongnon hache menu, du persil huille d'olyve du vinaigre & jectes sur vostre saulmon.

white salt. Then take your loach and gudgeon and throw them in alive. They will stuff themselves.[43]

Crayfish

Crayfish should be boiled in vinegar, verjuice, and salt, more so than other fish.

Roach and dace should be roasted on the grill and served in butter and verjuice.[44] Some prefer to fry them scaled ahead of time, garnished with verjuice, orange, fine salt.

Boiled trout

Trout should be boiled in wine, verjuice, vinegar, and salt. Then cook it with some parsley and vinegar. Some roast it on the grill larded with clove. Then make a sauce in this way with red wine, sugar, cinnamon, ginger, and vinegar. Salt to taste and boil it all together. Then pour said sauce over the trout. Otherwise, they are good in a pie.

Fresh roasted salmon

Fresh salmon should be prepared in the following way. Lard it with cloves and cook it in a pan in front of the fire with some fresh butter. Make the same sauce as for trout. Otherwise, cook said salmon with carp and pike. When it's done remove the fat that rises to the top. Add to it a splash of vinegar, verjuice, white powder, and some chopped parsley. Boil it all together and then pour it over your salmon with the juice of one orange.

Boiled salmon

Boil salted salmon in a large quantity of water. When it's cooked, remove it from the pot. Then add finely chopped onion, parsley, olive oil, and vinegar. Pour this over the salmon.

---

43. The relative cruelty of this practice notwithstanding, one does wonder about cooking these fish with all the innards left inside.
44. Cotgrave glosses *gardons* as 'fresh-water fish that resembles chevin'. In modern French, *gardon* is translated as roach, a freshwater fish similar to the North American sunfish. *Vendoyse* is referred to as dace or dare-fish, a small fish akin to a minnow.

❡ Saulmon en paste.
❡ Le saulmon frais est pareillement bon en paste.
❡ Mullet le mullet se veult rostir sur le gril puis faire la saulce en ceste facon prenez bon beurre et le fondes en la poelle tant qu'il commence a devenir roulx ayes persil hache du verjus vieil et nouve[a]u ung pe*[fol. 17v]*tit de saffran pouldre blanche & goustez de sel & faictes tout bouillir ensemble & jectes sur le mullet.

❡ La vive.
❡ Pareillement la vive se veult habiller sont aussi bonnes lesdictes vives boullues et mises au chauldumer le mullet est aussi fort bon en paste.

❡ Marsouin.
❡ Le marsouin se veult habiller en ceste facon mis par trenches & embrocher en la broche larde de claud de Giroffle puis quant sera cuyt fera la saulce en ceste facon prenez vinaigre verjus, et une tostee de pain bien noir sans brusler et passer par l'estamine avec ung petit de vin, & pour les espices muscades et menue espice et gostez de sel. Et faictes tout boullir ensemble, et jectez sur ledict marsouin.

❡ Marsouin en potaige.
❡ Ledict Marsouin se peult aussi bouter en paste, & il est fort bon, ledict marsouin se peult bouter en potage prenez ledict marsouin par petites pieces boutes en ung pot avec puree de poys & le faictes boullir ung boullon. Ce fait ayes de bon naveaulx paravant cuictz en bon boullon lesquelz bouteras en ton pot avec ton marsouin tu auras du pain hasle sur le gril bien noir *[fol. 18r]* sans brusler que tu feras tremper en vin vermeil, puis passer le tout par l'estamine & bouter

Salmon Pie

Fresh salmon is equally good in pastry.

Mullet

Mullet should be roasted on the grill. Then make a sauce in the following way. Take some nice butter and melt it in a pan until it starts to brown. Add some chopped parsley, old and new verjuice, a bit of saffron, and white powder. Salt to taste. Boil it all together and pour it over the mullet.

Weever[45]

Likewise, the weever should be prepared...[46] said weever are also good boiled and placed in a *chaudumé*. Mullet is also good in a pie.

Porpoise

Porpoise should be prepared in the following way. Cut it into slices and put it on the spit larded with clove. When it's cooked, make a sauce in the following way. Take vinegar, verjuice, and toasted bread, dark but not burned, and put them through a sieve with a bit of wine. For spices, add nutmeg, fine spice, and salt to taste. Boil it all together and pour over said porpoise.

Porpoise Pottage

Said porpoise can also be put in a pie and it is really good. Said porpoise can be put in a pottage. Take said porpoise cut into small pieces and put it in a pot with some puréed peas. Boil it for just a moment. Then take some good turnips cooked ahead of time in a nice broth, which you will put in the pot with the porpoise. Take some bread toasted dark on the grill but not burned and soak it in some

---

45. Cotgrave glosses this as 'The Quauiuer, or sea-Dragon.' The modern French *vive* is translated as weever, a fish with venomous spines (family *Trachinidae*). Rondelet discusses this fish in great detail in *Histoire entière des poissons*, chapter 10 (pp. 238–241).
46. There seem to be some missing words in this recipe because it is not explained how this fish should be prepared. For the *chaudumé*, see note 41, above.

en ton pot. Pour espices, muscades cloud batu gingembre [canelle] et menues espices troyes ou quattre ongnons bien cuictz et passer par l'estamine & bouter en son dict pot & gouster de sel. Et faire tout boullir ensemble et est fort bon en ceste maniere il se peult aussi saller & faire cuyre puis bouter aulx poys passes & est fort bonne. Et pareillement la balaine.

⁋ Esturgeon boully.
⁋ L'esturgeon est le poisson de la mer qui est prefere aulx aultres & ce doit cuyre en ceste facon, prenez bon vin verjus & vinaigre & sel saulge & ysope fenoil & le faire fort cuyre & quant il est cuyt laisses le refrioidir & mengez au persil & vinaigre.

⁋ Turbot.
⁋ Le turbot se cuyct pareillement. Et aussi faict la barbue.

⁋ La plye.
⁋ La plye se peult cuyre en pareil boullon. Mais elle ne se veult pas tant cuyre. Le torbot aussi L'esturgeon sont bons en paste. *[fol. 18v]*

⁋ Huytres frittes.
⁋ Les huytres escaillees se veullent laver puis faire ung boullon en sel & de l'ongnon & eaue. Puis les tirer & essuyer et frire en bon beurre et bouter menue espice par dessus.

⁋ Huytres a l'estuvee.
⁋ Aultrement les peult faire estuver entre deulx platz avec du beurre & poyvre & gouster de sel aultrement les peulx apres qu'ilz sont parboullies hacher menu avec ung ongnon ou deulx. Puis les bouter en ung pot avec du beurre menues espices Gingembre Cloud & muscades. Et gouster de sel. Et le faire cuire comme ung paste en pot.

red wine. Put it through a sieve and then into your pot. For spices, add nutmeg, ground clove, ginger, cinnamon, and fine spice along with three or four well-cooked onions and put it all through a sieve before adding to your pot and salting to taste. Boil it all together and it is very good in this way. It can also be salted and then cooked with garlic and puréed peas and that is very good. Likewise for whale.

Boiled sturgeon

Sturgeon is the fish of the sea preferred before all others and it should be cooked in the following way. Take good wine, verjuice, vinegar, salt, sage, hyssop, and fennel and cook them together thoroughly. When the fish is cooked, allow it to cool and eat with parsley and vinegar.

Turbot

Turbot can be cooked in the same way. Same for brill.[47]

Plaice

Plaice can be cooked in the same kind of broth. But it should not be cooked as long. Turbot as well as sturgeon are good in a pie.

Fried oysters

Shelled oysters should be cleaned in water. Then cook them in a broth of salt, onion, and water. Then remove them and wipe and fry them in good butter. Sprinkle some fine spice on them.

Stewed oysters

Otherwise, you can stew them between two plates with some butter and pepper; salt to taste. Otherwise, after blanching them, you can chop them up finely with one or two onions. Then put them in a pot with some butter, fine spices, ginger, clove, and nutmeg. Salt to taste. Cook them as you would a potted pie.

---

47. Cotgrave explains *barbue* as 'a kind of lesse Turbot, or Turbot-like fish, called by some, a Dab, or Sandling.' A dab is a flat fish resembling a flounder, but brill – the usual modern translation of *barbue* – is somewhat better to eat.

❡ Huytres en escailles.
❡ Lesdictes huytres en escailles sont bonnes quant sont fresches aulcuns apres qu'elles sont ouvertes boutent ung petit de beurre et de poyvre dessus puis les boutent ung petit dessus les Charbons avec les escailles pour les amortir.

❡ Seiches frittes.
❡ Les seiches se veullent peller & nectoyer puis les faire parbouillir & y bouter du sel & les faire boullir tant qu'ilz soyent bien tendres puis quant seront parboul*[fol. 19r]*lus les tirer & essuyer & frire en bon beurre avec de l'ongnon puis quant seront frites bouter par dessus pouldre blanche ou menues espices. Et le jus de l'orenge aultrement quant les dessusdictes seiches sont parboullyes les peulx hacher comme tripes & faire frire en beuree blanc & y bouter de la moustarde & pouldre blanche et de l'ongnon hache ensemble que se soyent tripes.

❡ Paste de coste de blettes.
❡ Lavez des costes de blettes faictes les blanchir avec oygnons, puis tirez sur ung aix & les hachez bien menu avec gresse de beuf peu de lart hache apart, puis bon bouillon que mettres en une poelle a frire avec voz costes. Et gresses faictes faire sur les charbons & mettes au pot pouldre blanche bien peu de saffran verjus boully sur charbon en remuant et y passes de mye de pain avec deulx ou troys moyeulx D'oeuf pour le lyer et ce faict comme paste en pot aulcuneffoys y mettes des moyeulx d'oeulx avecques larde de cloud de Giroffle mouelle de beuf y est bonne beurre aux jours maigre comme dessus.

❡ Abremont de laict.
❡ Prenes Laict gras boully en pot avec Bouillon gras avec amidon ou mie de pain pouldre blanche petit de saffran, passes tout avec vostre laict. Et quant *[fol. 19v]* [i]l sera boully verses voz oeufz dedans en remuant tous[j]ours sucre sel assez lye, dressez sur chappons ou poul[l]es ou en plat en facon de dragee.

Oysters in the shell

Said oysters in the shell are good when they're fresh. After the shells have opened, some throw in a bit of butter and pepper and then put them directly over coals in the shell to kill them.

Fried cuttlefish

Cuttlefish should be peeled and cleaned before blanching them. Add some salt and boil them until they are tender. When they are so boiled, remove them and then wipe and fry them in good butter with some onion. When they are fried, sprinkle on some white powder or fine spices along with the juice of one orange. Otherwise, when said cuttlefish are boiled, you can chop them up like tripe and fry them in white butter. Add some mustard, white powder, and chopped onion to them as if they were tripe.

Chard pie

Clean the chard ribs and blanch them along with some onions. Spread them out on a chopping block and chop them finely with some beef fat and a little salted pork fat chopped separately. Then put some nice broth in a pan to cook your chard and fat in. Cook over the coals and add to the pot white powder, just a bit of saffron, and verjuice. Boil it over the coals while stirring. Add some breadcrumbs sieved with two or three egg yolks to thicken as you would for a potted pie. Sometimes you can add egg yolks to it spiked with clove. Beef marrow is good in it, butter on fast days as above.

White milk sauce [48]

Take some creamy milk boiled in a pot with some rich broth, starch or breadcrumbs, white powder, and a bit of saffron. Sieve it all with your milk. When it has come to a boil, pour your eggs in while stirring constantly. Add sugar and salt. It should be rather thick. Serve it over capons or chicken or in a dish with sugared almonds.

---

48. The word *abremont* does not appear in any standard dictionaries. Given the details of the recipe, it would be a white sauce somewhat akin to a béchamel with no butter.

❡ Brochet.
❡ Prenez brochet vif de la longueur de deulx piedz, despeces le par troncons sans l'escharder et le mettes bouillir tout incontinent avec moytie eaue & vin blanc peu de bon verjus et vinaigre mettes six cloux de giroffle entiers demy noix de muscat pouldre en este romarin marjolaine, sarriettez groiselles, en yver deux ongnons coupes par rouellles assembles sesdictes herbes & les faictes bouillir en la casse ou poelle a bon feu cler ung petit avant que on se mette a table & tournez en cuysant une foys ou deulx & le faictes tant cuyre qu'il n'y demeure gueres de murettes le main que pourres sans boullir serves tout chault avec vostre boullon ou murette par dessus carpes barbeaulx excepte qu'il fault du vin vermeil aulx carpes le tout sans escharder.

❡ Poree.
❡ Prenes bettes espinars laictues Borraches persi[l] serfueil savoree Blanchissez en eaue boullante hachez bien menu Broyez fort au mortier ayes lart coupps en riblette & le faictes fondre en poelle a petit feu puis *[fol. 20r]* renverses en ung plat & remettes vostre lart en vostre poelle pour faire voz porees sur charbon en le remuant ensemble de bon boullon de beuf doit estre asses espez. Mettes en pot et mettes sur le charbon pour achever de cuyre sel. Et quant la servires mettez voz Riblettes par dessus ou lart par lesches pour este & printemps les plus vertes sont belles.

❡ Poreaulx.
❡ Poreaulx le blanc parboully avec ongnons hachez menus assemblez de bon boullon en pot pouldre blanche saffran assez lye cuict en remuant oyes sallees d'ung jour ou de deulx boully par quartiers. Et quant seront cuyctz tires les & mettes poreaulx dessus perdris rostyes du lievre rosty cuictz par quartiers.

Pike

Take a two-foot long live pike and chop it into steaks without skinning first. Put it on to boil immediately in half water and half white wine, a little good verjuice and vinegar. Add six whole cloves and half a nut of powdered nutmeg. In summer, use rosemary, marjoram, savory, and gooseberries. In winter, two onions cut into rounds. Combine said herbs and boil them in a dripping pan or pot over a bright fire shortly before sitting down to dinner. Turn [the pike] once or twice while cooking and let it cook until hardly any fish broth remains, the least possible without boiling. Serve it hot with your broth or fish broth[49] poured over top of carp or barbel except that you must use red wine with carp, all of it without skinning them first.

Herb pottage

Take chard, spinach, lettuce, borage, parsley, chervil, and savory and blanch them in boiling water. Chop them up finely and grind in a mortar. Take some salted pork cut in slices and melt them in a pan over low heat. Then turn them out onto a dish and retain the fat in the pan in order to cook your herbs over the coals. Stir them together along with some nice beef broth. It should be rather thick. Put it in a pot and on the coals to finish cooking. Salt. When you serve it, put your slices of salt pork on top or slices of lard. In summer and spring, the greenest are beautiful.

Leeks

Blanch the white parts with finely chopped onion. Add them to a pot of nice broth along with white powder and saffron. It should be rather thick. Cook while stirring some goose salted for one or two days and boiled in quarters. When they are cooked, remove them and put your leeks over roast partridge or hare cooked in quarters.

---

49. Cotgrave translates *murette de poisson* as 'Fish-broth, or sawce wherein fish hath been throughly boyled.'

⁌ Couldres Cocombres.
⁌ Couldre blanches cocombres jaulnes pour faire couldre il fault du lait pouldre blanche verj[u]s ou moyeulx d'oeufz Cocombres avec moyeulx D'oeufz ou avec laict, passez par l'estamine avec verjus Saffran boully ensemble.

⁌ Ris.
⁌ Prenez d[u] boullon de Chappon ou aultre pouldre blanche sucre sel & quant sera cuyt dress[e]s sur chapons *[fol. 20v]* boully. Et en pourrez faire la moitie jaulne que servires sur la moytie du chapon & l'aultre avec grosse dragee & qu'elle ne soit trop espesse.

⁌ Naveaulx.
⁌ Naveaulx au mouton beuf peu de lart devant que les tires mettes y une branche de saulge pour bailler goust a toute venaison sallee.

⁌ Poys de lundy.
⁌ Poys quant avant peu boully, prenes le premier boullon & mettes cuire avec eaue froide et peu de lart entrelarde. Et quant ilz seront presque cuyctz retirez les du feu & les mettes sur charbon en remuant puis bon boullon mettes dedans avec menue herbe hachez. Asses espices saffran si vous voulez au servir coupez lart par rides & serves par dessus ou eschinee ou venayson de sanglier salle bien cuict.

⁌ Paste en pot de mouton.
⁌ Prenez gigot de mouton et ostes le peau par dessus & tires la chair d'avec les os & la hachez le plus menu que pourrez avec gresse de beuf ou de mouton et peu de lart gras avec oygnons nouveaulx. Mettez en pot avec bon boullon faictes cuyre sur charbon en remuant aucuneffoys casses les os par petis morceaulx & laissez *[fol. 21r]* cuire tout ensemble, menues espices. Pouldre blanche saffran avec cloudz de Giroffle quatre ou cinq entiers, destrempes avec peu de verjus &

Gourds, cucumbers[50]

White gourds and yellow cucumbers. To make gourds, you need milk, white powder, verjuice, or egg yolks. Cucumbers with egg yolks or milk, put through a sieve with verjuice and saffron and boiled together.

Rice

Take some capon broth or other kind and add white powder, sugar, and salt. When it's cooked, serve it over boiled capons. You can also make half of it yellow, which you will then serve over half of the capon and the other with large candies. It should not be too thick.

Turnips

Turnips with mutton, beef, and a bit of salted pork fat. Before removing them, add a branch of sage to give it flavour. Eat with all salted venison.

Monday peas

After an initial boil, strain the first broth and put them on to cook with some cold water and a bit of streaky bacon added. When they are almost cooked, take them off the fire and put them over the coals while stirring. Add some nice broth along with finely chopped herbs. Add some spices, saffron if you wish. When serving, chop up the bacon into strips and serve them on top or with fatback or well-cooked salted boar venison.

Mutton potted pie

Take a leg of mutton and remove the skin from it and then the meat from the bone. Chop it as finely as you can along with beef or mutton fat and a bit of salted pork fat and some new onions. Put it in a pot with some nice broth. Cook it over the coals, stirring occasionally. Break up the bones into small pieces and let them cook along with it. Add some fine spices, white powder, saffron, and four or five whole cloves moistened with a bit of verjuice. Add some fine herbs and

---

50. Cotgrave defines *couldre* or *coudre* as 'A Hasell Nut,' both of which seem unlikely in this context. The word is perhaps a misspelled version of *gouhourde*, which Cotgrave glosses as a gourd.

mettez dedans avec menues herbes groiselles aussi de chair de beuf du maigre de la cuisse, mettes du verjus si n'avez de groiselles.

⁌ Paste en pot de gigot de mouton rosty ou longe de veau rostye froide.
⁌ Fault hacher la chair de gigot bien menue & sousfrires oygnons bien habille bien menue en sain de lart ou beurre, puis fondes le tout ensemble avec bon boullon pouldre, blanche menue espices cloud de Giroffle entier petit de saffran. Destrempe le tout avec petit de verjus assaisonne de sel. Faictes le tout boullir en ung pot sur le charbon. Aulcuns le lient de deulx ou troys moyeulx d'oeufz passees avec ung petit de boullon. Puis versez au pot en remuant servez tout chault.

⁌ Souppes a la capilorde.
⁌ Prenes Chappon ou perdrix rostie et en tires les aesles et les cuisses & toutes la chair par dessus les os. Pouis tirez la ch[a]ir aulcun hasle coste chair. Et puis y prenez pain couppe en soupe en ung plat. Et faictes ung lict de soupe ung lict de chair & de fromaige ga*[fol. 21v]* lase fin & aussi de cynamomon menue espice, puis recommancez a faire ung lict come dit est dessus. En tousjours rencontrant l'ung sur l'aultre jusques a troys ou quatre lict. Aulcuns y mettent moyeulx d'oeulx bien cuictz coupes par rouelles froict avec lart ou beurre & mettes parmy ledict lict quant vouldres servir trempes de bon boullon.

⁌ Choulx.
⁌ Prenez choulx et ostes les fueilles mortes tout entour de la pomme. Et la couppes par ung bout devers la poincte le plus parfond que pourres haches chair de veaulx & fort de gresse assaysonne de sel espice deulx ou troys moyeulx d'oeufz, cuictz, mesles parmy & mettes dedans ladicte pomme en reserrant & l'enveloppe d'une coiffe de mouton ou de veaulx & hachez avec petites brochetes & la mettes boullir avec boullon assaisonne de sel pouldre blanche. Et servir quant elle sera bien cuycte. Et au lieu de la farce on y peult mettre perdrix rostye avec peu de gresse hachez assaisonnee de sel pouldre blanche.

gooseberries along with some lean beef from the leg. Add verjuice if you don't have any gooseberries.

A POTTED PIE OF ROAST LEG OF MUTTON OR COLD ROAST LOIN OF VEAL
You must chop the mutton finely and fry some finely chopped onions in lard or butter. Then meld everything together with nice broth, white powder, fine spices, whole clove, and a bit of saffron. Moisten it all with a bit of verjuice, season with salt. Bring it all to a boil in a pot over the coals. Some thicken it with two or three egg yolks put through a sieve with a bit of broth. Then add this mixture to the pot while stirring. Serve it hot.

SOPS À LA CAPIROTADA

Take some roast capon or partridge and remove the wings and thighs. Remove the meat from the bones. Some sear this meat. Then put bread sliced into sops in a dish. Make one layer of sops and a layer of meat and fine rich cheese. Add also some cinnamon and fine spices and then continue making layers as above, one on top of another, until you have three or four layers. Some add to the layers hard-boiled egg yolks cut into rounds and fried in lard or butter. When you are ready to serve, moisten with nice broth.

CABBAGE

Take some cabbage and remove the dead leaves from around the head. From one end, cut into it towards the deepest point.[51] Chop up some fatty veal and season it with salt, spices, and two or three cooked egg yolks. Mix it all together and put it inside said head of cabbage, closing it up and wrapping it with mutton or veal caul fat. Attach the latter with little spits and put it on to boil in a broth seasoned with salt and white powder. Serve it when it's done. And instead of the stuffing, one can put in roasted partridge with a bit of fat, chopped up and seasoned with salt and white powder.

51. This instruction is not entirely clear. The recipe seems to be for a stuffed cabbage, but it's not clear whether one is to carve out a hole in the middle of the cabbage, or if the cabbage is to be cut it two and later joined back together around the stuffing and held together with caul fat.

❡ Pommes de choulx.
❡ Prenes pommes de choulx couppes plus menus que pourrez & les cuises avec bon boullon dans ung pot avec peu de lart entrelarde, puis y mettes peu de *[fol. 22r]* pouldre commune sel pourres servir avec perdrix rostie et lievre par quartiers choulx au large se mettent cuyre ❡ Idem.

❡ Mettes choulx par quartiers bien menues mettes boullir avec ongnon environ six puis purez sur ung aix. Mettez eaue froide par dessus haches bien menu ensemble avec bon boullon. Aulcuns y mettent du lart pouldre blanche. ❡ Idem.

❡ Prenez oyes plumee embroche faictes rostir, puis prenez pain hasle & mettez tremper avec bon boullon vin, verjus Vinaigre & moustarde passez tout par l'estamine & mettes bouillir sans le couvrir en pot, ensemble menues espices cloudz de giroffle entier succre une branche de saulge entiere pour donner goust sel. Et quant vostre oye sera cuycte mettes la en plat & mettez de vostre potaige dessus tout chault.

❡ Paste en pot.
❡ Fault oster les peaulx par dessus & chasser l'os par derriere. Puis le larder comme paste de venaison de cloux de giroffle canelle en broche comme les cloux & aussi de petites branches de romarin marjolaine. Fueilles de laurier de plus tendres herbes que pourres trouver. Puis mettes dans ung pot boullir avec *[fol. 22v]* Boullon verjus vin vermeil vinaigre & faictes boullir tout ensemble sur des charbons. Prenez ung peu de pain passe trempe avec b[o]ullon & mettes bouillir en pot avec menues espices cynamomon et fault qu'i[l] ne demeure que ung

Cabbage hearts [52]

Take some cabbages cut up as finely as you can and cook them in a pot of nice broth with a bit of streaky bacon mixed in. Then add a bit of common powder and salt. You can serve it with roasted and quartered partridge and hare.[53]

[The same]

Add finely quartered cabbages and set them to boil with about six onions. Then chop them finely on a cutting board. Add cold water to them after they are finely chopped along with some good broth. Some add salted pork fat and white powder.

[The same]

Take a goose, remove the feathers, put it on a spit and roast it. Then take toasted bread and soak it in good broth, wine, verjuice, vinegar, and mustard. Put it through a sieve and set it to boil in a pot without covering it. Add to it fine spices, whole clove, sugar, a whole branch of sage for flavour, and salt. When your goose is done, put it in a dish and pour your hot soup over it.

Potted pie [54]

Remove the skin from on top and take out the bone from behind. Then lard it as you would a venison pie with cloves, cinnamon cut into 'nails' like cloves, and also little branches of rosemary and marjoram. Add bay leaves and the most tender herbs you can find. Then put it in a pot to boil with broth, verjuice, red wine, and vinegar and boil it together over the coals. Take a bit of bread sieved and moistened with broth and boil it in the pot with fine spices, cinnamon, and powdered

---

52. The previous recipe, though entitled *Choulx* alone, is also for a hearted cabbage, such as a Savoy.
53. The end of the last sentence in this recipe ('...*choulx au large se mettent cuyre*') seems to be unfinished. In the following two recipes, the titles ('Idem') are misplaced, appearing in the last line of the previous recipes. Given these typographical mistakes, it is possible that some of the text from this recipe has dropped out.
54. The type of meat used in this recipe is not mentioned, but its skin and bones are to be removed.

plain plat de boullon & une noix muscade mise en pouldre servez tout chault & ung peu de cler.

⁋ Pomme.
⁋ Prenes foyes de veaulx mouton chevreaulx haches du foye de veau selon la quantite que vouldres faire avec lart gras gresse de beuf ou de mouton de la grosseur du foye. Une poignee de menues herbes haches tout ensemble puis .vij.ou.viij. moyeulx d'oeufz et de sel menue espices, puis prenes coiffes de veaulx de mouton & de chevreau des plus maigres, lesquelz feres tremper en eaue tyede, puis estandres sur ung aix, puis prenez de vostre farce la grosseur d'une pomme. Puis envelopes de ladicte coiffe & le lyez asses lasche affin qu'il ne creve & le faconnes comme une pomme [e]t le mettes boullir avec bon boullon verjus vinai[g]re a petit feu et assembler comme potaige de venayson. Et si voules faire desdictes pommes crues avec lart a doulx feu serves les avec oranges tous chaulx ou sauffereaulx de venaison ou pouldre de duc par dessus.

[fol. 23r] ⁋ Paste en pot de langue de beuf.
⁋ Prenes langues de beuf cuittes, couppes les par rouelles ou aultrement d'une coste de beuf couppes par lesches & ayes gresse de beuf hachee menue puis prenez vostre chair & la faictes cuyre en ung pot avec gresse bon boullon vin verjus, puis prenes pain hasle sur charbon et le trempes avec vostre boullon. Puis passes avec petit de vin vermeil vinaigre verjus et mettes le tout boullir avec vostre paste et qu'il ne soit pas fort lye. Celuy de beuf veult estre mieulx cuyt que celluy de langue & pour espices menues espices cynamomon noix

nutmeg. And there should only remain a full dish of broth. Serve hot with a splash of claret.[55]

'Apples'[56]

Take the livers of calf, mutton or kid and chop them up with calf's liver according to the quantity you want to make along with lard and beef or mutton fat in the same amount as the liver. Add in a handful of chopped fine herbs along with 7 or 8 egg yolks, salt, and fine spices. Then take some caul fat from veal, mutton, or the leanest kid, which you will soak in tepid water. Then spread it out on a cutting board and add the stuffing in an amount equal to the size of an apple. Then wrap it in said caul fat and secure it loosely so that it will not burst. Fashion it in the shape of an apple and put it on to boil in good broth, verjuice, and vinegar over a low flame. Put it together like a venison stew. And if you want to cook said apples with salted pork fat over a low flame, serve them hot with oranges and with *sauffereaulx* of venison or Duke's powder on top.[57]

Potted pie of ox tongue

Take cooked ox tongues and slice them into rounds or otherwise use a beef rib roast cut into slices and add some finely chopped beef suet. Take the meat and cook it in a pot with fat, good broth, wine and verjuice. Then take some bread toasted over the coals and soak it in your broth. Sieve it with a bit of red wine, vinegar, and verjuice and set it to boil with your crust. Make sure it is not too thick. Made with beef, it should be cooked longer than with tongue. For spices, add

---

55. The final phrase of this recipe is *ung peu de cler*, which is not entirely clear. If the last word is simply misspelled and/or cut off (the previous page contained a number of printing mistakes), this could be '*cleret*' or claret.
56. This recipe is not for the fruit itself, but for a sort of liver pâté shaped into the form of an apple.
57. The last sentence of this recipe is difficult to interpret. First, when it says '*si voules faire desdictes pommes crues*' it is difficult not to read the last word as 'raw' but that sense is meaningless in the context of a cooked meat pâté shaped like an apple. *Sauffereaulx* (which should possibly have been printed *Saussereaulx*) could be a misspelling of '*saulce realle*' the recipe for which appears below on pp. 228–229.

muscade peu bruslee & en pouldre cloux de giroffle entier assaisonner de sel espices sucre.

⁋ Pastez de veau.
Faictes blanchir vostre veau puis hache le avec gresse de beuf autant de gresse que de chair petit de lart gras mettez boullir en ung pot sur le charbon avec peu de bon boullon, vin blanc si voules assaison[n]e menues espices pouldre blanche saffran destrempe, avec peu de verjus & mettes dedans sel. Et quant vouldres servir ayes moyeulx d'oeufz cuictz lardes de cloudz de girofle entiers & mettez en vostre pot avec groiselles.

⁋ Friteaulx de fleur de sux.
[fol. 23v] ⁋ Prenes de la fleur de sux une plaine escuelle environ aut[a]nt de roses rouges. Mettes bouillir & estraignez tout ensemble peu de farine de la fleur huyct moyeux d'eufz sucre deux ou troys z et ung quart de z Cynamomon & y mettez peu de saffran en pourdre et assaisonnez de sel mesles le tout ensemble avec vostre cueiller. Et puis les faictes comme les aultres friteaulx bugueslez.

⁋ Beurre frays frit.
⁋ Prenes pain blanc dur & en faictes miettes bien menu prenez de l'amidon z ij, sucre z ii. avec peu de cynamomon. Et broyes avec autant de beurre frais que desdictes drogues ou plus puis refaictes en sorte de pain de beurre. Et soit destrempe avec la farine moyeulx d'oeufz, peu d'eaue Rose, sucre, sel, sans mettre d'aultre eaue pui destrempes le tout ensemble cler comme paste d'oublies. Et quant sera destrempez fondez ung peu de beurre frays puis mettez de vostre poelle comme si voulliez faire ung maleffrain puis mettez vostre pain de beurre en vostre poelle surladicte croste & l'enveloppe d'huille. Et les tournez d'ung coste et d'aultre en les faisant cuyre. Servez tout chault a l'entree sucre par dessus.

fine spices, cinnamon, slightly toasted ground nutmeg, and whole clove. Season with salt, spices, and sugar.

Veal pies

Blanch your veal then chop it up with some beef fat, as much fat as meat, and a bit of salted pork fat. Boil it in a pot over the coals with some good broth and white wine. If you want to season it, add fine spices, white powder, and saffron soaked in a bit of verjuice. Add salt. When you want to serve it, take some hard-boiled egg yolks studded with whole cloves and add them to the pot along with some gooseberries.

Elderflower fritters

Take about a bowlful of elderflowers and as many red roses. Put them on to boil and then strain them. Add them together with some fine flour, eight egg yolks, two or three ounces of sugar and a quarter ounce of cinnamon. Add in a bit of powdered saffron and season with salt. Mix it all together with your spoon. And then make them as you would other fritters.[58]

Fried fresh butter

Take stale white bread and crumble it finely. Add two ounces of starch and two ounces of sugar along with a little cinnamon. Grind it up with as much fresh butter as said drugs, or more, and then reform it into a kind of butter loaf. Mix some flour with egg yolks, a bit of rosewater, sugar, and salt without adding any other water. Then mix it together as you would for wafer batter. When it's mixed, melt some fresh butter in a pan and then put your [batter] in the pan as if you were making a *maleffrain*.[59] Then add your butter loaf to the pan on top of said crust and baste it with oil. Turn them over and over as you cook them. Serve them hot as a first course with sugar sprinkled on top.

58. The reference to fritters at the end is followed in the French text by the word '*bugueslez*' which seems on the surface to function as an adjective. It is not clear what the word refers to. Cotgrave does gloss the word *bugnet* as a variant of *bignet* (pastry, fritter), so perhaps this word is just another reference to similar pastries.

59. This word seems similar to a *matefaim*, a sort of thick crêpe or omelette.

Aultre beurre.

[fol. 24r] ☙ Prenes beurre frays & le faictes fondre en une poelle, puis prenes de vostre paste que feres estendre la le plus deslye que pourres en ladicte poelle, faictes la cuire, puis prenez d'aultre beurre ung petit & le faictes fondre sur vostre croste. Ayes vostre pain & frises dessus avec ledict amydon sucre cynamomon et la pouldre, parmy vostredict beurre sur ladicte croste, & le faictes cuyre en demenant. Et luy donnes couleur par dessus avec une poelle de fer toute chaulde. Et de telle crostes pourres faire crostes. Tartes de telles cresmes qu'il vous plaira.

☙ Jaspe de laict.

☙ Prenes bon laict gras & autant de Glaire D'oeufz passees par l'estamine. Persil ung petit hachez. Ung peu de pouldre blanche, assaisonne de sel, puis mettes tout ensemble & faictes bouillir. Et quant il sera cuyt & que vous l'aures bien remue le pressures en une serviette jusques a ce qu'il soit froit & assez froit d'ung jour en l'aultre puis coupes en petites lesches et le frises avec beurre serves tout chault sucre dessus a l'entree de la table & semble iaspe.

☙ Potaige blanc de chappon ou de poulles.

☙ Prenez chapon ou poullet et le faictes cuyre comme *[fol. 24v]* dict est au potaige dessus pour assembler prenes amandes bien broyez & passes avec vostre boullon de vostre chapon peu de verjus de pouldre blanche de vin blanc de menues herbes hachees. Et quant vostre chapon sera cuyct mettes vosdictes amandes pouldre herbes, vin en vostre pot en remuant avec groiselles sel. Et en povez faire de hamoste de veaulx poictrine collet, poullailles poulletz cuyctz en pieces.

☙ Potaige vert.

☙ Prenes chapon poulles ou veaulx despeces par pieces ou entiers. Mettes boullir en bo[u]llon de beuf ou de mouton avec peu de lart

Another butter

Take fresh butter and melt it in a pan. The take your batter and spread it as thinly as possible in said pan, cook it, then take a little more butter and melt it on top of your crust. Take your bread and fry it on top with said starch, sugar, cinnamon, and powder, on top of said butter on top of said crust and move it about while it cooks. Brown it on top by placing a hot iron pan on top of it. With such crusts you can make pies and tarts with any kinds of cream that you wish.

Milk jasper

Take nice rich milk and the same amount of egg whites put through a sieve. Add a bit of chopped parsley, a little white powder, and season with salt. Then mix it all together and bring it to a boil. When it's cooked and you have stirred it well, squeeze it in a cloth until it has cooled for a day or so. Then cut it into slices and fry it in butter. Serve it hot with sugar on top as a first course and it will look like jasper.[60]

White pottage of capon or hens

Take a capon or chicken and cook it as in the previous pottage recipe.[61] To put it together, take finely ground almonds and put them through a sieve with some of your capon broth, a bit of verjuice, white powder, white wine, and chopped fine herbs. When your capon is cooked, put said almonds, powder, herbs, and wine into your pot, stirring it along with some gooseberries and salt. You can also make it with *hamoste*,[62] veal breast or neck, hens or chicken cooked in pieces.

Green pottage

Take capon, hen, or veal cut in pieces or whole. Put them on to boil in beef or mutton broth with a bit of fatty or lean salt pork chopped

---

60. Jasper is a type of quartz consisting mostly of silica and having an opaque, variegated appearance. Here, it would look like a green variety of jasper given the use of parsley in this recipe.
61. This recipe must have been taken out of another context because there is no immediately preceding pottage recipe.
62. The word *hamoste* does not appear in any of the standard dictionaries. It could be a misspelled word referring to a particular part of veal, perhaps a *jarret de veau*.

gras ou maigre hache bien menu & estuvez bien & pour assembler prenez bled vert force persil & aultres verdures selon le temps pilles comme saulce verte et l'estraignes & retenes le jus dedans ung plat avec peu de Mye de pain de moyeulx d'oeufz cuictz, ou crudz peu de pouldre blanche le tout passez avec peu de boullon et de verjus, et quant sera cuict que la vouldres servir mettes dedans vostre pot vostre verdure avec menues herbes haches en remuant & mettes groiselles & sel & font plus honneste les chapons entiers que en pieces & toutes viandes aussi que ne soyent trop lyez.

⁋ Potaige rouge.
[fol. 25r] ⁋ Prenes chappons, poulles ou veaulx par pieces ou entiers boullys comme dessus est dict. Et quant ilz seront asses cuyctz. Prenes pouldre de ris avec amendes broyes peu d'eaue rose, et de pouldre blanche, passes le tout par l'estamine & mettez a vostre pot. Et quant aures tire voz chapons en remuant, puis prenes de larcamiecte & mettes tremper avec vin blanc ou verjus ou du boullon. Et apres qu'il sera destrempe et aura rendu sa couleur mettes ladicte couleur dedans vostredict potaige en le remuant pour donner couleur rouge, sel sucre, servez en plat, & grosses dragees par dessus. Et qu'il soit assez lye. Ilz sont plus honnestes entier que par pieces.

⁋ Potaige violet.
⁋ Faictes comme desus sinon qu'il fault prendre du tornesson violet au lieu de larcamiette, il fault que ses potaiges soyent plus lyees que cleres Vous pourrez faire Ris de telle couleur que ainsi est dit.

⁋ Pommes de veaulx ou de chevreaulx de ventre.
⁋ Fault cuyre lesdictz ventres avec boullon de beuf ou de mouton, ung peu de lart gras avec menues herbes une poignee. Et quant ilz seront cuictz purez les desus ung aix et les haches bien menu tout ensemble *[fol. 25v]* puis prenez moyeulx d'oeufz crudz, pouldre blanche menues espices, saffran et sel, apres prenes des coeffes de veaulx, de chevreaulx, ou de mouton les plus maigres que pourres trouver & les mettes tremper en eaue tyede pour les ad[o]ulcir, puis

finely. Stew it well. To put it all together, take some new wheat, a lot of parsley, and other greens according to the season and pound them as you would for green sauce. Squeeze them and retain the juice in a dish with some breadcrumbs, cooked or raw egg yolks, and a bit of white powder. Sieve it all with a bit of broth and verjuice. When it's cooked and you want to serve it, put the greens in your pot with finely chopped herbs and stir, adding gooseberries and salt. The capon is better served whole rather than in pieces, as is the case for all meats. It should not be too thick.

Red pottage

Take capons, hen, or veal, split or whole and boiled as above. When they are just about done take some rice flour, ground almonds, a bit of rosewater, and some white powder. Put it all through a sieve and add it to your pot. After you've removed your capon and stirred, take some alkanet[63] and soak it in white wine, verjuice, or broth. When it has soaked and given off its colour, put this coloured liquid into your pottage and stir it to make it red. Add salt and sugar and serve it in a dish with large candies on top. It should be rather thick. The meat is better served whole than in pieces.

Violet pottage

Do as mentioned above, except use violet turnsole instead of alkanet. These pottages should be thicker rather than thin. You can also make rice with this same colour as mentioned above.

Apples made from calves' or kids' stomachs

Cook said stomachs in beef or mutton broth with some salted pork fat and a handful of fine herbs. When they are cooked, deposit them onto a cutting board and chop them finely altogether. Then add raw egg yolks, white powder, fine spices, saffron, and salt. Next, take the leanest veal, kid, or mutton caul fat that you can find and put it on to soak in tepid water to soften it. Then spread it out and put your

---

63. Alkanet is a plant (*Alkanna tinctoria*) that can be used as a dye or food colouring.

les estendes et mettez de vostre farce dessus du gros d'une grosse pomme puis reserres vostredicte coeffe & la lyes de fillet assez lasche affin qu'elle ne creve en boullant, puis faictes boullir comme ci apres est escript. Faictes les boullir tout ensemble a petit feu assaisonne de sel. Et coupez les filletz quant les vouldres servir et serves voz pommes en platz, et de vostre potaige mettes par dessus faict comme cy apres en pourres faire saulce. Et en ferez rostir sur le gril au servir peu de pouldre de duc dessus ou la moustarde a l'entree.

℃ Potaige de ventre de veaulx ou chevreaulx.
℃ Faictes boullir voz ventres & pieds de veaulx avec petit de [l]art & sel, & quant ilz seront cuictz pures les et les mettes par pieces les piedz en deulx, puis les mettes boullir en bouillon de beuf ou de mouton. Prenez moyeulx d'oeufz crudz ou cuitz avec petit de pain mettes tremper lesdictz oeufz & pain avec vostre boullon: puis passes par l'estamine assemblez peu de pouldre blanche menues espices, saffran, peu de vin blanc, et *[fol. 26r]* verjus. Et mettes tout boullir ensemble a l'heure que vouldres servir avec menues herbes haches groiselles en remuant sel & est du potaige. Et ne fault que soyt gueres lye.

℃ Cretonnee de poys nouveaulx ou febves.
℃ Prenes poulletz veaulx ou chevreaulx par pieces mettes cuyre avec boullon de beuf ou mouton & quant ilz auront boully mettes dedans peu de lart gras hache. Et quant ilz seront demy cuictz mettes poys ou febves dedans esgrenes pouldre blanche menues herbes haches sel & faictes cuyre le reste sur les charbons & demeurant groisselles.

℃ Potaige cretonne.
℃ Prenes grains comme dessus poulletz veaulx, ou chevreaulx, mys par pieces, mettes boullir avec bon boullon. Et autant de bon laict.

stuffing on it, the same amount as a large apple. Then wrap the caul fat around it and tie it with string loosely so that it won't burst when boiling. Then boil it as is described hereafter. Boil them all together over a low flame and season with salt. Cut the strings off when you are ready to serve and serve your apples on dishes. Pour your soup from the next recipe over the top as you would a sauce. And you can roast it on the grill, serving with some Duke's powder on top or mustard when served as a first course.

Calves' or kids' stomach pottage

Boil your stomachs and calves' feet with a bit of salted pork fat and salt. When they are cooked, remove them and cut them into pieces, the feet in half. Then boil them in beef or mutton broth. Take raw or cooked egg yolks and a bit of bread and soak said eggs and bread with your broth. Then put them through a sieve and incorporate some white powder, fine spices, saffron, a little white wine, and verjuice. Bring it all to a boil when you are ready to serve with chopped fine herbs and gooseberries, stirring in some salt. It is a pottage and it should not be terribly thick.

Cretonnée[64] of new peas or fava beans

Take chicken, veal, or kid, split into pieces and put them on to cook in beef or mutton broth. When it comes to a boil, add some chopped salted pork fat. When it's about half cooked, add hulled peas or fava beans, white powder, chopped fine herbs, and salt. Let it cook the rest of the way over the coals and add gooseberries to finish.

Cretonné pottage

Use meat as above – chicken, veal, kid – split into pieces and put on to boil in some nice broth and an equal amount of milk. Bring it to

---

64. The origin of this term is somewhat mysterious, but may have some relation to the use of bacon in similar recipes. Cotgrave glosses *cretons* as 'The crispie peeces, or mammocks, remaining of lard, that hath beene first shred, then boiled, and then strained through a cloth.' Similar recipes appear in many medieval and Renaissance cookbooks, particularly the *Viandier* (Scully, 1988, recipes 11 and 11a) and the *Ménagier de Paris* (1994, recipe 94).

Et faictes boullir avec bon lart hache menu. Et quant vouldres estuvez bien. Et quant il sera demy cuit, mettes poix dedans cuyre avec pouldre blanches herbes hachez faictes cuyre a demeure sel la ou il y a laict il n'y fault point d'aigreur.

℄ Laict cretonne.
[fol. 26v] ℄ Prenes comme dessus faictes boullir et assembles comme dessus excepte laict & au lieu du laict prenez bon boullon et moyeulx d'oeuf crudz petrix de verjus, pouldre blanche, menues herbes groselles, et quant il sera cuyt et que vouldrez servir mettes tout b[o]uillir ensemble. Aulcuns fryent lesdictz grains, et en sont plus frians.

℄ Cyve de lyevres.
℄ Carpes de lievre despece par pieces avec bon boullon vin vermeil vinaigre & le frisez en saing de lart et prenez pain haslez trempe en vostre boullon avec le foye de lievre. Passe avec peu de vin vermeil et mettez en pot & quant sera demy cuyt menues espices noix de m[u]scade peu boustee en pourdre avec o[n]gnons fris menues aulcuns le font rostire sur le gril les aultres le lardent tout creud au long et aussi le font rostir en broche a demy cuyct & puis le despecent & aussi en font cyvez de porceaulx hasle en la broche ou agnis hasle ou fritz il[s] veullent estre ung petit plus cler que espes.

℄ Sanglier cerf.
℄ Sanglier salle ou cerf, trempes et boulles eaue et peu de bon boullon quant il est cuyct mettes en belles cernes avec naveaulx cuictz que vous mettrez de*[fol. 27r]*dant quant sera demy cuyct et quant la venaison

a boil with some nice finely chopped salt pork. Stew it well. When it is half cooked, add peas to cook with it along with white powder and chopped herbs. Let it cook for the remainder and then add some salt. When using milk, you should not use anything sour.

Milk cretonné [65]

Take the ingredients used above and boil and incorporate them as above except for the milk. Instead of milk, use good broth and raw egg yolks whipped up with verjuice, white powder, fine herbs, and gooseberries. When it's cooked and you are ready to serve, bring it all to a boil. Some fry said meats and they are tastier that way.

Hare civet

Take some hare cut into pieces and fry it in salted pork fat and add nice broth, red wine, and vinegar.[66] Take some toasted bread and soak it in your broth along with the hare's liver. Put it through a sieve with a little red wine and then add it to your pot. When it's half done, add fine spices, nutmeg that has been ground, and some fried chopped onions. Some roast it on the grill and others lard it when raw and whole and roast it on a spit until half cooked and then divide it into pieces. Others make it with young pig roasted on a spit or lamb roasted or fried. They want the dish to be slightly thinner, not thick.

Boar or stag

Salted boar or stag should be soaked and boiled in water and a bit of broth. When it's cooked, put it in rounds with cooked turnips that you will add when it's half cooked. When the venison is cooked, cut

---

65. This title belongs to the previous recipe and vice versa. The previous recipe calls for milk whereas this one expressly says not to use it.
66. Since this is clearly a meat dish, the first word '*Carpes*' seems unlikely to refer to the fish of that name. This is perhaps a Latinism (seize, take) although there are relatively few uses of Latin throughout the text. The first sentence is also odd in that it refers to the meat and then a list of liquids (broth, wine, vinegar) before giving the instruction to fry 'it' (presumably the hare) in bacon fat. We can perhaps assume that the meat is fried before the liquids are added, a change reflected in the translation.

est cuycte couppes par cernes Dresses naveaulx cuictz en bon boullon doulx par dessus la venaison ensemble dudict boullon. Naveaulx ne cuysez ny en vin ny en aigreur.

⁋ Venaison contrefaicte en potaige.
⁋ Prenes hault coste ou poyctrine de mouton hasle sur le Gril despeces par pieces asses grandes. Mettes les boullir avec bon boullon et vin vermeil peu de vinaigre verjus oygnons. Couppes par rouelles foye & mettes dedans avec lart hache par deulx ensemble. Prenez pain hasle passe par estamine avec v[o]stre Boullon vin vermeil menues espices le tout boullyr ensemble sel. Puis y mettez des naveulx quant ilz seront cuyctz en vin. Boullon doulx, quant on veult servir.

⁋ Broet georget.
⁋ Prenes veaulx poulles co[n]gnins & despeces par pi[e]ces & faictes blanchir ou hasler en la broche ou frire en lart, puis boully en boullon avec peu de bon vin vermeil verjus vinaigre lart bien menu ensemble.
⁋ Prenez pain hasle trempe de vostre boullon passer par l'estamine avec foyes de congnins ou poulles me*[fol. 27v]*nues espices cynamomon. Six cloux de giroffle boully tout ensemble sel menues herbes.
⁋ Item pourrez faire des congnins poulles et foye rostye.

⁋ Aultre brouet.
⁋ Prenes veaulx poulle ou congnins & despeces par pieces & faictes les blanchir foyes avec lart, puis faictes boullir avec vinaigre vin vermeil puis prenez amandes avec escorces passes par estamine avec bon boullon, et mettez avec voz congnins ou poulles que vous aurez faict cuyre avec bon boullon menues espices cynamomon tout ensemble boully, & quant sera cuyct avec six cloulx de giroffle et sucre sel iij herbes haches Groyselles vous en pourres faire de chair rostye froydes.

it into rounds. Serve the cooked turnips in nice sweet broth over the venison along with said broth. Turnips should not be cooked in wine or in sour liquids.

Counterfeit venison pottage

Take the upper rib or breast of mutton browned on the grill and cut into large pieces. Put them on to boil in a nice broth with red wine, a little vinegar, verjuice, and onions cut into rounds. Take the liver and put it in with some salted pork fat, both of them chopped together. Add some toasted bread put through a sieve with your broth, red wine, and fine spices, all of it boiled together. Add salt. Then add turnips after they have cooked in wine.[67] Serve with sweet broth.

Brouet georget [68]

Take veal, hen, and rabbit and cut them into pieces. Blanch them or brown them on a spit, or fry them in salted pork fat. Then boil them together in broth with a bit of good red wine, verjuice, vinegar, and finely chopped salted pork fat.

Take toasted bread soaked in your broth and put it through a sieve with the livers from the rabbit or hen, fine spices, cinnamon, and six cloves. Boil it all together then add salt and fine herbs.

You can roast the rabbit, hen, and liver.

Another *brouet*

Take veal, hen, or rabbit, cut into pieces and blanch them along with the liver and some salted pork fat. Bring it to a boil with vinegar and red wine. Take some almonds with their skins put through a sieve with nice broth. Add them to your rabbit or hen that you have cooked in nice broth, fine spices, and cinnamon, all of it boiled together. When it's cooked, add six cloves, sugar, salt, 3 chopped herbs, and gooseberries. You can also make it with cold roasted meat.

---

67. Cooking the turnips in wine seems to contradict the dictum appended to the end of the previous recipe.
68. Like the preceding recipes for *cretonnées* and *civets*, the *brouet*, a type of stew, is a stalwart of medieval cuisine. The *brouet georget* appears in *Le Viandier*.

❡ Prenes z iiij de Gingembre z iii s de canelle z i s de poyvre rond z i de poyvre long ij de noix de muscade z i de cloux de Giroffle z i de Graine de paradis z i de muscade z i de Garingal et i le tout mis en pouldre & passes par l'esset.*

❡ Pour assembler demye livre de menues espices d'aultre sorte.

❡ Prenes z ii s de gingembre z ii de Poyvre rond z i de canelle z i muscade z s de cloux de giroffle z i de *[fol. 28r]* graine de paradis. Elle n'est pas si excellant que la dessusdicte. Ces deulx pouldres servent a deulx potaiges Noirs & bruns gras & maigres, et toutes saulces & a toutes patisserie requerant menues espices apres declaree & a gellee comme maigres et graces. Et vault mieulx pour gellee ne fire concace, pource qu'elle ne noircist pas toute la gellee et est plus claire.

❡ Fault Rape de Gingembre autant que vouldries faire de Pouldre blanche & aussi mettes en pouldre, et passes par le saffel avec ung peu D'amydont pour une livre Amidon z i pour la blanchir & sert a tout potaiges blanc jaulne & saulce blanche l'on s'en sert en aulcunes patisseries cy apres declairees.

❡ [Li]B z viii de Gingembre z viii de poyvre rond & le tout mesles en pouldre & passes par le saichet. Elle est bonne a patisseries de venaison.

❡ Pouldre de duc.
❡ Lib z nicari z s canelle le gros d'une febve de Gingembre deulx

---

* The letter 'z' denotes 'ounce' (our abbreviation 'oz' was expressed in medieval manuscripts as a single character, a somewhat convoluted 'z'; the abbreviation itself derives from the Italian *onza*). The letter 's' after some of the ounce-measures signifies *semi-* or half.

[Fine spices] [69]

Take 4 ounces of ginger, 3½ ounces of cinnamon, 1½ ounces of round pepper, 1 ounce of long pepper, 2 ounces of nutmeg, 1 ounce of clove, 1 ounce of grain of paradise, 1 ounce of nutmeg,[70] 1 ounce of galingale, all of it ground into a powder and sifted.

To make half a pound of fine spices in another way

Take 2½ ounces of ginger, 2 ounces of round pepper, 1 ounce of cinnamon, 1 ounce of nutmeg, ½ ounce of clove, 1 ounce of grain of paradise. It's not as excellent as the previous one. These two powders can be used in black and dark soups, whether meat day or fast day, as well as in all sauces and pastries requiring fine spices mentioned hereafter and in meat or meatless jellies. And for jellies, it is better that the spices not be ground up because that way it will not darken up the jelly and it can remain more transparent.

[White powder] [71]

You need grated ginger, as much as how much white powder you want to end up with. Grind it into a powder and put it through the sifter with a bit of starch. For one pound of powder, 1 ounce of starch to whiten it. It can be used in white and yellow soups and white sauce. It can also be used in some pastries mentioned hereafter.

[Another]

8 ounces of ginger, 8 ounces of round pepper, all of it mixed into a powder and put through a sifter. It's good with venison pies.

Duke's powder

One pound of sugar, half an ounce of cinnamon, a bean-sized piece

---

69. There is no title for this recipe, but the following recipe refers to *menues espices d'aultre sorte* [fine spices of another sort]. We can thus assume that these are two versions of the often-used spice mixes called 'fine spices.'
70. Since nutmeg has already appeared in the list, we can assume that this is an undesired repetition.
71. There is no title listed, but the first line of the recipe clearly states that this one is for white powder.

ou troys cloulx de Giroffle le tout bastille ensemble & passee par lesusdict.

℃ Toutes les pouldres dessusdict se gardent a ij sepmaines ou ung moys sans corrumpre.

℃ Prenes persil effueille deulx poignees marjolai*[fol. 28v]*ne effueillee deux poignees et demye saulge demye poignee ysope autant sarriette autant sarpollet une poignee soulcye une poignee. Et quant c'est pour faire farce aulcuns y mettent soulcye et peu de Baselicque. Elles servent a tous potaiges et les fault faire seicher environ la sainct Jeahn baptiste.

℃ Pour faire eaue d'emande.

℃ Faictes boullir deulx ou troyes quartes d'eaue de fontaine, puis plumez deulx ou troys z d'amande et les broyez & passes avec vostredicte Eaue & mettes le tout en fiolle de voirre quant sera froide ou en aultre vaisseau & se gardera deulx ou troys jours en une eaue elle est bonne pour maladies chauldes.

℃ Entree de table a jours gras pour faire blanchir foye de veau Rosty de mouton & de chevreaulx.

℃ Il fault blanchir vostre foye de veau tant de lart que de cloud de giroffle & l'envelopper de la coiffe & le faire rostir. Il convient saulce de venaison ou verjus vert. Vous pourres farcir tous foyes comme foyes de pourceaulx rostye & le servir a l'orange ou pouldre blanche par dessus ou ainsi que dict est au farcy n'y fault point de saulce.

of ginger, two or three cloves, all of it pounded together and sifted as above.

All the above powders can be kept from four to six weeks without going bad.

[MENUES HERBES][72]

Take parsley leaves two handfuls, of marjoram leaves two and a half handfuls, of sage a half-handful, the same of hyssop, the same of savory, wild thyme a handful, and marigold a handful. When used to make stuffing, some add marigold and a little basil. They can be used in all pottages and they should be dried around the feast of John the Baptist.

TO MAKE ALMOND MILK

Bring to a boil two or three quarts of water from the fountain. Remove the skins from two or three ounces of almonds. Grind them up and put them through a sieve with your water. After it cools, put it all in a glass vial or some other container and it will keep for two or three days. Mixed with water, it's good for fevers.

FIRST COURSE ON MEAT DAYS[73]
TO MAKE BLANCHED ROAST LIVER OF CALF, MUTTON, OR KID

You have to blanch your calf's liver along with as much salted pork fat as clove. Wrap it in caul fat and roast it. Venison sauce or green verjuice is appropriate with it. You can stuff any liver as suggested for roast pig liver and serve it with orange or white powder strewed over the top or in the same way as suggested for the stuffed liver. There's no need for any sauce.

---

72. There is no title for this recipe, but since it involves a variety of herbs and comes on the heels of several recipes for generic spice mixtures, we might assume that this is a recipe for the '*menues herbes*' used throughout the text. This assumption is strengthened by the use of the subject '*Elles*' in the last sentence, which in its feminine and plural form would be a logical pronoun for *menues herbes*.

73. In what is perhaps a printing mistake, this title is conflated with the title of the following recipe. It was perhaps meant as a chapter title since many of the following recipes are referred to as first course dishes.

[fol. 29r] ❧ Pour faire hastereaulx de foyes de veaulx.

❧ Il les fault couper comme les aultres hastereaux de veaulx & les trancher le plus deslye que pourrez et hacher lart. Groiselles saulges bonnes herbes & assaisonne de menues espices sel. Apres vostredicte farce faictes les comme les aultres frises les en saing de lart de mouton de beuf. Ou les faictes rostir en broche si voulez servez chault a L'orenge ou a quelque aultre saulce qu'il vous semblera comme de venaison verjus vert. Ou saulce roulx giroffles.

❧ Pour faire saulce de foyes de veaulx ou d'aultres.

❧ Prenes foyes de veaulx et les faictes cuyre avec gresse lart mouton beuf et menues herbes bon boullon de Beuf ou de mouton. Et quant ilz seront assez cuictz purez ledict boullon dessus ung aix & hache tout ensemble assaysonne de Sel et d'espices. C'est assavoir pouldre Blanche menues espices avec moyeulx d'oeufz puis les envelopps de lart coiffes & les faconnez en facon d'andouilles & les cuyses en brochettes de boys. Puis les feres rostir dessus le gril a petit feu de longue main au servir pouldre de Duc dessus. S'i[l] vous reste de ladicte farce vous en pourres faire friteaulx. Mais fault avoir de la glaire d'oeufz & la bien *[fol. 29v]* battre puis faconnez ladicte farce en friteaulx & les Trempes dans ladicte glaire D'oeufz & les frises en lart ou aultres gresses. Servez les a l'entree de la table tous chaulx pouldre de duc dessus.

❧ Item pourrez faire de semblable des requestes de chapons poullailles & aultres voullatailles.

To make calf's liver HASTEREAUX [74]

You need to cut them up like other veal *hastereaux* and slice them as finely as you can. Chop up salted pork fat as well. Add gooseberries, sage, and good herbs. Season with fine spices and salt. After your stuffing is ready, make them up as the others. Fry them in pork, mutton, or beef fat. Some people roast them on a spit. If you want to serve them hot, garnish with orange or some other sauce as you see fit such as venison sauce or green verjuice. Or red sauce with cloves.

To make a sauce with calf's or other kinds of liver

Take calves' livers and cook them in pork, mutton, or beef fat, fine herbs, and good beef or mutton broth. When they are sufficiently cooked, strain them from said broth onto a cutting board, and chop everything up together. Season with salt and spices such as white powder and fine spices. Add some egg yolks and then wrap them up in salted pork fat and caul, shaping them like sausages and cooking them on wooden skewers. Then roast them on the grill over a low flame for a long time. When serving, sprinkle Duke's powder on top. If you have said stuffing left over, you can make fritters with it. But you will need well-beaten egg whites. Form the stuffing into fritters, dip them in said egg whites, and then fry them in lard or some other fat. Serve them hot as a first course with Duke's powder on them.

You can also do the same with leftover capon, chicken, or other poultry.

---

74. Cotgrave glosses this term as a part of a hog's throat or neck, but also provides a recipe that is similar to several versions to be found in our cookbook: 'also, one liver or more of a calfe, etc., wrapped (whole, or sliced, and seasoned with good hearbes, and spices) in the call of the beast, and afterward roasted, or fried and served up hot with Oranges, or in some good sauce: (This dish, as also another (if not more) dressed in another fashion, is called *Hastereaux*).' Godefroy refers to a *hasterel* as 'le foie, et grillade de foie de porc; tranches de viande que l'on mange rôties' [the liver, grilled pork liver; slices of meat eaten roasted]. He also refers to a *haterel* as part of the pig: 'nuque du cou, partie postérieure du cou, quelquesfois la tête' [the nape of the neck, the back of the neck, sometimes the head]. Huguet glosses a *hastereau* as a 'Sorte de grillade' [a sort of grilled meat]. See also note 102, below.

⁋ Pour faire cuyre foyes de cerf chevreaulx ou de beuf.
⁋ Faictes bouillir voz foyes en vin et peu, & de vinaigre eaue & force sel menues herbes saulge. Et quant ilz seront assez cuictz tires les et les Lardez de cloux de Giroffle, puis pouldre de menue Espice et de Sel ou aultre saulce qu'il vous plaira.

⁋ Entree de table.
⁋ Foyes de poulletz chapons chevreaulx oyes cochons ensemble les piedz et les aesles se doibvent servir a l'entree de la table a la vinaigrette & persil par dessus & vinaigre qu'ilz seront bien cuyctz en bon boullon.

⁋ pour farcir foye de veau de mouton & chevreaulx.
⁋ Prenes gresses de mouton ou de beuf lard gras menues herbes haches tout ensemble asses menu assaisonne de sel menues espices & les farcisses comme saul*[fol. 30r]*ce de porc & les enveloppes de leurs coiffes & les pourres faire rostir au four en lichefrites en les tournant souvent & aussi en broche rosty & les serves avec oranges & pouldre blanche par dessus.

⁋ Saulcisses de gigot de mouton.
⁋ Pour faire des saulcisses de gigot de veaulx comme pourceaulx & sont meilleurs de huyct jours que fraichement faictes en z mettez du saffran et les trempes bien en verjus en les faisant. Si prent l'on aulx saulcisses de la cuisse de porc andouilles incontinent que aures tire le ventre du porc lavez le et le fendes les boyaulx le plus menus que pourres ou en quatre et puis les escacherez dessus le fil avec sel, puis faictes voz andouilles & le mettes seicher a la cheville en l'air & se gardent longuement sans rostir.

To cook stag, kid, or ox liver

Bring your livers to boil in just a little wine, water, and vinegar. Add a good bit of salt, fine herbs, and sage. When they are sufficiently cooked, take them out and lard them with cloves. Then add fine spice powder and salt or some other sauce as you wish.

First course

Livers from chicken, capon, kid, goose, and pig, along with feet and wings should be served as a first course in vinaigrette style [75] with parsley and vinegar sprinkled on top. They should be thoroughly cooked in a nice broth.

To stuff calf's, mutton, or kid's liver

Take mutton or beef fat, salted pork fat, and fine herbs and chop them up together rather finely. Season with salt and fine spices. Stuff them as you would a pig's liver and wrap them up in their caul fat. You can roast them in the oven, in the dripping pan turning them often, and also on the spit. Serve them with oranges and sprinkle white powder on top.

Mutton leg sausages

To make veal leg sausage as with young pig.[76] And they are better after eight days rather than freshly made the same day. Add saffron to them and soak them in verjuice while making them. If you prefer to make pork leg sausages or andouilles, as soon as you remove the pig's stomach, wash it and chop the intestines as finely as possible or into four pieces. Then tie them up with string and salt them. Then make them into sausages and leave them to air dry on a peg. They can be kept for a long time without cooking.

---

75. It should be noted that these livers are not to be served with what we would consider a modern vinaigrette (a sauce made of oil, vinegar, salt, pepper, herbs, etc.). Beginning with the *Ménagier de Paris*, and continuing through to at least the end of the sixteenth century, a vinaigrette is typically a spiced stew of pork innards that only incidentally contains vinegar, as in so many other recipes here. As is the case on several menus of this period, the vinaigrette is served as a first course.

76. The title refers to mutton, but the recipe discusses only veal and pork.

❧ Testes de chevreaulx frictes dorees.

❧ Prenes moyeulx d'oeufz et de toutes menues herbes haches avec peu de pouldre blanche assaisonne de sel puis battes le tout ensemble & endores ladicte teste. Et la frises en saing de lart, au servir verjus vert pouldre de duc, & fault paravant qu'elle soit cuicte en bon boullon avant que la fricasses prenes veau cuyct *[fol. 30v]* rousty poulles ou aultre gibier, et frises en saing de lard, puis prenes boullon pouldre blanche verjus moyeulx d'oeufz et passes le tout par l'estamine, menues herbes hachees & le tout faire boullir ensemble mais avant ostes la gresse avec groiselles ou aigretz. Et ainsi de poulle poulletz cuitz mys en pieces.

❧ Prenes poulles poulletz cuitz & les despeces par pieces frises les en saing de lard hache bien menu, Quant seront cuictz espurez la gresse, puis prenes ung fillet de verjus, vinaigre, et ung peu de bon boullon & de moustarde menues espices faictes le tout ensemble boullir, & assaisonne de sel, servez tout chault & ainsi pourres faire de toutes aultres chairs froides boullies ou rosties & aussi de requestes de poullailles et tout aultres gibiers.

❧ Entree de table de trippes.

❧ Coupes tripes bien cuyctes & les frises en saing de lart assaisonnez de Sel serves les toutes chauldes et pouldre blanche dessus avec moustarde.

❧ Paste de veau ou de mouton a la saulce chaulde. Et toutes sortes d'entree de table.

❧ Paste de veau ou de mouton a la saulce chaulde faictes de langues de beuf ou de costes a l'entree de table *[fol. 31r]* venayson froide pour l'entree hure de sanglier venaison rostye froydes & oyes rosties froydes, Et aussi vollailles saulvaiges rostyes froydes.

❧ Pour faire bouldin.

❧ Prenez ung foye de veau, moutons, et le faictes blanchir & ostez les filletz qui sont par dedans et couppes menu broyez en mortier puis

Kid's head, fried and gilded

Take egg yolks, all kinds of chopped fine herbs, along with a little white powder, and season them with salt. Then whip it all together and gild said head with it. Fry it in lard. Serve with green verjuice and Duke's powder. It needs to be cooked in a nice broth prior to frying.

[no title] [77]

Take cooked veal, roast hen, or some other game and fry it in lard. Then take some broth, white powder, verjuice, and egg yolks and put it all through a sieve. Add chopped fine herbs and bring everything to the boil. After skimming the fat, add some gooseberries or unripe grapes. The same can be done with cooked hen or chicken cut into pieces.

Take cooked hen or chicken, split them into pieces and fry them in finely chopped salted pork fat. When they are cooked, strain out the fat. Then take a splash of verjuice, vinegar, a bit of good broth, mustard, and fine spices and bring it all to a boil. Season with salt and serve hot. You can do likewise with other meat – cold, boiled, or roasted – and also with leftover poultry or other game.

Tripe as a first course

Cut well-cooked tripe and fry it in salted pork fat. Season with salt and serve hot with white powder and mustard on top.

Veal or mutton pie in hot sauce.
And all kinds of first courses.

Veal or mutton pie with hot sauce. Make ox tongue or beef ribs as a first course. Cold venison as a first course. Cold boar's head or roast venison. Cold roast goose. And also cold roast wildfowl.

To make pudding

Take calf's or mutton liver and blanch it. Remove any strings from inside it, chop it finely, and grind in a mortar. Then take about a

---

77. The following recipe appears with no title and no separation at the end of the previous recipe (three words before the end of fol. 30r), although there is no obvious connection between the two. We can assume this is a printer's mistake.

prenes environ une livre de gresse de beuf ou de mouton et autant de lard gras faictes cuyre en bon boullon ou avec toutes herbes menues & quant il sera cuict prenez sur ung aix & le haches tout ensemble & broyes avec vostre foye et aussi deulx moyeulx d'oeufz cuictz assaisonne de sel, & menues espices hachees six ongnons avec groiselles ou aigretz & faictes voz bouldins en telz boyaulx que vous vouldres.

ℂ Bouldins blanc.
ℂ Prenes ung peu de chair maigre de porc ou de veau hachee bien menu avec autant de gresse d'oye & ung peu de bon laict gras avec moyeulx d'oeufz mettes lesdictz oeufz & laict en sorte qu'il se puisse bien lyer en cuysant avant que le faire cuyre il fault passer par l'estamine laict oeufz & assaisonne de sel de pouldre blanche puis mettre le tout ensemble et faictes comme a ceux de porc qui sont faictz de saing & se cuysent en telle sor*[fol. 31v]*te que boudin de foye de veau ou de porc.

ℂ Aultres boudins.
ℂ Prenes foye de porc hache bien menu avec autant de gresse de pourceaulx comme de foye & peu de menues herbes sans persil & prenez autant de Saing de pourceau comme de foye et de gresse et assaisonne de menue espice de sel & de graine de fenoil & le tout mesles ensemble & faictes comme les aultres comme piedz de mouton fricassees foye a saing de lart et ongnon quant ilz seront bien cuictz & couppes par morceaulx avec groiselles ou aigret, servez tout chault pouldre blanche dessus & sel.

ℂ Piedz de mouton pour le gousier.
ℂ Piedz de mouton bien cuictz couppes menu avec ongnons bien menu & persil hache & vinaigre, servez au gouster.

ℂ Carbonnades pour souppe.
ℂ Souppes assaisonnes de sel, prenes costellestes de porc bien cuictes et les faictes peu rostir sur le Gril puis prenes ongnons couppes bien menu faictes estuver avec verjus en telz vaisseaulx que vouldres quant

pound of beef or mutton fat and as much salted pork fat. Cook this in a nice broth with finely chopped herbs. When it's all cooked, remove it to a cutting board and chop it all up and then grind it along with your liver and two cooked egg yolks. Season with salt, chopped fine spices, six onions, and gooseberries or unripe grapes. Make your puddings in whatever casings you like.

White puddings

Take a bit of lean pork or veal and chop it finely with the same amount of goose fat and a little rich milk and egg yolks. Add said eggs and milk so that it will bind as it cooks. Before cooking, make sure to put the milk and eggs through a sieve and season with salt and white powder. Then put everything together and make them as you would for pork sausages that are made with pork fat. They can be cooked like calf's or pig's liver sausages.

Other puddings

Take pig's liver chopped finely with the same amount of pork fat as liver along with a bit of fine herbs but no parsley. Take as much pork fat as liver and fat and season with fine spices, salt, and fennel seed. Mix it all together and make them like the others, like fricassee of sheep's trotters and liver cooked with lard and onion.[78] When they are cooked, cut them into pieces, garnish with gooseberries or unripe grapes, and serve hot with white powder and salt sprinkled on top.

Sheep's trotters for a snack

Sheep's trotters cooked well, cut into small pieces, served with finely chopped onions and parsley, vinegar; serve as a snack.

Carbonades for sops

Take sops seasoned with salt. Take well-cooked pork cutlets and roast them on the grill. Then take finely chopped onions. Stew with verjuice in any pot that you want. When they are stewed, add a bit of

---

78. This line does not make sense in context.

seront estuvees ung peu de moustarde avec peu de poul*[fol. 32r]*dre blanche, puis couppes voz coustellettes Serves chault vostre ongnon, pouldre dessus ou en sel de toutes rosties seiches a la moustarde.

⁌ Fricassees.
⁌ Coupes voz foyes par lesches & aussi des ongnons par rouelles & saupouldrez de sel puis frises en saing de lart serves tout chault pouldre blanche dessus, et ainsi pourrez faire de tous aultres foyes comme il[s] ont vue saulce appellee barbe robert.

⁌ Hastereaulx.
⁌ Couppes voz hastereaulx du maigre du gigot de veaulx le plus deslye que pourres puis hastes d'ung cousteau: prenes lart gras gresse de beuf ou de mouton avec menues herbes, & le tout haches ensemble assaisonne de menues espices, pouldre blanche, sel pour faconner voz hastereaulx & les faictes rostir serves tout chault verdelet a la pomme d'orenge ou ung saultereau de venaison ou en giroffle: ou en p[o]taige noir. Et le tout faictes a l'orange ou verjus vert.

⁌ Jambon.
⁌ Faictes tremper jambon puis le faictes cuyre avec saulge et toutes bonnes aultres herbes et quant il sera bien cuyct levez la peau par dessus & y mettes for*[fol. 32v]*ce bonnes herbes & puis le laissez refroidir. Aussi a tous aultres jambons de venaison et aultres sallees. Bresil bien trempe veult cuyre en eaue seullement, servez froit le tout a la moustarde.

⁌ Saulcisses de boulongne.
⁌ Prenes chair de beuf et de porceau maigre autant d'ung comme d'aultre, une livre des deulx ostez les peaulx hachez bien menu avec une livre de lard gras nouveau, et pour assembler prenes cinq z de pouldre tant de poyvre que gingembre & environ z [ii] de poyvre entier sel menu z i ou environ le tout bien mesles ensemble puis le tous meslez dans boyaulx de beuf bien nectz bien serre & presse

mustard and a bit of white powder. Then cut up your cutlets. Serve your onions hot with powder or salt on top along with dry toast spread with mustard.

Fricassees

Cut your livers into slices and your onions into rounds. Sprinkle them with salt and then fry in salted pork fat. Serve them hot with white powder on top. You can do the same with all other kinds of liver that one uses. See the sauce called Robert's beard.

Hastereaulx [79]

Cut your *hastereaulx* from the lean part of the veal leg, as finely as you can. Then pound with the side of a knife. Take salted pork fat, beef or mutton fat, and fine herbs and chop them all together. Season with fine spices, white powder, and salt to form your *hastereaulx*. Roast them and serve them hot but a little rare with orange or a *saultereau* [80] of venison, or with cloves, or in a black soup. And all of it made with orange or green verjuice.

Ham

Soak the ham then cook it with sage and all kinds of nice herbs. When it's cooked, lift up the skin on top and put in a lot of nice herbs and then allow it to cool. Likewise for all other venison hams, or other salted meats. Salted beef should be soaked well and cooked in only water. Serve it cold with mustard.

Bologna sausages

Take the flesh of beef and lean piglet, the same amount of one as the other, a pound of each, remove the skin, chop very fine with a pound of fat fresh lard, and to assemble take five ounces of ground spices, as much of pepper as ginger and about two ounces of whole pepper, fine salt about one ounce or thereabouts and mix everything well together. Then stuff the mixture into the beef casing that has been

79. See note 74.
80. See note 57 for a similar misspelling of what might be *saulce realle*.

& les lyez d'ung grant demy piedz de long chascun a par soy, & les mettes par l'espace de deux jours au sel, puis les mettez seicher a la cheminee.

⁋ Saulcisses de lombardie.
⁋ Prenes chair de chapons cuycte, perdrix becasses ou de oyseaulx de riviere, & ung peu de chair de pourceau avec Lard gras a larder hachees le tout ensemble bien menu assaisonne de menues espices & sel et ung de poyvre rond tout entier puis faictes voz saulcisses en boyaulx de beuf de plaine main bien nectz longz de demy pied le plus plain que pourrez, & les mettes *[fol. 33r]* seicher hors de la cheminee au long du feu, & se gardent deulx ou troys ans tous crudz. Et les fault faire tremper, puis les mettre cuyre en eaue et en vin longuement.

⁋ Cocombre contrefaict saulcisse, pomme, poire.
⁋ Prenes une rouelle de veau et la hachez bien menu sans gresse et assemble pouldre blanche, menues espices, peu de saffran de sel avec le gros d'un oeuf de farine que vous saulpouldrez par dessus. Et acheves de hacher tout ensemble comme saulcisses au espices & sel & les

cleaned well and dried, and press, and tie separately a good half-foot long each one, and place them for two days in salt, then place them to dry in the chimney.[81]

Lombard sausages

Take cooked capon flesh, partridges, woodcock or river fowl, and a bit of young pig flesh with fat lard to lard it, chop everything together very finely and season with fine spices and salt and one of round whole pepper then make your sausages in beef casings, a handful, well cleaned the length of a half foot, as full as you can and let them dry outside the fireplace far from the fire. And these can be kept two or three years entirely raw. And they must be soaked, then cooked in water and wine a long time.[82]

A counterfeit cucumber sausage, apple, pear

Take a round of veal [83] and chop it very fine without fat and assemble white powder, fine spices, a little saffron, some salt with an egg-sized amount of flour which you will sprinkle on top. And having thoroughly chopped everything together like sausages with the spices

---

81. Three pounds of meat will make about 3 or 4 six-inch sausages using beef middles, whose diameter is about 2¼ inches. These are not thus the very wide bologna that in Italy are traditionally made in a beef bung, which is about 4½ inches wide and would hold about 7 or 8 pounds of meat. Chopping even extremely finely would also not give you an absolutely smooth texture, or batter, from which bologna is made today. Nor are these poached before smoking. The end result is closer to a bratwurst. The *Grand Cuisinier* of 1576 spells out the abbreviation ('z') as *drægmes*, but more correctly this text has it as ounces. An ounce of salt is 5 teaspoons, which is roughly what would be used in a modern recipe. A very large quantity of spice goes into these sausages.

82. We are not given measurements or proportions here, though it seems as if a measure of pepper was intended but omitted (perhaps a handful?). In any case, for every five pounds of meat, use 4 tablespoons of salt. They were to be air-dried away from the fireplace or chimney.

83. The round is the rear thigh, cut in a round form, the equivalent of the round of beef on a younger animal, often sold as a roast in modern markets.

faconnes comme cocombres, ou une pomme ou de saulcisse longues, mis en gros boyaulx. Et aussi vous en pourres faire sans boyaulx. Le tout faconnez avec farine ung petit en poires ou en pommes. Ausdictes pommes et poire il fault mettre des queues. Il fault cuyre les cocombres et saulcisses en vin, eaue, sel saulge. Lesdictes pommes et poires se doyvent mettre ou cuire en bon boulion & assembler comme ung potaige de chapon lye pour donner couleur a voz cocombre, prenes moyeulx d'oeufz avec ung peu de farine aussi avec peu de jus de bledz, et de ce dores vosditz cocombres en les faisant seicher de longue main devant le feu.

⁋ Les saulcisses sont bonnes a menger fraydes. Et *[fol. 33v]* ne se gardent point plus de hault huyct jours & les cocombres aussi, haches* voz foyes et pomons quant seront cuytz avecques peu de menues herbes frises tout avec ung peu de saing de lard et puis quant ilz seront cuictz fort, prenes deulx ou troys moyeulx d'oeufz ung peu de boullon verjus pouldre blanche menue espice saffran faictes le tout boullir ensemble en le remuant & mettes dans ung petit pot groiselles ou Aigretz et assaisonne de sel et fault qu'il soit lye comme paste en pot.

⁋ Galimaffree.
⁋ Prenes ung gigot de mouton cuict fraichment et le haches le plus menu que pourres en ung plat d'ongnons parmy & le assembles comme est dit dessus parmy les herbes il fault coupper ledict gigot de mouton asses grossement & aussi rompre les os par morceaux & les ongnons bien menu & mettes le tout estuver avec peu de verjus & du beurre et pouldre blanche le tout ensemble et assisonne de sel.

⁋ Saulce d'enfer.
⁋ Faictes boullir voz piedz de porceaulx bien cuitz avec bon boullon. Et quant ilz seront bien cuictz tires les et les mettes rostir sur le gril, puis couppes les a gros morceaulx en plat & saulce verte dessus. Quant

---

* Here begins a different recipe; the preceding line should presumably have gone with the recipe above it.

and salt, form them like cucumbers or an apple or long sausage, and place in a big casing. And you can also make them without casings. Form everything with a little flour into pears or into apples. For these apples and pear you must make stems. The cucumbers and sausages must be cooked in wine, water, salt and sage. The apples and pears should be cooked in good broth and arranged like a thickened capon stew. To give colour to your cucumber, take egg yolks with a little flour also with a little wheat grass juice, and with this paint the cucumbers, while letting them dry a long while in front of the fire.

These sausages are good to eat cold. And don't keep them more than eight days, the cucumbers as well.

Chop your livers and lungs when they are cooked with a little fine herbs all fried with a little melted lard and then when they are well cooked, take two or three egg yolks, a little broth, verjuice, white powder, fine spice, saffron and let everything boil together while stirring and place gooseberries or unripe grapes in a little pot and season with salt, and it should be thick like a potted pie.

Gallimaufry [84]

Take a leg of mutton freshly cooked and chop it as finely as you can on a plate with onions along with it, and assemble as is said above about herbs. It is necessary to cut the said leg of mutton coarsely enough and also to break the bone into pieces, and the onions very finely, and place it all to stew with a bit of verjuice and butter and white powder, everything together, and season with salt.

Hell sauce

Boil your pig's trotters until well cooked in good broth. And when they are well cooked remove them and place to roast on a grill, then cut them into large pieces on a plate and put green sauce on them.

---

84.   This word means a hodge-podge, a kind of stew.

[fol. 34r] voz pied seront cuictz hasles les sur le gril: prenez oygnons haches bien menu et les mettes dedans ung plat, faictes estuver avec verjus, et quant ilz seront estuves asses mettes y moustarde peu, puis prenes voz piedz de pourceaulx mys par pieces & les mettez en plat tout chaulx & des charbons tous vifz par dessus, & puis verses vostre saulce d'aigreur par dessus et serves a l'entree de la table.

⁂ Cochons.
⁂ Prenes cochons bien plumes non gueres gras mis par pieces par l'espesseur de deulx doigtz en carre faictes bouilir avec eaue vin blanc sel et ung petit de saulge, puis pures le boullon quant il sera cuyct et le gardes & mettes en plat troys pieces dudict cochon en chascun plat & quant seront froictz mectes de vostre bouillon saulce & saulge comme dict est au chapitre des saulces dessus vostre cochon entree de table ou l'yssue si voules garder vostre cochon en saulge. Prenes autant dudict boullon que avez garde que de vostre saulce & mettes bouillir ensemble avec peu de menue espice & pouldre blanche ensemble vostredicte graine dedans ung pot quant sera froict estouppes le bien et se gardera sept ou huyct jours. Et en pourres servir comme Galentine quant en aures affaire.

⁂ Prenes cochon bien nect despeces le par pieces com*[fol. 34v]*me dessus. Et le mettes Bouillir avec vin blanc eaue & ung peu de verjus & de vinaigre assaisonne de sel a l'assemblee fault menue espice Saffran et quant il sera cuyct prenes amandes bien broyes et prenes vostre dict boullon quant sera cuyct & en passes de vosdictes amandes bien Broyes ensemble voz foyes dudict cochon qui seront cuitz. Puis quant sera passe faictes bouillir le tout ensemble & en dresses en plat a chascun trois pieces. Et puis les emplisses de vostre boullon & les lairres [laisses] froidir comme Gellee. Aulcuns n'y veulent point de saffran et demeure en sorte de blanc menger. Les aultres le laissent dedans le pot tout ensemble. Et se garde quatre ou cinq jours.

⁂ Laict gras larde.
⁂ Prenes bon laict gras ayes de lart gras cuyt mis par petites bandes

When your trotters are cooked brown them on the grill: take onion chopped finely and put them on a plate, let stew with verjuice and when they are stewed enough add a little mustard, then take your pig's trotters chopped in pieces, and place on a very hot plate with hot coals on top, then pour your sour sauce on top and serve as a first course.

Pigs

Take pigs well skinned and not too fat and chop into pieces the thickness of two fingers squared. Boil with water, white wine, salt and a little sage, then strain the broth when it is cooked and save, and place on a plate three pieces of the said pork in each plate and when it is cold pour your broth, sauce and sage, as is said in the chapter on sauces, over your pig and present for the first course or the last course if you want to keep your pork in sage. Take the said broth that you have kept from your sauce and boil it together with a little fine spice and white powder together with your said meat in a pot. When it is cooled, stop it up well and keep for seven or eight days. And you can serve it like a galantine when needed.

Take a pig well cleaned and cut into pieces as above. And place to boil with white wine and a bit of verjuice and vinegar, season with salt together with fine spices, saffron and when it is cooked take almonds well pounded and take your said broth when it is cooked and sieve with your said almonds well pounded together with your livers of the said pig which will be cooked. Then when it is sieved, boil everything together and place in plates three pieces each. And then fill them with your broth and let them cool like jelly. Some do not use any saffron and it remains a kind of blancmange. Others leave it in the pot all together. And it keeps for four or five days.

Fat larded milk

Take good rich milk, and cooked salted pork fat cut into little strips.

pour lyer puis moyeulx D'oeufz crudz passe par l'estamine avec vostre laict pouldre Blanche & faictes Boullir tout ensemble aussi vostre lart assaysonne de sel en le remuant qu'il ne se caille. Et quant il sera cuict verses dedans une estamine ou serviette et le pressures. Et laisses degouster une nuyct. Le landemain couppes le par lesches frises le en lart gras mettes Pouldre blanche de duc dessus ou sucre.

   [fol. 35r] ℂ Tortues.

ℂ Tortue leur fault Coupper la teste oultre et les fault laisser mortifier d'ung jour en ung four. Puis les faire cuyre avec les cuysses dans ung pot de terre & sel l'espasse de deulx ou troys heures & si [s]ont des dures elle veullent plus cuyre si se sont de jeunes trois heures. Puis quant elles seront cuyctes tires les, et les mettes dans eaue froide ostes les cruses et peaulx entaillee reserve le foye & les oeufz & plumes les jambes & piedz et puis si les mettes par pieces ensemble oeufz & foyes et ostes l'amer & frises en saing de lart ou beurre selon le jour* avec groiselles ou aigretz puis pouldre blanche par dessus et menges avec l'orange. Aulcuns prennent ung moyeuf d'oeuf et ung peu de verjus boullon et mettes dans en fricassant avec groiselles ou aigretz & en peult on faire estuver dedans ung petit pot comme de pigeons aussi habilles grenolles quant selle eront [elles seront] escorchees frittes ou estuvees aussi escargotz tires hors des creuses et veullent fort cuyre avec soree [force] sel.

   ℂ Les maigres friteaulx.

ℂ Prenes jeunes herbes comme espinars laictues persil marjolaine, fueille de maulve & toute aultees bonnes herbes haches bien menu les estraignez fort entre voz mains le plus que pourres & l'assaisonnes prenez *[fol. 35v]* farine de la grosseur de la quarte partie de herbes et moille la grosseur d'ung oeuf et moyeulx d'oeufz six peu de menue espice & de canelle z de succre assaisonne de sel en remuant tresbien avec une cuillie puis faictes fondre deulx ou troys coings de beure en une poelle, puis prenes avec une cueiller et mettes en vostre poelle en

---

*   *Jour*, in this instance, is making reference to whether it is for a *jour maigre* (fast day), or *jour gras* (when animal fats and meat were permitted).

To thicken, take raw egg yolks passed through a sieve with your milk, white powder and let everything boil together as well as your salt pork fat seasoned with salt while stirring so it doesn't curdle. And when it is cooked place in a sieve or napkin and press it. And let it drain for one night. The next day, cut it into slices, fry in salt pork fat and place white Duke's powder or sugar on top.

Tortoise

You must cut the head of the tortoise off and leave it to age for a day in an oven. Then cook it with the thighs and salt in an earthenware pot for two or three hours, and if they are tough, they should be cooked longer, if they are young, three hours. Then when they are cooked remove them and place in cold water, remove the shell and cut out the skin, reserve the liver and eggs, and clean the legs and feet and then place them in pieces together with eggs and livers. Remove the gall bladder and fry in melted lard or butter according to the season with gooseberries or unripe grapes then add white powder on top and eat with orange. Some take an egg yolk and a bit of verjuice and broth and make it in a fricassee with gooseberries and unripe grapes and you can stew in a little pot like pigeons. Also dressed frogs when they are skinned, fried or stewed, also as snails removed from the shells, to be cooked well with a lot of salt.

Lean fritters

Take young herbs like spinach, lettuce, parsley, marjoram, leaves of mallow and all other good herbs chopped very finely and squeeze them hard between your hands as much as you can. To season, take flour by weight a fourth part of the herbs and marrow the weight of an egg and 6 egg yolks, a little fine spice and cinnamon and an ounce of sugar seasoned with salt and stirred very well with a spoon, then melt two or three pounds[85] of butter in a pan, then take a spoon and place in your pan the way you make '*buqueste*' fritters and fry over

---

85. Cotgrave calls this a cake or dish of butter but says, 'In the ordinary fashion of our pound,' so we have translated it as a pound; a lot of butter, but certainly enough for deep-frying.

façon de buquestes & frises a petit feu et les tournes & quant seront asses cuyctes serves toutes chauldes succre par dessus.

℃ Ris.
℃ Prenes jeunes herbes la[i]ctues persil marjolaine deulx ou troys fueille de mante & faictes blanchir lesdictes herbes & hacher bien menu et les estraindre bien fort pour les assembler fort bon fromaige broye ou fraye aussi gros que les herbes & que de farine espandu parmy peu de menue espice trois ou quatre moyeulx d'oeufz assaisonne de sel le tout bien poictry ensemble & faconne en petites pieces saulcisses en les roullant avec la main & avec farine et quant les vouldres servir faictes les cuyre en eaue Bouillant peu sallee et les faictes boullir jusques ad ce qu'elles viendront par dessus l'eaue boullant puis tires les et les mettes en platz avec beurre frais fondu & fromaige jectes dessus serves chauldes.

[fol. 36r] ℃ Saulcyrion en may.
℃ Saulcyrion il les fault bien nectoyer laver essuyer essuyer & mettre en ung plat ou en ung petit pot avec beurre verjus Cynamomon pouldre blanche, six cloux de giroffle & faire estuver de longue main a petit feu & y mettre petit de saffran sel et quant ilz seront cuictz serves tous chaulx et aussi a jour gras avec lart menu pareillement.

℃ Champignons.
℃ Champignons au moys de Septembre comme dessus vous les feres peller & les plus jeunes raynes & haches oygnons naenu [menu] parmy. Il fault peller laver faire blanchir en eaue avec oygnons peu de sel, puis les esprindre et frire en beurre ou lart tout chault serves pouldre blanche dessus sur les charbons. Sel beurre pouldre blanche tous chaulx. Faictes cuyre pastenades entre deulx brayses. Puis plumes et les couppes par roelles assaisonnez de sel d'huylle d'olyve vinaigre.

a low flame and turn them, and when they are cooked serve all hot with sugar on top.

Rice [86]

Take young herbs, lettuce, parsley, marjoram, two or three leaves of mint and blanch the said herbs and chop very fine and squeeze very hard. To assemble, strong good cheese pounded or crumbled as much as the herbs and some flour mixed throughout, a little of fine spice, three or four egg yolks seasoned with salt, all well mixed together and fashioned into little bits of sausages by rolling with your hands, along with flour, and when you want to serve, cook them in boiling water, lightly salted, and let them boil just until they come up to the top of the boiling water. Then take them out and place on a plate with fresh melted butter and cheese sprinkled on top. Serve hot.

Mushrooms in May

Button mushrooms must be well cleaned, washed, wiped and placed in a dish or a little pot with butter, verjuice, cinnamon, white powder, six cloves and stewed a long while on a low fire, and add there a little saffron, salt and when they are cooked serve them very hot and also likewise on meat days with a little salted pork fat.

Mushrooms

Mushrooms in the month of September as above, you peel them, and the youngest are scraped, and chop onions finely with them. You must peel, wash and blanch in water with onion and a bit of salt, then squeeze out and fry in butter or lard and serve hot with white powder on top, over the coals. Salt, butter, white powder, all hot. Cook parsnips between two coals.[87] Then peel and cut into rounds, season with salt and olive oil and vinegar.

---

86. The title of this recipe is obviously wrong. These are actually a kind of dumpling or gnocchi.
87. It is not clear if these parsnips are to be included with the mushrooms or are a separate recipe that was accidentally included here.

❡ Oygnons.
❡ Faictes cuyre oygnons entre deulx cendres. Puis quant seront cuyctz plumes les et les mettes par quartiers roelles assaysonne de Sel d'huylle d'olyve vinaicre pouldre blanche tout chault. Toutes sallades au [fol. 36v] tant d'este & d'iver este requiert harentz soretz. Il fault oster les queues bien lavees en eaue tyede. Et puis les laisses tremper. Et changes par deulx ou troys foys ladicte eaue & bien dessallee. Puis assembles d'huylle d'olyve vinaigre & succre en les remuant les jours avec membre. De mouton rosty.

❡ Mesles.
❡ On faict cresme de mesle avec succre cynamomon passe non par trop espesse mettes vin vermeil ostes les queues desdictes mesles & les frises pouldre de duc dessus servez chault.

❡ Cresson & jeunes herbes.
❡ Tordes cresson & le laves essuyes & mettes huylle d'olyve dessus & peu de bon vinaigre en remuant fort le tout ensemble avec huylles oygnons haches et les frises avec persil on les contrefaict de harenc blanc escache.

❡ Prenes beurre moyeulx d'oeufz cuyctz en eaue passez le tout par estamine avec peu de cynamomon succre eaue rose sel peu & faconnes comme ung coing de beurre.

❡ Fault faire boullir oeufz de Carpe ou layctance avec eaue & vin blanc ou verjus sel & quant et [elles] seront cuictz mettes les dessus ung Aix & les couppez par gros [fol. 37r] morceaulx & les poudroyes de farine de tous costes & les frises en huylle ou beurre avec Oygnons aussi coupes a gros morceaulx. Et quant seront cuictz servez chaulx pouldre blanche dessus ou orange.

Onions

Cook onions between two cinders. Then when they are cooked, peel them and cut in quarter rounds seasoned with salt, olive oil, vinegar, white powder served hot. All salads both in summer and winter require dried herrings. It is necessary to remove the tails, and wash in tepid water. And then let them soak. And change the water two or three times, so they are well desalted. Then add to them olive oil, vinegar and sugar and stir them each day with your hand. On Roast Mutton.[88]

Medlars

You make cream of medlars with sugar, cinnamon. Sieve without pressing too much, add red wine, remove the stems of the said medlars, and fry them, with Duke's powder on top. Serve hot.

Cress and young herbs

Wring out cress and wash, dry and add olive oil on top and a little vinegar and toss everything well together with oil. Chop onions and fry them with parsley. You counterfeit them with crushed white herring.[89]

Take butter, egg yolks cooked in water and pass it all through a sieve with a little cinnamon, sugar, rosewater, a little salt and fashion like a cake of butter.

Boil carp eggs or milt with water, white wine or verjuice, add salt and when they are cooked place them on a board and cut them into large morsels and dust them with flour on all sides and fry them in oil or butter with onions, also cut into large pieces. And when they are cooked serve hot with white powder or orange on top.

---

88. This was certainly meant to be another recipe, but was accidentally included here.
89. This line probably belongs somewhere else since it is hard to imagine how herring could be used to counterfeit cress. In the 1576 edition of the *Grand Cuisinier*, the person who reset the type separated these into two lines.

⁌ Cerises confittes.
⁌ Prenes cerises ou griottes & leur ostes les queues & les mettes dedans une petite casse avec peu de vin blanc ou d'eaue necte sucre a l'equipollent de la saulce faictes bouillir a petit feu. Et quant le boullon viendra en sorte que elles seront cuyctes mettes les refroidir, puis passes le tout par estamine et mettes le jus dedans ung voirre Ou aultre vaisseau si Voulles. Et ce sera Gellee de Cerises ou de Griottes. La Chair que sera demouree en vostre estamine serves la succre dessus a l'entree de la table ladicte Gellee se garde troys ou quatre jours febves nouvelles a l'entree de table des oygnons pouldre blanche Huictres a l'entree. Mesles a l'entree frictes avec beurre & pouldre de duc.

⁌ Friteaulx.
⁌ Prenes chair de carpes ou brochetz & le haches bien menu avec menues herbes pour l'assembler moyeulx d'oeufz peu de cynomomon de menu espice sel, puis achevez de le hacher apres frises a petit feu comme aulx *[fol. 37v]* friteaulx avec beurre & tournes .ii. ou .iii. foys serves tout chault pouldre de duc dessus faictes bouillir vos chapons prenez moyeulx d'oeufz cuictz ou creud avec peu de mye de pain blanc pouldre Blanche. Le tout passes avec vostre boullon par l'estamine avec peu de vin blanc verjus puis haches menues herbes mettes en vostre pot petit de saffran groiselles aigret Remuez souvent affin qu'il ne se tourne servires avec ledict chapon chault broet par dessus & aussi de veaulx mys par pieces.

⁌ Haricot de foyes de veaulx.
⁌ Foye de veau de mouton ou aulters foyes de veaulx coupes & les mettes boullir avec bon boullon en ung pet[i]t pot de terre avec oygnons lart couppe menu verjus vin vermeil vinaigre le tout mys tremper avec ung Peu de pain hasle menues Espices, goustes de sel, aussi si voulles menues herbes bien menu hachees.

Preserved cherries

Take cherries or morellos and remove the stems and place them in a small pot with a little white wine or clear water, add sugar of the same amount as the sauce and boil over a low fire. And when the liquid gets to the point that they are cooked, cool them, then pass everything through a sieve and place the juice in a glass or other vessel if you like. And this will be cherry or morello jelly. The pulp that will remain in your sieve, you serve with sugar on top as a first course. The said jelly keeps for three or four days, along with new fava beans as an appetizer, onions, white powder and oysters as a starter. Medlars as a first course, fried with butter and Duke's powder.[90]

Fritters

Take flesh of carp or pike and chop it finely with fine herbs. To assemble, add egg yolks, a little cinnamon, fine spices, salt and then having finished chopping, fry, over a low flame like the fritters with butter and turn 2 or 3 times. Serve very hot with Duke's powder on top.[91] Boil your capons, take egg yolks, cooked or raw with some white breadcrumbs, and white powder. Pass everything with your broth through a sieve with white wine, verjuice, then finely chop herbs, place in your pot a little saffron, and some gooseberries. Stir often until it can't be stirred. With the said capon, serve hot broth on top and also with veal cut into pieces.

Haricot[92] of calf's liver

Calf's liver, of mutton or other livers. Cut calves' livers and place to boil with good broth in a little earthenware pot with onions and salted pork fat chopped fine, verjuice, red wine, vinegar, and soak everything with a little toasted bread, fine spices, salt to taste. Also if you like, fine herbs finely chopped.

90. This is either an alternate version of the above recipe made with medlars or it should be another recipe, with the directions missing.
91. Another recipe starts here randomly, for a kind of thick capon stew.
92. This term comes from *herigoter*, to shred or cut up finely. By one of the strangest and long-perpetuated mistakes in culinary history, it was assumed to have something to do with haricot beans, with which the dish *haricot de mouton* is made today.

⁂ Allouettes.

⁂ Prenes allouettes bien habillees et les faictes reffaire & les frises en sain de lard et les faictes boullir en bon boullon petit verjus de vinaigre de de vin vermeil, pain hasle destrempe de vostre boullon & passe par l'estamine puis faictes boullir avec voz allouettes *[fol. 38r]* pour assembler, prenes cynamomon menues espices cloud de giroffle entier, noix de muscade peu haslee mise en pourdre & y mettez du succre du sel, & pas trop d'espice.

⁂ Paste en pot de trippes.

⁂ Prenes trippes quant elle[s] seront bien cuyctes et les haches bien menues avec oygnons, puis mettes en ung pot avec ung peu de boullon gras, & les faictes cuyre sur les charbons en remuant et a l'assembler prenes peu de men[u]es espices pouldre blanche, saffran destrempe avec peu de verjus, et mis en vostre pot groisellez ou aigretz.

⁂ Potaige.

⁂ Prenes trippes quant elles seront bien cuyctes coupez par morceaulx puis mettes les boullir avec bon boullon, ung peu de verjus vinaigre peu de menues espices pouldre blanche saffran & sel, groiselles, aygret aussi des piedz de beuf et tous aultres.

⁂ Chauldeau.

⁂ Prenes bon boullon doulx avec moyeulx d'oeufz peu de verjus pouldre blanche le tout passe par l'estamine assaisonne de sel.

Larks

Take larks well dressed and twice cook them, fry them in melted lard and then boil them in a good broth, with a little verjuice, vinegar and red wine, toasted breadcrumbs moistened with your broth and passed through a sieve and then boil with your larks. To assemble, take cinnamon, fine spices, whole cloves, a little toasted nutmeg made into powder, and add sugar and salt, and not too much spice.

Potted Pie of Tripe

Take tripe when they are well cooked and chop them very finely with onions, then place in a pot with a little fatty broth, and let them cook over the coals, while stirring, and to assemble take a little fine spices, white powder, saffron soaked in a little verjuice and place in your pot gooseberries or sour grapes.[93]

Pottage

Take tripe and when they are well cooked, cut into morsels then let them boil with good broth, a little verjuice, vinegar, some fine spices, white powder, saffron and salt, gooseberries, sour grapes. Also for cowheel and other things.

Caudle

Take good light broth, egg yolks, a little verjuice, white powder and pass everything through the sieve, season with salt.[94]

---

93. This tripe recipe and the next are essentially the same, the only major difference is that the former, being very finely chopped, forms in the end a kind of spreadable pâté, or something like a *rillette*. The pottage implies large bits in a kind of liquid stew, or what in Italy would be called a *minestra*, into which you can also put other meats. Notice how tomatoes replace the sour fruit in what will eventually be *Tripes à la provençale*.

94. The final effect of this is a thick, sour and refreshing soup, very much like Greek *avgolemono*, made exactly the same way except without lemon. It's not clear whether this is beef or chicken broth, but when the author calls for beef broth, as in the next recipe, he specifies it. Chicken broth would be more pleasant in this recipe in any case.

[fol. 38v] ℂ Potaige.

ℂ Prenes queues, costes de mouton ou poictrine despeces par pieces apres que aures ostes la peau mettes boullir par pieces avec bon boullon doulx de beuf ou de mouton mettes lard entrelarde. Et quant ilz seront cuycts prenes deulx ou troys moyeulx d'oeufz et les passes par l'estamine avec peu de verjus pouldre blanche et mettes dans vostre pot quant vouldres servir en remuant aussi groiselles aigret sel herbes menues hachees.

ℂ Le brochet se veult fendre et oster les tripailles pour le cuyre vin blanc, verjus & ne le tirez chault.

ℂ La perche se cuyt entiere & aultres poissons.
ℂ Pour faire boullir carpes perches, Saulmons & aultres poissons, faictes boullir vostre eaue, vin vermeil sel saulge bonnes herbes et quant bouldra mettes vostre poisson dedans et le faictes cuyre a bon feu, et le couvres d'ung plat & mettes peu de beurre.

ℂ Turbot Grevot* Rouget comme Brochet Saulmon & Aloze, mais il ne les fault pas tirer si chaulx.

ℂ Andouilles d'oeufz.
ℂ Il fault faire comme une humblette excepte qu'il fault froisser mye de pain blanc avec force succre & ca[*fol. 39r*]nelle & aussi mettes y force bonne pouldre de duc. Et quant ilz seront bien batues faictes fondre en une poelle ung coing de beurre et mettez voz oeufz dedans et mettes sur charbons, puis de vostre pouldre pouldroyes par dessus voz oeufz, & puis quant elle sera cuycte en rouelle & la faconnes comme une andouille serves chaulde avec moustarde pour gens debilles vieulx faictes comme dessus excepte que au lieu de pouldre de duc bon formaige.

* The *Livre de cuisine*, from which the *Livre fort excellent* was reprinted, has this word as *grenot*. Although old dictionaries define *grenot* as 'a fish that is good to eat', none specifies what sort of fish it is. The word *grenault* crops up later, on p. 206, where we have translated it as monkfish, which this might indeed be.

Pottage

Take tails, ribs of mutton or breast, cut into pieces. After you have removed the skin, place to boil in pieces with good light beef or mutton broth. Add pork belly. And when they are cooked, take two or three egg yolks and pass through a sieve with a little verjuice, white powder and place in your pot. When you want to serve it, stir in also gooseberries, sour grapes, salt and finely chopped herbs.

Pike should be split and the intestines removed. To cook, white wine, verjuice, and don't remove it while hot.[95]

Perch is cooked whole like other fish

To boil carp, perch, salmon and other fish, boil your water, red wine, salt, sage, good herbs and when it boils place your fish in and let it cook over a good fire, and cover it with a plate, and add a little butter.

Turbot, *grenot*, mullet, like pike, salmon and shad, but you should not remove them while hot.

Andouille sausages of egg

You should make this like an omelette except that you should crumble white bread, with a lot of sugar, cinnamon, and also with a lot of good Duke's powder. And when they are well pounded, melt in the bottom of a pan a pound of butter and pouring in your eggs and put it over the coals, then with your powder, dust the top of your eggs, and then when they are cooked, roll them up like an andouille, serve hot with mustard, but for weak old folks as above except that in place of Duke's powder use good cheese.[96]

---

95. The logic here is that the fish should be cooled in the broth, so it firms up and doesn't fall apart, as it would if removed hot.
96. It seems as if the author intends the spiced breadcrumb mixture to go on top of the eggs and then be rolled up, much like any other omelette filling.

⁋ Andouillette verte.
⁋ Prenez blettes, bledz persil marjolaine, broyes en mortier, et puis pressures fort pour avoir le jus, surccre, sel cinamomon. Et passes le tout par l'estamine, et la faictes cuyre comme les aultres, et elle sera verte.

⁋ Ooeufz poches au beurre en plat.
⁋ Oeufz poches au beurre en plat quant ilz seront presque cuictz, prenes une poelle de fer chaulde et la mettes dessus lesdictz oeufz pour leur bailler couleur ou en faictes ou il n'y ait que les moyeulx.

⁋ Oeufz cuytz en eaue.
⁋ Faictes cuyre oeufz en eaue et qu'ils soyent durs et *[fol. 39v]* les Plumes et fendes par le millieu boutes les en plat avec beurre petit de verjus pouldre blanche peu de saffron avec peu de menues espices & herbes hachees, sel et quant les vouldres servir faictes les boullir sur du charbon entre deulx platz serves tous chaulx en este. En yver au lieu des herbes mesles de la moustarde.

⁋ Oeufz de plusieurs couleurs.
⁋ Pour rougir oeufz il les fault cuyre en eaue avec racine de Garence jusques ilz soient bien coulourez & bien durs.
⁋ Jaulne. Cuyses en Eaue avec force Pellasses d'ongnon.
⁋ Violet, il fault chauffer l'eaue qu'elle soit tiede, et puis y mettez z.v. d'or fueille. Et le tout faire ensemble jusques ilz seront bien cuyctz.

⁋ Oeufz cuictz sans feu.
⁋ Prenes ung pennier mettes chaulx vive dedans au fons dudict pennier & puis mettez oeufz tant que vouldres & les mettes par dessus ladicte chaulx, puis remplisses ledict pennier de chaulx par dessus lesdictz oeufz. Et quant vous les vouldres faire cuyre mettes ledict

Little green andouille

Take chard, green wheat, parsley, marjoram, grind them in a mortar, then press them vigorously to extract the juice. Then add sugar and cinnamon. And pass everything through a sieve and cook it like the others. It will be green.

Eggs poached in butter on a plate

Eggs poached in butter on a plate, when they are nearly cooked, take a hot iron pan and place it above the said eggs to give them colour or make them only with yolks.

Eggs cooked in water

Cook the eggs in water and when they are hard, peel them and split down the middle from end to end, put them on a plate with butter, a little verjuice, white powder, a little saffron with fine spices and chopped herbs, and salt. When you want to serve them let them boil over the coals between two plates and serve hot in summer. In winter in place of the herbs, mix in mustard.

Eggs of many colours

To redden eggs you should cook in water with the root of madder until they are well coloured and hard.

Yellow. Cook in water with a lot of onion skins.

Violet, you must heat the water until it is tepid and then place in 5 ounces of gold leaf.[97] And put everything together until they are well cooked.

Eggs cooked without fire

Take a basket and place in it quicklime at the bottom of the said basket and then add eggs as many as you like, and place on top of the said quicklime, then fill the basket with quicklime on top of the said eggs. And when you want to cook them place the said basket in

---

97. While this word does mean gold leaf, it seems unlikely that it would colour eggs, or that one would squander 5 ounces of gold on such a project. It may perhaps be a plant.

pennier en l'eaue et puis l'en ostes & les oeufz cuyront tousjours. Mettes lesdictz oeufz hors de ladicte chaulx & ilz se cuyront d'eulx mesmes. ☙ Saulce

[fol. 40r] ☙ Barbe robert.
☙ Prenes oygnons menues fritz en saing de lard ou Beurre selon le jour* verjus vinaigre, moustarde menues espices sel, et faictes bouilir tout ensemble. Ceste saulce sert a congnins rostys poisson frit tant de mer que d'aultre & oeufz fritz.

☙ Rappe.
☙ Prenes six moyeulx d'oeufz, puis de bon boullon peu de pouldre blanche verjus asses passes le tout par l'estamine mettes boullir avec groiselles ou aigretz & menues herbes hachees assaisonnes de sel.

☙ Pour chappons oysons poulles, poulletz fricasses.
☙ Faictes comme dessus au lieu de boullon fault puree de poys clere ung peu de beurre ou boullir en este au poisson bouilly dressees en Escuelle en lieu de Verjus verd ou Vinaigre, principallement aulx barbeaulx.

☙ Poys nouveaulx.
☙ Prenez poys nouveaulx esgoustez et les faictes bouillir avec bon laict & beurre, et quant seront cuyctz prenez moyeulx d'oeufz passes par l'estamine avec peu de laict pouldre blanche. Et saffran. Et quant les vouldrez dresser mettes voz moyeulx d'oeufz dedans le *[fol. 40v]* pot et recullez dudict feu en le remuant tousjours, assaisonne de sel, de menues herbes haches, ainsi pourrez faire de febves.

---

* Here again, the reference to *jour* indicates that the cook should choose either butter or lard depending on whether it is a fast day (*jour maigre*) or not.

water and then take it out of the water and the eggs will always be cooked. Remove the eggs from the said quicklime and they will cook on their own. Sauce.[98]

Robert's beard sauce [99]

Take onions finely [chopped] fried in melted lard or butter according to the season, verjuice, vinegar, mustard, fine spices, salt and boil everything together. This sauce works with roast rabbits and fried fish, both saltwater and others, and fried eggs.

Verjuice sauce

Take six egg yolks, then some good broth, a little white powder, enough verjuice, pass it all through a sieve and let it boil with gooseberries or sour grapes and finely chopped herbs, season with salt.

For capons, goslings, hens, chickens fried

Do as above but in place of broth, you should use thin pea purée and a bit of butter when boiling. In summer boiled fish, dressed in a terrine, in place of green verjuice or vinegar, principally for barbel.

New peas

Take new peas drain and boil them with good milk and butter, and when they are cooked take egg yolks passed through a sieve with a little of the milk, white powder. And Saffron. And when you want to dress them, place your egg yolks in the pot and move away from the fire, stirring always, season with salt, finely chopped herbs. You can even do this with fava beans.

---

98. Here is yet another compositor's error.
99. *Sauce Robert* is one of the classic French sauces, made of lightly sautéed onions with demi-glaze and mustard. Early editions of the *Larousse gastronomique* claim that it is named for one Robert Vinot in the sixteenth century, but there are older versions. Why this particular version is named for Robert's beard is unknown, unless it was brown? In Rabelais' *Fourth Book* he mentions this sauce and that it goes well with rabbit, pork and duck, eggs, excellent evidence that he knew this cookbook.

⟦ Fault que voz poys soyent cuyctz en eaue et beurre et quant seront presque cuictz assaisonnez de sel, peu de pouldre blanche, saffran, menues herbes, groiselles. Il n'y fault point d'espice.

⟦ Saulgrenee de poys.
⟦ Prenes poys rouges bien lavez & tirez puis mettes les baullir sans tremper en eaue tyede. Si c'est pour gens graveleux mettes cuyre avec racine de persil & fenoil. Et en ostez les cueurs assaisonne de beurre ou d'huylle d'olyve peu de verjus menues herbes, sel saffran a fievres porchalles ou petites ozeilles point de saffran humez de boullon a jeun au matin.

⟦ Febves.
⟦ Faictes boullir febves en eaue et quant elles seront bien cuyctes mettes des oygnons bien menus fris en sel beurre ou huylle et les mettes ung peu refroidir & quant elle seront refroidies mettes les dans ung pot les choses dessus et les faictes rebouillir sur le feu la saulce en les remuant souvent peu de saffran on les sert avec harencs marsouin salle et aultre saulce.

[fol. 41r] ⟦ Escrevisses.
⟦ Faictes cuyre escrevisses avec vin sel et eaue ainsi comme il appartient. Puis broyes des amandes avec l'escorche & aussi les corps desdictes escrevisses. Puis le tout passes par l'estamine avec le beurre puree de poys claire & de vin vermeil. Peu de vinaigre. Menues espices, cynamomon, & le tout boullir ensemble en petit pot. Assaisonne de Sel, puis cernes piedz des Escrevisses et les frises & les plumes en beurre. Et quant ilz seront fritz mettes une partie dans vostre potaige La reste est bon a menger au verjus verd a l'orange. Escrivisses bailles avec vinaigre a toutes gens desgoustees.

⟦ Huyctres au cyve.
⟦ Prenes huyctres bien lavez et les mettes cuyre en eaue et sel frises les avec oygnons et quant elles seront frictes prenes pain hasle passe par

It is necessary that your peas be cooked in water and butter and when they are nearly cooked, season with salt, a little white powder, saffron, fine herbs, gooseberries. It doesn't need any spice.

Pease pottage [100]

Take red peas well washed and sorted then set them to boil without soaking in tepid water. If it is for people with stone, cook with parsley root and fennel. And remove the hearts, season with butter or olive oil, a little verjuice, fine herbs, salt, saffron. For fevers, add purslane or a little sorrel, a touch of saffron, moisten with broth, for breakfast in the morning.

Fava beans

Boil the beans in water and when they are well cooked and add finely chopped onions fried in salted butter or oil, and cool them a bit and when they are cooled place in a pot with things on top, and let the sauce come back to a boil over the fire, stirring often, and add saffron. Serve them with herring, salted porpoise or another sauce.

Crayfish

Cook the crayfish with wine, salt and water as appropriate. Then crush almonds with the skin and also the bodies of the said crayfish. Then pass everything through a sieve with butter, thin pea purée and red wine. A little vinegar. Add fine spices, cinnamon, and boil everything together in a little pot. Season with salt, then crack and shell the claws of the crayfish and fry in butter. And when they are fried, place some in your pottage. The rest is good to eat with green verjuice, and orange. Give crayfish with vinegar to people with blunted taste.

Oyster stew

Take oysters wash well and place them to cook in water and salt. Fry them with onions and when they are fried, take breadcrumbs passed

---

100. Cotgrave translates *saugrenée* as 'porridge, or meat of pease'. It seems as if the author intends the parsley root and fennel to lend a smoother texture to the final dish, which would explain removing the woody centre of the parsley root.

l'estamine avec puree de poys claire vin vermeil vinaigre verjus puis bouillir tout ensemble huyctres & potaiges z iii espices saffran.

⁋ Estuvee.
⁋ Prenes petit brochetons eschardes mis en pieces ou anguilles escorchees par troncons mettes dedans ung pot avec puree de poys claire peu de vin blanc ver*[fol. 41v]*jus vinaigre peu de beurre menues espices, pouldre blanche saffran. Deulx ou troys cloudz de giroffle entiers menues herbes en yver de l'oygnon en lieu des herbes, aigret.

⁋ Estuvee noire.
⁋ Eschardes carpes ou brochetons couppes par troncons mettes dans ung pot de terre asses menu peu de puree oygnons vin vermeil vinaigre verjus menues espices Cynamomon. Deulx cloudz de giroffle beurre Huylle d'olyve Sel, cuyre le tout sur charbons et le couvrez en cuysant et qu'il n'y demeure gueres de boullon en cuysant Menues herbes groiselles aigret sel. Ainsi faictes d'anguille.

⁋ Oeufz en paste en pot.
⁋ Prenes oeufz selon la quantite que voul[d]res et les bates tres bien peu de sel: prenez oygnons nouveaulx foyes avec beurre bien menu herbes hachees. N'y fault point de saulge ny d'ysope. Et les faictes cuyre avec vostre oygnon bien peu, puis mettes vos oeufz dedans et en faictes une amelete puis quant il sera cuycte mettes la sur haist et la hachez menue, mettez la puis dans ung pot nect avec puree de poys claire & beurre. Faictes cuyre sur charbons en remuant comme autre paste ensemble menues espices pouldre blanche saffran en poul*[fol. 42r]*dre destrempe en verjus et mettes dedans et prenes moyeulx d'oeufz entrelarde de cloux de giroffle comme pour ung aultre paste de groiselles aigretz. Et en yver largement de verjus D'oygnons frictz en lieu d'herbes serves chaulx.

through a sieve with thin pea purée, red wine, vinegar, verjuice, then boil everything together, oysters and pottage, with three ounces of spices, saffron.

Stew

Take small pikes, scale, and chop into pieces or sliced, skinned eels, place in a pot with thin pea purée, a little white wine, verjuice, vinegar, a little butter, fine spices, white powder and saffron. Two or three whole cloves, fine herbs, in winter onion in place of the herbs, unripe grapes.

Black stew

Scale carp or pike and cut into sections, place in an earthenware pot small enough, some puréed [peas], onions, red wine, vinegar, verjuice, fine spices, cinnamon. Two cloves, butter, olive oil, salt, cook everything over the coals and cover while cooking, and let most of the broth cook off. Fine herbs, gooseberries, unripe grapes, salt. You can also make this with eels.

A potted pie of eggs

Take eggs according to the quantity you wish and beat them very well with a little salt. Take young onions, livers with butter, and very fine chopped herbs. Except not sage or hyssop. And let it cook with your onion just a little, then place your eggs in and make an omelette, then when it is cooked place it on a board and chop finely. Then place it in a clean pot with thin pea purée and butter. Let it cook over the coals while stirring like other pies together with fine spices, white powder, powdered saffron soaked in verjuice and placed in, and take egg yolks stuck with cloves as for another pie and gooseberries, sour grapes. In winter more verjuice, fried onions in place of the herbs, serve hot.

ℂ Mesles

ℂ Prenes mesles lardes et les faictes boullir en eaue apres qu'elles seront cuyctes ostes l'eaue & la mettez dans ung plat rassoir affin que l'escaille & pierres demeurent au fonds dudict plat. Prenes moyeulx d'oeufz puis Saffran verjus pouldre Blanche le tout passe par l'estamine menues herbes vostre bollon pour destremper le tout en Kareseme du laict d'amande.

ℂ Chauldume pour le cerveau.

ℂ Prenes peu de puree de poix claire petit d'eau, et deulx ou troys moyeulx d'oeufz peu de pouldre blanche tout passe par l'estamine, puis prenes menues herbes boutes boullir dans ung pot verjus sel avec beurre en remuant.

ℂ Anguille viande exquise et qui est fort bonne.

ℂ Prenes anguilles escorchees mises par troncons peu de saulpouldre de sel, frises d'huylle ou beurre, puis *[fol. 42v]* prenes pain hasle trempe en puree de poix claire & en vin vermeil broye avec l'escosse passe par l'estamine vinaigre verjus boutes boullir avec chardon menues espices cloud de giroffle cynamomon avec huylle d'olyve ou beurre sel serves chaulx.

ℂ Prenes puree de poix bien claire avec beurre ou huylle. Oygnons bien menu & mettes bouillir avec naveaulx. Et quant ilz seront cuictz passes mye de pain trempe avec le boullon & mettes dedans avec peu de saffran sel. Aulcuns n'y mettent point de puree, mais du laict & n'y fault point d'ongnon ny pain passe.

ℂ Espinars.

ℂ Prenes espinars & les faictes Blanchir puis haches les sur ung ayst. Prenes beurre frises oygnons bien menues et voz Espinars sur le charbon mettes puree de poix avec en ung petit pot peu de laict D'amande de sel pouldre blanche verjus en les remuant ilz sont pour la Karesme.

Medlars

Take medlars, lard them and leave to boil in water. After they are cooked, take them out of the water and let them sit on a plate so that the skins and stones fall to the bottom of said plate. Take egg yolks then saffron, verjuice, white powder, and pass it all through a sieve with fine herbs and your broth to moisten everything. During Lent, make with almond milk.

Chowder[101] for the brain

Take a little thin pea purée, water and two or three egg yolks, a little white powder and pass through a sieve, then take fine herbs and let boil in a pot, adding verjuice, salt, and butter while stirring.

Eel, an exquisite food that is very good

Take skinned eels and slice into sections and sprinkle with salt, fry in oil or butter, then take toasted bread soaked in thin pea purée and red wine, beat with the [pea] pods, pass through a sieve with vinegar, verjuice, and let boil over the coals, fine spices, cloves, cinnamon, with olive oil or butter, salt, serve hot.

Take very thin pea purée with butter or oil. Onion very fine and place to boil with turnips. And when they are cooked, pass [through a sieve with] breadcrumbs soaked in the broth and put in with a little saffron, salt. Some don't add purée at all, but some milk, and some don't add either onion or sieved bread.

Spinach

Take spinach and blanch, then chop on a board. Take butter and fry finely chopped onions and your spinach over the coals, add to it pea purée in a little pot with a little almond milk and salt, white powder, verjuice and stir. For Lent.

---

101. This would have been called a caudle in English of the sixteenth century, but the relation to a thick soup which we now call a chowder, something made in a cauldron, suggests this translation as well.

❧ Espinars.
❧ Faictes boullir eaue dedans ung pot avec beurre sel Puis prenes Espinars Laictues persil Bourrache Ozeille lavez & Tordez mettez en pot ledict potaige & ne veult point boullir comme une onde ainsi pourrez faire de jeunes blettes persil.

[fol. 43r] ❧ Choulx cabutz.
❧ Prenes choulx cabutz & ostes les fueilles mortes & qu'ilz ne soyent en boytes despecees bien menu les blettes. Et les mettes Blanchir avec oygnons environ demye heure pures sur ung haist & mettes de l'eaue froide dessus & estraignes entre voz mains & haches bien menu & les mettes dans ung pot de terre avec bon laict gras beurre peu de pouldre blanche sel. Et faictes boullir sur la braise en remuant souvent et l'en pourrez assembler au lieu du laict de la puree de poix.

❧ Aultre choulx.
❧ Prenes choulx & en ostes les fueilles mortes puis ostes la teste des pommes le plus menu que pourres avec oygnons ayes puree de poys bien claire eaue chaulde, & le tout mettes dedans ung pot de terre avec beurre ou huille sel et faictes bouillir puis y mettes voz choulx hachez & les faictes cuire & quant ilz seront presque cuictz mettez peu de pouldre blanche aulcuns y passe mye de pain par l'estamine avec puree de pois ou eaue & fort bien lye.

❧ Poissons en saulce sallemine.
❧ Prenes poissons brochetz carpes ou aultres eschardes de poissons frit en Beurre qui sera ung peu saulpouldre de sel pour assembler a faire ladicte saulce, pre*[fol. 43v]*nes amandes broyees avec l'escorce peu de pain hasle passe avec puree de poys claire peu de vin vermeil vinaigre verjus menues espices cynamomon faictes boullir & remuez dresses sur vostre fricture quant vouldres servir.

❧ Poreaulx.
❧ Prenes poreaulx apres qu'ilz sont bien trayes et laves couppes menu tant que pourrez et ung petit oygnon aussi bien menu & mettez boullir tout ensemble dans ung pot de terre avec puree de poys claire

Spinach

Boil water in a pot with butter, salt, then take spinach, lettuce, parsley, borage, sorrel, wash and wring out, place said pottage in a pot and do not let it boil, just a ripple. You can also make this with young chard, parsley.

Cabbage heads

Take cabbage heads and remove the dead leaves, and they should not be chopped in very small pieces like chard. And let them blanch with onions about half an hour, drain on a board, and put cold water on top, and squeeze between your hands. Chop finely and place in an earthenware pot with good fat milk, butter, a little white powder and salt. And boil them over coals, stirring often and you can assemble, in place of milk, with pea purée.

Another cabbage

Take cabbage and remove the dead leaves then remove the cores and chop as finely as you can, with onions, then add very thin purée of peas, hot water, and put everything in an earthenware pot with butter or oil, and salt and let it boil. Then put in your chopped cabbage and cook it. And when they are nearly cooked, add a little white powder. Some add breadcrumbs and pass through a sieve with pea purée or water and it should be thick.

Fish in *sallemine* sauce

Take fish, pike, carp or other, scaled fish, fried in butter and sprinkled with salt. Upon serving, make said sauce, take almonds ground with the skins, a little toasted bread, passed [though a sieve] with thin pea purée, a little red wine, vinegar, verjuice, fine spices, and cinnamon. Let it boil and stir. Pour over your fried fish when you want to serve.

Leeks

Take leeks after they have been well sorted and washed, cut as finely as you can and a little onion also very finely chopped, and boil everything together in an earthenware pot with thin pea purée,

beurre huille sel & quant ilz seront presque cuictz mettez petit de pouldre Blanche Saffran ilz veullent cuyre a estroit aulcuns y passent mye de pain & en sont plus doulx & lye.

prenes le blanc des Poreaulx mettes boullir avec oygnons purees & hachees menu ensemble, faictes fondre du Beurre en une poelle et frises ladicte ensemble puree de poys claire bon lart gras en Karesme laict d'amande pouldre blanche saffran sel tout mys dans ung pot & le faictes achever de cuyre sur le charbon en remuant fort on les sert avec anguilles ou saulmon salle.

⁌ Marrons.

⁌ Prenes marrons, et les faictes cuyre entre deulx *[fol. 44r]* braises et ne les fault comme rien cuyre mais que on les puisse plumer, puis apres passez ung peu de Cynamomon par l'estamine avec vin vermeil puis mettez lesdictz marrons dans ung pot de terre tout neuf avec ledict vin Cynamamon et succre et le tout faictes cuyre ensemble tant que le jus soit ung peu lie comme Syrop, & en cuysant mettez deulx ou troys cloux de giroffle entiers et servez tout chault en plat.

⁌ D'aultres marrons vin blanc succre sans cynamomon vous les ferez cuyre comme dessus est dict. Et aussi en pourrez faire Cresme quant ilz seront cuytz passe par l'estamine avec peu de cynamomon et fault qu'elle soit lyee. Et est bonne & belle.

⁌ Cocombres.

⁌ Prenes cocombres & les plumes par rouelles & les faictes cuyre avec Oygnons comme aulx pouldre hachez les dessus ung haist. Et les pressurez dans une estamine puis frises les avec beurre.

⁌ Ensemble Moyeulx d'oeufz crudz peu de puree de poys claire peu de pouldre blanche le tout passer par l'estamine. Saffran verjus sel menues espice, le tout mettez boullir sur charbon dans ung pot. Et serves tout chault.

⁌ Faictes bouillir bon laict gras en pot avec beurre ensemble, prenez moyeulx d'oeufz et passes par l'esta*[fol. 44v]*mine avec laict & verjus en remuant persil dedans sel pouldre blanche en remuant tousjours affin qu'il ne se prenne point.

butter, oil, salt, and when they are nearly cooked, add a little white powder and saffron. They should cook until well done. Some sieve with breadcrumbs and they are sweeter and thickened.

Take the white of leeks, boil with onion purée and chop everything together finely, melt butter in a pan and fry the said mixture with thin pea purée, good fat lard, or in Lent, almond milk, white powder, saffron, salt, everything put in a pot. Let it finish over the coals, stirring frequently. Serve with eels or cured salmon.

Chestnuts

Take chestnuts and cook them between two coals and they must be barely cooked, just until you can shell them. Then pass a little cinnamon and red wine through a sieve, then place the said chestnuts in a new earthenware pot with the said wine, cinnamon and sugar and cook everything together until the juice is a little thick like syrup. While cooking, add two or three whole cloves and serve very hot on a plate.

Otherwise chestnuts, white wine, sugar without cinnamon, cooked as above. And you can also make a cream. When they are cooked, pass through a sieve with a little cinnamon until they are thick. It is good and pretty.

Cucumbers

Take cucumbers and peel, cut into rounds, and cook them with onions as [in cucumbers] in powder. Chop them on a board. And press them in a sieve then fry with butter.

Together raw egg yolks, a little thin pea purée, a little white powder, everything passed through a sieve. Saffron, verjuice, salt, fine spices, everything boiled over the coals in a pot. And serve very hot.

Boil good fat milk in a pot together with butter, take egg yolks and pass through a sieve with milk, verjuice, stir it, add parsley, salt, white powder all the while stirring, so that it doesn't stick to the bottom.

⁕ Trippes.

⁕ Prenes trippes cuyctes & couppez de la grandeur de hastereaulx et si vous y mettes les boyaulx il ne les fault que fendre pour assembler vostre farce prenes lart Gras avec gresse de beuf ou de Mouton avec herbes hachees menu. Le tout ensemble assaisonne de menues espices sel puis faconne voz hastereaulx comme les aultres & y mettes vostre farce & les embrochez en une petite branche & les faictes rostir serves tous chaulx pouldre blanche dessus.

⁕ Chapitre de rost.

⁕ Veaulx chevreaulx aigneaulx faictes blanchir en eaue boullante, puis tremper en eaue froide lardes rost de long & les menger a l'orange verjus dessus sel menu.

⁕ Chappons poulles poulletz oysons pigeons se doibvent plumer en eaue chaulde blanchir comme dessus est dict.

⁕ Toutes vollatilles saulvaiges se veullent revenir sur les charbons.

[fol. 45r] ⁕ Oyseaulx de riviere.

⁕ Canars a la dodine oyes cines grues cygoignes butors faisans pans N'y fault point de lart Mais veullent estre lardes de cloulx de giroffle il fault pour arrouser ses oyseaulx que estaches* de lardon petites brochetes dessus lesdictz oyseaulx en rotissant arrouse de vinaigre & de sel menu pouldre commune et ceulx qui sont ainsi Assaisonnez doibvent estre mengees froides. Ceulx que vouldres menger chauldes il les fault larder & rostir comme dessus serves les seiches au sel menu point arrouse.

---

*   This word is close to *estaca* in Spanish, a stake or skewer, and it seems this is what is intended here.

Tripe

Take cooked tripe and cut the size of *hastereaux*[102] and if you add the intestines, they can just be split. To assemble your stuffing, take fat lard with beef or mutton fat and finely chopped herbs. Season everything with fine spices, salt and then fashion your *hastereaux* like the others and put in your stuffing and skewer them on a small branch and let them roast. Serve very hot with white powder on top.

Chapter on roasts

Veal, kid, lamb, blanch[103] in boiling water, then soak in cold water, lard, roast lengthwise and eat with orange, verjuice and fine salt on top.

Capons, hens and chickens, goslings, pigeons must be plucked, blanched in hot water as said above.

All wild fowl should be browned over the coals.

River fowl

Ducks in dodine, geese, swans, cranes, cygnets, bustard, pheasants, peacocks. They should not be larded but should be stuck with cloves. It is necessary to baste the birds that you skewer with little strips of bacon on the spits, on top of the said birds. While roasting, baste with vinegar and salt, ordinary fine spice powder, and those that have been thus seasoned ought to be eaten cold. Those that you would wish to eat hot should be larded and roasted as above. Serve them dry with only fine salt, not basted.

---

102. For *hastereaux*, see note 74 above. *Hastereaux* are mentioned in Rabelais' *Gargantua and Pantagruel*, book IV, ch. LIX. They are slices of pig's liver or organ meats, larded and roasted on a skewer. So the size is probably about 2 or 3 inches. It seems that these are stuffed into casings with fat as well.

103. This blanching procedure before roasting is very typical of medieval cooking. There are several possible reasons for it. A medicinal logic suggests that it purges the flesh of crude humours making it more digestible, but more sensibly, the blanched flesh firms up, stays on a spit better and does not immediately drip fat as it melts before the fire, so there may be purely gastronomic reasons for this technique. Meat blanched first is not, as one might suspect, drier or any less flavourful than if it were roasted raw.

❧ Perdrix.

❧ Perdrix rostyes a la Tonnellette ou aulx choulx poreaulx a l'ongnon sel menu orange pigeons ramees aulx choulx pigeons cresartz perdre aulx pluvier revenu sans laver au sel a l'orange les lapins aussi blanchir & revenu.

❧ Mouton.

❧ Le mouton rosty ce sert avec carpes* viande farcies il n'y fault point de saulces.

❧ Item a gybiers rostyes & farcies il ne les fault faire blanchir mais que les plumez en eaue il ne fault que quatre lardons aulx aelles, et aulx cuisses la ou il n'y a point de farce.

[fol. 45v] ❧ Rosty sanglant.

❧ Quant vostre rosty sera cuict & quant le vouldrez servir prenes ung peu de saing de liepvre en pouldre & en mettes dessus et quant on le couppera il sera sanglant.

❧ Chapon barbe.

❧ Fault plumer habiller larder et Embrocher rostir chapon. Et quant sera presque cuyct ostes les lardons, puis destrempes de la farine avec moyeulx d'oeufz eaue rose Succre assaysonne de sel & fault qu'elle soit asses clere comme pastes de friteaulx. Puis en mettez dessus ledict chapon avec une cuillier en rotissant et fault qu'il soit assez loing du feu affin qu'il seiche petit a petit & qu'il ne brusle et l'arrouses par trois ou quatre foys affin qu'il soit couvert de vostredicte paste & le [f]aire cuyre petit a petit puis apres qu'il sera cuyct arrouses le de saing de lard & le servez tout ainsi.

❧ Pan revestu.

❧ Fault escorcher pan & se garder de rompre sa peau. Et le faire revenir en eaue chaulde boullante larde de cloud de giroffle & lard puis le faire rostir & envelopper les piedz en cuysant & quant seront

---

* It seems unlikely the author intended carp; it may be a misprint for *capres*, capers.

Partridge

Partridge roasted *à la tonnelette*[104] or with cabbage, leeks and onion, fine salt, orange. Wood pigeons with cabbage, domesticated pigeons, partridges or plovers browned without washing with salt, orange. Rabbits also blanched and browned.

Mutton

Roasted mutton is served with [capers] and stuffed meats. It doesn't need any sauces.

Item for roasted and stuffed game, you must not blanch them but pluck them in water. You need only four lardons for the wings and for the legs where there is no stuffing.

Bloody roast

When your roast is cooked and when you want to serve it, take a bit of powdered hare's blood and place on top and when it's cut it will be bloody.

Barbed capon

It is necessary to pluck, clean, lard and skewer roast capon. And when it is nearly cooked, remove the lardons, then paint with flour mixed with egg yolks, rosewater, sugar, seasoned with salt, and it should be thin enough like the batter for fritters. Then put it on said capon with a spoon while roasting and it should be far enough from the fire so that it dries little by little and don't let it burn, and baste it three or four times so that it will be covered with the said batter and let it cook little by little. Then after it is cooked, baste with melted lard and serve it as is.

Redressed peacock

You must skin the peacock and be careful not to break the skin. And cook it in boiling hot water, stick with cloves and lard, then let it roast and cover the feet while cooking and when it is cooked baste it

---

104. In modern French this means a little keg. The recipe reappears in *L'Escole parfaite des officiers de bouche* in 1662; and see also note 114.

cuictz arrouses les de vinaigre pouldre comme sel et quant seront froytz mettes les sur ung tranchoir de boys une bro*[fol. 46r]*che fendue qui le soustiendra par l'estomach & le revestez de peau en sorte comme s'il estoyt en vie & fault prendre lard brochette & tranchoir. Et fault attacher le col & queue de fil d'archet & luy faire la roue comme s'il estoit en vie. Et luy pourres faire jecter feu par la gueulle.

⁋ Pans et chapons bardez a porc espic.
⁋ Faictes rostir chapons pans & aultres gibiers comme il appartient & barbe comme dessus est dict pour assaisonner la saulce menue espice cynamomon eaue rose vinaigre cloud de giroffle & mettes le tout soubz le rosty a la lechefritte & faictes boullir. Puis ayez de la canelle bien deslyee chargee de succre comme dragee bien longue de troys ou quattre doys que vous picquetes sur lesdictes Glaire* comme plumes de porc espic vous mettres vostre saulce au fonds du plat & qu'elle ne touche point a vostre confiture.

⁋ Paste de gigot de mouton.
⁋ Faictes couper vostre Gigot de mouton comme ung de veau puis ostez la chair de dedans et gardes de rompre la peau puis haches ladicte chair avec gresse ou lard assaisonne de sel, et d'espices groiselles aygretz, en yver force Oygnons. Puis remettez tout audict gigot. Et couses a petites brochettes de boys *[fol. 46v]* ou fillet & les faictes cuyre a petit feu servez tout chault.
⁋ Le fault mettre tremper en bon vinaigre deulx ou troys jours & le boullir ou rostir et vous les trouvez sains au menger.

⁋ Pour mettre les mains en eaue boullante.
⁋ Prenes mocelle boubarde plantain Bursa pastoris, victu pastoris petit de canfre parmy. Et en oignez voz mains puis les mettes seurement dedans ladicte eaue bouillante.

---

*   Corrected as *gibiers* in the 1576 *Grand Cuisinier*.

THE MOST EXCELLENT BOOK OF COOKERY

with vinegar, powder as well as salt, and when it is cold place it on a trencher of wood with a split skewer which supports it through the stomach and put it back in the skin as it would be in life, and you need lard, a skewer and trencher. You must stitch the neck and tail with thread and make it fan its tail as if it were alive.[105] And you can make it spit fire from its mouth.

PEACOCK AND CAPONS BARDED LIKE PORCUPINES

Roast capons, peacocks and other game as they require, and barded as indicated above. For seasoning the sauce, fine spice, cinnamon, rosewater, vinegar, cloves and place it all under the roast in the dripping pan and let it boil. Then take very slender cinnamon sticks, covered in sugar like candy, as long as three or four fingers, that you stick in the said game like the spines of a porcupine. Place your sauce on the bottom of a plate so it doesn't touch at all your confection.

MUTTON LEG PÂTÉ

Cut your leg of mutton as one of veal then remove the flesh within and be careful not to break the skin, then chop the meat with fat or lard seasoned with salt and with spices, gooseberries, sour grapes, in winter with a lot of onions. Then put everything back in the said leg. And close with little wooden skewers or sew and cook it on a slow fire. Serve very hot.

It must be soaked in good vinegar for two or three days and boil it or roast and you will find it healthy to eat.

TO PLACE YOUR HANDS IN BOILING WATER

Take *mocelle, boubarde*,[106] plantain, shepherd's purse, shepherd's meal, a little comfrey together. And anoint your hands then you can really place them into the boiling water.

---

105. It seems as if one would pass the string through the feathers, held taut with a stick behind, like a violin bow.
106. These two terms completely elude us. The first may be *moelle* or marrow, or it may be related to the word *moscellin*, 'of musk', and the second perhaps rhubarb? Plantain is a plant from the genus *Plantago*; shepherd's purse is *Capsella bursa-pastoris*; while *victu pastoris* or 'shepherd's meal' as we have translated it, is unknown to us.

◖ Croste de paste de papier.
◖ Prenes une fueille de papier et la faconnes en maniere de croste de paste et engresses bien d'huylle & mettes vostre paste dedans et le faictes cuyre sur le gril ou au four.

◖ Paste a troys.
◖ Fault faire la rostye grande en sorte que on y puisse mettre troys dedans sans y toucher aulx rives. Et fault remplir ledict paste de bran pour le cuyre & aussi l'ung des petis. L'ung des aultres deulx remplir de chair de beurre, faiche assaisonne comme il fault.
◖ Avec moyeulx d'oeufz. Et l'autre de langue ou coste de b[e]uf couppe par petites pieces & assaisonne de saul*[fol. 47r]*ce chaude. Et faictes cuyre ensemble. Et quant ilz seront cuictz couppes ceulx qui seront plains de bran & mettes hors ledict bran. Apres mettes les petis pastez dedans le grant. Et mettes des oyseaulx tous vifz dedans.

◖ Naige contrefaicte.
◖ Prenes une quarte de bon laict gras. Et fault qu'il y ait ung an que la vache ay faict le veau mettez parmy vostredict laict six aulbins d'oeufz z i ou deulx de farine de ris ung quarteron de succre en pouldre tout assemble batu comme beurre. Et l'escumes ce que vient par dessus. C'est la naige mettes la en plat.

◖ Beurre.
◖ Prenes beurre salle ou frais dedans ung pot et le mettes sur le charbon & le faictes fondre loing du feu, & toute l'ordure yra au feu a faire le potaige.

◖ Brochet & carpes.
◖ Prenes brochet carpes. Ou aultre poisson de doulce eaue, et le habillez & despeces comme il appartient, & ung petit saulpouldre de

Crust for pastry made of paper

Take a sheet of paper and fashion it like a pastry crust and grease it well with oil and place your dough inside and let it cook on the grill or in an oven.

Triple pie

You must make a large piecrust such that you can put inside three without touching the edges. You must fill the said piecrust with bran to cook it and also one of the small ones. One of the other two fill with meat, butter, season as appropriate.

With egg yolks. And the other with tongue or beef rib meat cut into little pieces and seasoned with hot sauce and let them cook together. And when they are cooked cut those which are full of bran and take out the said bran. Afterwards, place the little pies inside the big one. And put living birds inside.[107]

Counterfeit snow[108]

Take a quart of good rich milk. And it must have been a year since the cow had a calf. Add to your milk six egg whites, one ounce or two of rice flour, a quarter pound of powdered sugar all whipped together like butter. And skim off what comes to the top. That's the snow. Put it on a plate.

Butter

Take salted or fresh butter in a pot and place over the coals and let it melt far from the fire, and all the impurities will sink down toward the fire. Use to make pottage.[109]

Pike and carp

Take pike, carp. Or some other fresh water fish, and dress it and cut up as necessary. Add a little seasoning of salt and heat your butter

---

107. One is a big pie; the others are small. And the live birds go inside with them.
108. This is a recipe that shows up in all cookbooks of this era, the *Proper Newe Booke of Cokery* has it arranged on an apple stuck with a sprig of rosemary. Messisbugo includes it and there is an illustration of a man making it in Scappi.
109. This recipe seems to be an early version of clarified butter.

sel & faictes que vostre beurre ou huille soit moyennement chaulde puis faictes a petit feu a longue main, Tournes souvent. Il est meilleur a petit feu. Et vostre beurre ou huylle demourra *[fol 47v]* bon et servir plusieurs foys. Et si est bon en potaige & aussi a tous poissons saulpouldre, a loches de la farine & du sel serves a l'orange verjus vert en este.

❡ Chapon.
❡ Cuyses chapon en broche prenes une pomme de fer grosse comme uog [ung] oeuf, et qu'elle soit toute rouge puis mettes dans ledict chapon enveloppez d'une serviette.

❡ Frictures de mer.
❡ Solles chardes & laves les trippes saulpouldres de sel et de farine frittes en huylle ou au beurre en remuant souvent de limandes Merlans aussi les tripes ostees & le bout de la teste saulpoudre de sel et farine ainsi pourres faires de tous aultres bons a frire menges a l'orenge, merland a la saulce barbe Robert.
❡ Prenes de belles paillettes deulx ou troys douzaines et les couppes d'ung pied et demy de long devers le gros bout & les mettes dans vostre huylle moyennement chaulde & mettes vostre poisson cuiyre dessus en remuant et ne les frises gueres, verjus dessus ou orange.
❡ Seiches ny trop fresches ny trop trempes plus d'ung jour frises oygnons pouldre blanche dessus au servir orange.

[fol. 48r] ❡ Alozes.
❡ Alozes vuydes cest le boyaulx ostez & l'amer lavez les & saulpouldres faictes rostir sur le gril en les tournant arrouses de beurre & verjus

or oil at a medium heat then cook over a small fire for a long while, turning often. It is better over a small fire. And your butter or oil will stay fresh and can be used many times. And this is good in pottage and also for all seasoned fish. For loaches use flour and salt, serve with orange, green verjuice in summer.

Capon

Cook capon on a spit. Take a ball of iron as big as an egg, and heat it red hot and then place it in the said capon and wrap it in a napkin.

Seafood fritters

Sole, scale and clean out the guts, sprinkle with salt and with flour, fry in oil or butter, stirring often. For dab [110] and whiting also, remove the guts and head, sprinkle with salt and flour. Thus you can make all others that are good for frying. Eat with orange, or whiting with Robert's beard sauce.[111]

Take some pretty *paillettes*[112] two or three dozen and cut them one foot [113] and a half from the large end and place them in your moderately hot oil and let your fish cook, turning them, and just barely fry them, verjuice on top or orange.

Cuttlefish neither too fresh nor soaked too much more than a day, fry onions, white powder on top, serve with orange.

Shad

Gut the shad, remove the intestines and gall bladder, wash and season. Roast on a grill and while turning baste with butter and verjuice with

---

110. In modern French, *limande* means dab, however Cotgrave translates it as 'A Burt or Bret-fish' which was a common name for brill or turbot. The texture of dabs is more akin to that of whiting.
111. This is the onion-based sauce mentioned above. It has an interesting history, with later versions evolving in the same direction as French cuisine in general, veal stock replacing the lard and breadcrumb thickener.
112. This word normally means 'glittering sequins', so it seems safe to say that this is a shiny small fish. Today, however, the term in a culinary sense refers to cheese straws.
113. An inch and a half from the large end would make more sense if these are small fish.

avec une branche de sauge puis mettes en plat beurre verjus & menues herbes haches menu saffran, avec groiselles aigretz boullir le tout entre deulx platz ou terrasses sur le charbon. Ainsi peult on faire de maquereaulx ou moys d'apvril avec rommarin, marjolaine estuvee en yver au brochet du verjus beurre, pouldre blanche.

⁋ Tenches.
⁋ Tenches. Il les fault esmoucher en eaue boullante rapee & nestoyez bien et laver coupes toutes les aslles a l'entour le plus pres du corps que pourres, puis les fendes du long du dos depuis la teste jusques a la que[ue] escorchez les plus pres des os que pourrez d'ung coste & d'aultre, puis quant aurez leve la chair prenes meenues herbes haches avec beurre Menues espices, sel puis estendez voz tanches et mettes de vostre saulce sur ladicte chair et peaulx puis l'arousez, en facon d'andouille. Et lyez le fillet tant que la chair soyt par dehors & faictes rostir sur le gril et arrousez de beurre en tournant souvent & la mengez avec la tonnelette ou girofflee ou saulce muscadet.

[fol. 48v] ⁋ Alozes ou carpes a la castille.
⁋ Il les fault escarder & oster les ventrailles puis mettes en une casse ou brosse avec beurre ou huylle, verjus, vinaigre ung petit fillet, beurre menues espices blanche saffran. Et cloud de girofle entier, romarin ou marjolaine ou branche de laurier, la fueille groiselles aygret. Faictes cuyre dedans ung pot ou sur les charbons avec sel, tournes souvent. Et aussi macquereaulx y pourres mettre.
⁋ Prenes amandes & les plumes & [l]es fendes par le meillieu & les faconnes comme vouldres selon l'escusson que vouldres faire, et les assaisonnes dessus vostre gelee en escusson ou en aultre sorte que vouldres lyes doulcement.

a branch of sage. Then place on a plate with butter, verjuice, fine herbs chopped finely, saffron, gooseberries, unripe grapes. Boil everything between two plates or earthenware casseroles over the coals. Thus you can make mackerel in the month of April with rosemary or stewed with marjoram; in winter, pike with verjuice, butter, and white powder.

Tench

Tench. It is necessary to blanch in boiling water with wine. Clean well and wash, you cut out all the spines around it as close to the body as you can. Then split it along the back from the head to the tail. Fillet it as close to the bone as you can on one side and the other, then when you have removed the flesh take chopped fine herbs with butter, fine spices, salt, then spread your fillets and place your sauce on the said flesh and skin and then baste like an andouille. And place the fillet so that the flesh will be on the outside and roast on the grill and baste with butter turning it often. Serve it with *tonnelette*[114] sauce or clove sauce or a Muscadet sauce.

Shad or carp *à la castille*

You must scale and remove the entrails then place in a casserole and brush with butter or oil, verjuice, a dash of vinegar, butter, fine white spice, saffron. And whole clove, rosemary or marjoram or a sprig of bay leaves, gooseberries, sour grapes. Let it cook in a pot or over the coals with salt, turning often. And you can also add mackerel.

Take almonds and shell them, and split down the middle and fashion as you like according to the escutcheon that you want to make and place them above your jelly to look like an escutcheon or in another shape that you would like. Thicken slightly.[115]

---

114. This is a typical medieval sauce of toast, wine, fried onions, spices, currants, in which partridges are often served.
115. This is either an entirely different recipe involving a coat of arms fashioned out of almonds and set in gelatin, or the gelatin itself comes from the shad recipe above, though this seems very unlikely as there is no broth, nor are the bones explicitly used, which would be necessary to make a kind of aspic. It may be a few sentences are missing, or the author assumed readers would recognize what the recipe involves.

⁌ Lamproye.

⁌ Escorches lamproye & les faictes seigner par les pertuys & mettes a part le sang que recepures & les laves en bon vin vermeil ou vinaigre dessus vostre sang puis embroches les & les faictes rostir a petit feu, receves ce qui en sortira en rotissant puis ayes du pain et le faictes rostir qu'il soit tout noir, puis le mettez tremper avec ce que aures Receu saing Vin. Et tout passe par l'estamine, avec pain & bon vinaigre Menues espices canelle, et noix muscade ung peu bruslee le tout *[fol. 49r]* soit mys en pouldre, & quant le tout sera passe ensemble faictes bouillir avec succre et cloux de giroffle entier. Et fault qu'elle soit asses claire assaisonne de sel. Puis mettes vostre saulce & lemproye en ung pot de terre & quant elle sera froyde estoupes tresbien ledict pot & se gardera huict jours.

⁌ Les ungs les mengent seiches a L'orenge chaulde sel par dessus, avec leur saulce chaulde dessus ou escuelles.

⁌ Saulce noire.

⁌ Faictes comme de la lamproye. Et n'y a a dire que le saingret & n'y mettent d'avantaige que ung petit de cloud de giroffle en pouldre elle sert a venaison, vollailles saulvaiges requierent avoir saulce noyre.

⁌ Muscade.

⁌ Faictes comme dessus, et sert a plusieurs choses Rost poisson frit Paste de langue de beuf et aultres pastes requierent saulce au lieu de cloux de giroffle, en yver de la muscade en pouldre.

⁌ Cougnins.

⁌ Prenes ung peu de pain hasle et les foyes desdictz chapons ou poulles aussi ung peu hasles sur les charbons. Le tout mettes tremper avec peu de vin bout*[fol. 49v]*tes & passes par estamine avec menues espices, canelle, vin rouge, verjus, vinaigre. Et mettes en la lescherfrite

Lamprey

Skin the lamprey and let them bleed from all orifices, and set the culled blood aside. And wash them well with good red wine or vinegar over your blood, then skewer them and let them roast over a low flame. Collect that which drops while roasting then take bread and toast it so it's all black, then place it to soak with the drippings, blood and wine. Pass everything through a sieve with bread, good vinegar, fine spices, cinnamon and slightly toasted nutmeg, everything ground into powder, and when all is passed together let it boil with sugar and whole cloves. It must be thin enough, seasoned with salt. Then take your sauce and lamprey in an earthenware pot and when it is cool, stop up the said pot well and it will keep for eight days.

Some eat them dry with hot orange and salt on top, with hot sauce on top or in a platter.

Black sauce

Make it like the lamprey. And there's no question of using lard, don't add more than a little powdered clove. It will work for venison. Wild fowl require a black sauce.

Nutmeg sauce

Make it like above and serve with many things, roast fish, fried. Ox tongue pie and other pies require a sauce in place of cloves, in winter some ground nutmeg.

Rabbits [116]

Take a little toasted bread and the livers of the said capons or hens also a little browned over the coals. Moisten everything with a little ropy [117] wine and pass through a sieve with fine spices, cinnamon, red wine, verjuice and vinegar. Place it in your dripping pan under

---

116. Either the author meant to say rabbits in the recipe and accidentally wrote capons, or it is a typesetter's mistake, but the recipe will work with either in any case.

117. Taillevent considered this a fault in wine to be corrected, *vin bouté* or *boucté*, which due to a kind of lactic acid spoilage gets little filaments floating in it. It is unclear why the author here would want to use it.

dessus voz chapons en rotissant avec branche de saulge, & faictes bouillir sur charbons assaisonnez de Sel et dresses sur voz chapons quant les vouldrez servir.

⁋ Saulce pour le beuf rosty.
⁋ Faictes rostir vostre beuf larde de cloux de giroffle & puis quant il sera quasi cuyct arrouses vostredit beuf de vinaigre et mettes vostre poelle dessus pour revenir vostre vinaigre & y mettez pouldre de menues espices et poyvre en pouldre et peu de pain hasle si voules & y mettes ung peu de saulge pour bailler goust & faictes bouillir & si le vinaigre est trop fort peu de verjus ou de bon boullon assaysonne de sel serves chault sur le beuf.

⁋ Saulce madame.
⁋ Prenes moyeulx d'oeufz verjus petit de boullon passe par l'estamine avec peu de pouldre blanche cynamomon boully avec sucre se elle sert a poulles poulletz chappons ung peu de canelle.

⁋ Saulce doulx au laict.
⁋ Prenes ung petit de pain hasle comme celle de ca*[fol. 50r]*meline trempe en bon laict d'amandre & pille avec demye douzaine de grosses d'aulx et passes le tout pour l'estamine avec peu de pouldre blanche & canelle petit vin vermeil vinaigre verjus sel boulles & dresses sur oyes & canars.

⁋ Saulce vert.
⁋ Prenes du ble auzeille salmonde et persil aulx nouveaulx peu de pouldre blanche passe par l'estamine puis trempe avec vinaigre dressees en escuelles.

⁋ Moulx de raisin.
⁋ Prenes des raisins bien menues & en ostes les grapes et quant seront esgrenees foulles les entre voz mains, puis mettes ung peu de vin vermeil et ung peu de pain & puis faictes boullir le tout ensemble et quant il sera bien cuyct mettes le refroidir en ung vaisseau & quant

your capons while roasting, with a sprig of sage, and let it boil over the coals, season with salt and dress your capons when you want to serve them.

Sauce for roast beef

Roast your beef stuck with cloves and then when it is nearly cooked, baste your said beef with vinegar and place your pan underneath to catch your vinegar and add ground fine spices and ground pepper and a little bit of toasted bread if you like and add a bit of sage to give flavour and let it boil, and if the vinegar is too strong a little verjuice or good broth, season with salt and serve hot over the beef.

Sauce madame

Take egg yolks, verjuice, a little broth passed through a sieve with a little white powder, cinnamon boiled with sugar. And if for hens, chickens and capons, a little cinnamon.

Sweet sauce with milk

Take a little toasted bread like for a cameline sauce, soak it in good almond milk and pound with half a dozen cloves of garlic and pass everything through a sieve with a little white powder and cinnamon, a little red wine, vinegar, verjuice, and salt. Boil and serve with geese and ducks.

Green sauce

Take wheat, sorrel, herb bennet and parsley, new garlic, a little white powder and pass through a sieve then moisten with vinegar and serve in platters.

Grape sauce

Take very small grapes and separate the clusters and when they are all seeded, press them between your hands, then take a little red wine and a little bread and then boil everything together and when it is well cooked place it to cool in a vessel and when it is cool pass though

il sera froit passes par l'estamine avec peu de canelle menues espices pouldre blanche et faictes qu'elle soit asses lyee et quant elle sera passee succre assaysonne de sel & pour le garder mettes dans ung vaisseau de terre elle se gardera six jours quant il est bien estoupe & en pourres faire de cerises ou pommes & sert a plusieurs rostz cochons poulletz chappons et aultres gibiers.

[fol. 50v] ⁌ Aulx blans.
⁌ Prenes Amandes broyees mettes tremper et peu de mye de pain blanc en bon boullon bien maigre, le tout ensemble passe par l'estamine avec huyt grosses d'oulx piller avec de la pouldre blanche, et fault qu'il soit lye.

⁌ Dodine blanche.
⁌ Prenez de bon laict de vache boutes boullir en une poelle dessus vostre rost pouldre blanche deux ou troys moyeulx d'oeufz passes par l'estamine avec vostre laict et mettez boullir tout ensemble avec peu de succre de sel & petit de persil effueille si voules mettre marjolaine haches dresses a tous oyseaulx de riviere avec rostyes dessoubz.

⁌ Chapons poulletz vollailles rostyes oyseaulx de riviere.
⁌ Mettes de verjus dessoubz le rost en une poelle puis prenes moyeulx d'oeufz durs et de foye de poullalle & vollailles ha[s]les peu sur le charbon puis passes par l'estamine avec verjus et peu de boullon pouldre blanche & mettes boullir avec bonnes herbes haches et servez mettes succre et rostie dessus si voules.

⁌ Aloze.
[fol. 51r] ⁌ Fault faire rostir l'alouze sur le gril quant elle sera ung peu saulpouldre de sel faictes rostir a petit feu arrouses souvent de beurre ou huylle verjus & quant elle sera asses cuycte & quant l'aures tourne souvent mettes la dedans le plat avec beurre verjus puree de pois claire pouldre blanche saffran rommarin marjolaine persil & toutes aultres bonnes herbes entieres assaisonne de sel vous la pourres faire cuyre en une lichefritte dedans le four. Mais il fault qu'elle soyt crue quant la

a sieve with a little cinnamon, fine spices, white powder so it will be thick enough and when it is sieved, add sugar and season with salt. And to keep it, place in an earthenware vessel; it will keep for six days when it is well sealed, and you can make it from cherries or apples and it will serve for many roasts, pigs, chickens, capons and other game.

White garlic

Take ground almonds, place to soak and add some white breadcrumbs and good lean broth. Pass everything through a sieve with eight cloves of garlic ground with white powder, and it should be thick.

White dodine sauce

Take good cow's milk and put on to boil in a pan under your roast, with white powder, two or three egg yolks passed through a sieve with your milk and boil everything together with a little sugar, some salt, and some parsley leaves. If you like, add chopped marjoram. Serve with all river fowl with the toasts underneath.

Capons, chickens, poultry roasted, river fowl

Put verjuice under the roast in a pan, then take hard-boiled egg yolks and some chicken and poultry livers, brown a bit over the coals then pass through a sieve with verjuice and a little bit of broth and white powder and let boil with good chopped herbs and serve. Add sugar and toast on top if you like.

Shad

You must roast your shad on the grill when it is seasoned a little with salt, let it roast over a low flame, baste often with butter or oil, verjuice and when it is cooked enough and when you have turned it often, place it on a plate with butter, verjuice, thin pea purée, white powder, saffron, rosemary, marjoram, parsley, and all other good whole herbs, seasoned with salt. You can cook it in a dripping pan in the oven. But it must be raw when you place it in the said oven. And

mettres audict four. Et couvrez souvent aigretz ainsi peult l'on faire potaige de macquereaux frais, aulcuns apres que l'alouze est boullye il la faict hasler sur le charbon et la mengent a L'orange ou au verjus vert ou a la saulce dessusdit.

⁋ Prenes vinaigre cloux de giroffle entier petit de canelle entiere despecee comme cloux de giroffle ou en pouldre avec menues espices faictes boullir avec succre & quant sera boully assaisonne de sel & mettes dessus voz viandes a saulmon boully rosty devant le feu en ung plat & truycte rostye devant le feu en ung plat en ceste sorte larde de cloux de giroffle en rotissant devant le feu pareillement l'alouze boullye rostye. Il ne fault point de cloux a L'alouze ny a oeufz frictz.

⁋ Saulce de venayson.
⁋ Prenes peu de pain hasle ou de cameline ou potai*[fol 51v]*ge de venayson passes par l'estamine vostre pain et en deffault de camelyne ou potaige avec vinaigre menues espices canelle & faictes boullir avec succre & une douzaine de cloux de giroffle entiers sel & elle sert a cerfz Biches chevreaulx Sangliers & toutes aultres venayson.

⁋ Cameline.
⁋ Faictes [h]asler des rostyes de pain Blanc devant le feu et qu'elles ne soyent gueres rostyes puis trempes les avec vin vermeil vinaigre et mettes sur charbon jusques a ce qu'elles soyent trempees puis mettes les refroidir et quant elles seront froides passes les par l'estamine canelle menues espices et qu'elle ne soit pas trop lyee mettes succre dessus dedans sel & la fault ung peu aigrette ne fault point boullon mettes en pot de terre estouppes bien & se garde sept ou huyct jours et sert a toutes rostyes & en yver dresses en escuelles pourres servir a plusieurs saulces.

⁋ Saulce vert.
⁋ Prenes pain blanc trempe en vinaigre puis mettes refroidir la plus souveraine verdure de saulge de fort laurier de blettes salmonde ozeille persil des gros choulx force persil au lieu d'aultres herbes en autonne pilles vostre ble ou herbes puis apres qu'elles se*[fol. 52r]*ront pillees

cover often with sour grapes. Thus you can make a pottage of fresh mackerel. After the shad is boiled, some brown it over the coals and eat it with orange or green verjuice or with a sauce on top.

Take vinegar, whole cloves, a little whole cinnamon broken up like cloves or ground with fine spices, let it boil with sugar and when it is boiled, season with salt, place on top of your meats, for boiled salmon, roasted before the fire on a plate, and trout roasted before the fire on a plate of this sort, stuck with cloves while roasting before the fire, equally shad boiled, roasted. There should not be cloves with shad nor with fried eggs.

Venison sauce

Take a little toasted bread or some cameline or pottage of venison, pass through a sieve your bread and if there's no cameline or pottage, with vinegar, fine spices, cinnamon, and let it boil with sugar and a dozen whole cloves, salt and it works on stag, doe, kid, boar and all other venison.[118]

Cameline sauce

Brown toasted white bread before the fire and it should only be slightly toasted, then soak in red wine, vinegar and place over the coals just until it is soaked. Then let it cool and when it's cool pass through a sieve, cinnamon, fine spice and it should not be too thick. Add sugar on top and salt within, and it must be a little sour, but do not boil it. Place in an earthenware pot, seal it well and it will keep for seven or eight days. Serve with all roasts, and in winter put it in dishes and you can serve it instead of many sauces.

Green sauce

Take white bread soaked in vinegar then let it cool. Add the best greens like sage, some strong bay, chard, herb bennet, sorrel, parsley, some big cabbages, a lot of parsley in place of other herbs and in autumn crush your wheat or herbs then after they are crushed soak

---

118. In this instance, and at other points through the text, the word 'venison' is used in its orginal meaning of 'flesh of game or other animal used as food' (*SOED*).

broyes vostre pain avec & assaysonnes ed [de] sel avec peu de pouldre blanche et de vinaigre & s'il est trop fort mettes peu de verjus passes le tout par l'estamine. Et qu'elle soit asses lyee. La plus verte est la meilleure & en celle de chair n'y a point de différence sinon que on y broye deulx ou troys fueilles de saulge parmy et l'appelle on saulge pour la cause et sert a tous boullons boullys tant de mer que de riviere, celle ou est la saulge est au chochons et piedz de pourceaulx mais en sangliers.

❡ Beccasse.
❡ Faictes rostir sans effondrer si elle est bien grosse ne la lardes point mettes une poelle dessoubz ainsi qu'elle rostira pour recepvoir le jus qui en tumbera & mettes dessus groiselles verjus petit d'eaue blanche de saulge entiere pouldre blanche sel serves avec rostyes et la saulce qui sera cuycte par dessus.

❡ Blanc menger.
❡ Prenes amandes bien broyees, puis passes par l'estamine avec peu de mye de pain peu d'eaue chaulde de vin blanc verjus pouldre blanche et fault qu'il soit asses lye sel succre faictes bouillir en pot de terre ou poelle sur les charbons en remuant tousjours, et quant [s]era presque cuyt assaisonne a vostre goust a chapons *[fol. 52v]* rostis et aultres rostz en jectant dragee dessus & toutes frictures de poissons en Karesme jaulne en mettant du saffran en cuysant.

❡ Aultre menger.
❡ Prenes amandes bien broyees avec l'escosse passe par l'estamine peu de cynamomon pouldre blanche eaue chaulde vin vermeil & verjus peu aigre. Passes du pain si voules qu'il soit lye comme dessus. Faictes boullir sur du charbon en remuant ses [si les] deulx saulces sont en dangier de bouillir et y mettes du succre & si vous voulles elle vous servira comme dessus.

❡ Paste a la saulce chaulde.
❡ Prenes langues de beuf cuyctes couppes par cernes ou d'ung os coste de beuf crue, aussi coppes avec gresse de beuf bien hachee, puis prenes

your bread with it and season with salt with a little white powder and vinegar, and if it is too strong, add a little verjuice, pass everything through a sieve. And it should be rather thick. The more green the better and the kind of flesh doesn't make a difference. Otherwise one can crush two or three leaves of sage in it and one calls it a sage for this reason and it works with all broths for both fresh and saltwater [fish]. That with sage in it is for pork and pig's trotters but also for boar.

Woodcock

Roast it without gutting. If it is quite big, don't lard it, place a pan underneath while it roasts, to receive the juices which drip, and place gooseberries above, verjuice, a little clear water, whole sage, white powder, salt. Serve with toast and the sauce, which will be cooked above.

Blancmange

Take finely ground almonds, then pass through a sieve with some breadcrumbs, a little hot water, some white wine, verjuice, white powder, and it should be rather thick. Add salt, sugar, let boil in an earthenware pot or pan over the coals, stirring constantly. And when it's nearly cooked, season to your taste. For roasted capons and other roasts, toss candies on top, and for all fried fish during Lent, if you want it yellow, add saffron while cooking.

Another blancmange

Take finely ground almonds with the skin, pass through a sieve with a little cinnamon, white powder, hot water, red wine and slightly sour verjuice. Pass with bread if you want so that it's thick like above. Boil it over the coals, stirring all the while if these two sauces are in danger of boiling and add sugar and if you like they will serve you as above.

Pie with hot sauce

Take cooked ox tongues cut into rings or a raw rib bone of beef, also cut with beef fat well chopped. Then take your tongues and make a

voz langues & faictes ung lict de gresse par dessu[s] la crouste, puis mettes ung aultre de voz langues par dessus vostre gresse [pouldres de] pouldres de menues espices quattres cloulx de giroffle entiers, puis faictes ung aultre lict comme dit est & tous aultres aussi jusques a ce que vostre paste soit pleine faictes le cuyre & quant il sera a demy cuyct emplisses de saulce chaulde: dessus syropt appelle muscadelle ou saulce chaulde puis le laissez achever de cuyre.

[fol. 53r] ❧ Chapon.

❧ Prenes chapon et le concassez & le mettes dans la croste avec menue espice sel saffran lart trenches par petites cernes faictes cuyre au four & le serves tyede mettes y saulce madame ou rape si voules.

❧ Paste d'alebran.*

❧ Prenes chair de chapon crue, assavoir le blanc hache avec gresse de beuf menue espice cynamomon saffran succre sel puis mettes en vostre croste avec moyeulx d'oeufz cuyctz larde de cloux de giroffle vous y pourres mettre de la mouelle de beuf, aussi ferez paste de faisant chapon cuyct ou crud serves chault. Et n'y mettes point de Succre si ne voules.

❧ Poullailles a la saulce robert.

❧ Faictes comme d'ung chapon en paste. Et quant seront demy cuictz prenes moyeulx d'oeufz verjus passe par l'estamine avec peu de boullon pouldre blanche mettes dedans & faictes cuyre a demourant mettez aussi aigret groiselles ainsi de poulletz et sans saulce comme chapon.

❧ Paste de veaulx.

❧ Faictes blanchir vostre gigot de veau apres que l'aures despece haches le bien menu avec gresse de beuf au *[fol. 53v]* tant que de chair et lart gras petit pour assaysonner menues espices cloux de Giroffle entiers saffran sel puis mettez en sa croste avec groiselles ou aigret moyeulx d'oeufz cuitz larde de cloux de giroffle.

---

* *Alebran* is most likely Cotgrave's *halebran*, which he translates as 'teal'. However, the recipe itself is for a chicken or a pheasant dish.

bed of fat on the crust, then place another of your tongues on top of your fat, dust with fine spices, four whole cloves, then make another layer as was said, and all the other ones likewise until your pastry is full. Cook it and when it is half cooked fill with hot sauce. On top, syrup called muscadelle or hot sauce then let it finish cooking.

Capon

Take a capon, joint it, and place it in the crust with fine spices, salt, saffron, slices of salted pork fat cut into little rounds, let it cook in the oven and serve it warm, placing on it sauce madame or verjuice sauce if you like. [119]

Teal pie

Take raw capon flesh, that is to say the white breast meat, chopped with beef suet, fine spice, cinnamon, saffron, sugar, salt, then put in your crust with cooked egg yolks, stuck with cloves. You can put in beef marrow, also you can make a pie with pheasant, cooked capon or raw. Serve hot. And don't add any sugar if you don't want it.

Hens with sauce Robert

Make it like a capon pie. And when it is half cooked take egg yolks and verjuice, pass through a sieve with a little broth and white powder, add and let it finish cooking. Add also sour grapes and gooseberries, for chickens, and without sauce like capon.

Veal pie

Blanch your leg of veal after you have cut it up, chop it very finely with beef fat so that the flesh and fat are small, for seasoning fine spices, whole cloves, saffron, salt then place it in its crust with gooseberries or sour grapes, cooked egg yolks stuck with cloves.

---

119.   See the recipe on pp. 188–189 above for sauce madame. The verjuice sauce is a suggested translation of the word *rape*. *Saulce rappee* is identified in the *Ménagier de Paris*, while Cotgrave defines *rapé* as 'A veri smalle wine comming of water cast upon the mother of grapes, which have been pressed [must]'.

❧ Paste de mouton.

❧ Prenez chair de mouton haches bien menu avec gresse de beuf oygnons ou a belles menues espices pouldre blanche sel Groiselles mettes du saffran si voules.

❧ Chevreaulx.

❧ Despeces voz cartiers de chevreaulx par morceaulx & les blanchisses et bouttes en paste pouldre blanche cynamomon saffran lart couppe par cerne sel groiselles mettes saulce robert si voules.

❧ Pinsons.

❧ Pinsons concassees piedz aesles testes pouldre de menue espices sel puis pouldres vostre croste apres mettez voz pinsons dedans piedz aesles testes, & pouldroyees de vostre pouldre par dessus il fault qu'il soit doulx d'espice et de sel par dessus lard gras menu hache, groiselles.

❧ Pigeons ramiers.
[fol. 54r] ❧ Ramyer comme dessus est dict avec peu de lard pouldre de menue espice, sel, saulce chaulde pour yver.

❧ Allouettes.

❧ Allouettes bien plumees blanchir peu conquassees croste de paste bien fine ayez pouldre de duc pour une douzaine d'allouettes .z. iiii. puis pouldroyes la croste & arrengez voz allou[e]ttes en vostre croste avec cloud de giroffle entier haches lard menu, mettes par dessus avec le reste de vostre pouldre assaisonne de sel avec peu de pouldre blanche faictes cuyre on peult mettre aussi passereaulx torterelles.

❧ Haches peu de veau ou de mouton [ou] beuf avec gresse de beuf meslee dedans assaisonnes vostre croste de menues espices sel, mettes voz marles par le meillieu de la chair hachee & acheves de remplir du reste de vostre chair vostre paste assaisonne de vostre pouldre sel avec peu de Lard gras menu mys par dessus.

Mutton pie

Take mutton flesh chopped very finely with beef fat, onions, or with nice fine spices, white powder, salt, gooseberries. Add saffron if you like.

Kid

Cut up your quarters of kid into pieces and blanch them and place them in the crust with white powder, cinnamon, saffron, salted pork fat cut into rounds, salt, gooseberries. Add sauce Robert if you like.

Chaffinch

Cut up chaffinches, feet, wings, heads, season with fine spices and salt. Then powder your crust after you place your chaffinches inside, feet, wings, heads, and season with your powder on top. It must be sweet with spice and salt on top, salted pork fat finely chopped, gooseberries.

Wood pigeons

Wood pigeons as above with a bit of salted pork fat, season with fine spice, salt, hot sauce for winter.

Larks

Larks, well plucked, blanched a little, broken down into pieces and encased in a crust of fine pastry. Use Duke's powder, for a dozen larks, 4 ounces, then season the crust and arrange your larks in your crust with whole cloves, finely chopped salted pork fat. Place on top of the rest with your powder, season with salt and with a little white powder, let it cook a little. You can also make this with sparrows and turtle doves.

Chop a little veal or mutton or beef with beef fat mixed in, season your crust with fine spices, salt, place your blackbirds in the middle of your chopped flesh and fill up the rest of your pastry with your flesh, powder, salt with a bit of fine salted pork fat placed on top.

⁌ Passereaulx.
⁌ Passereaulx faictes comme dict est des allouettes a la saulce chaulde mettes en paste tant seullement avec peu de menue espice & sel avec saulce chaulde pour gens qui sont froys.

[fol. 54v] ⁌ Canardz.
⁌ Canardz concassez & qu'ilz soyent reffaictz, mettez en paste Menues espice cloud de giroffle sel lard coupe en petites pieces. Dodine de verjus mettes dedans quant ilz seront presque cuyctz ou muscadelle.

⁌ Mouton en paste.
⁌ Concasses gigot & ostes petites peaulx par dessus & le lardes de lart cloux de giroffle puis le mettes en paste comme de venaison mettes menu espice sel et que la croste soit de grosse farine asses espesse & quant sera presque cuit peu de bon vinaigre serves tyede.

⁌ Oysons.
⁌ Concasses oysons mettes en paste avec peu de pouldre blanche sel puis prenez poix ou febves nouvelles en gosse & les faictes blanchir puis les essuyes mettez par dessus les oysons avec lart hache bien menu servez tyede.
⁌ Soit assemblee comme dessus mais il n'y fault point de febves mais des orenges plumes & du lart en pieces menues espices par dessus servez chault.

⁌ Perdrix.
⁌ Mettes perdrix en paste peu de menues espices sel cloux de giroffle entiers aulcuns y mettent saulce *[fol. 55r]* chaulde dedens au cuire, ou quant il est presque cuyct il n'y fault point de saulce quant on les veult menger froitz.

Sparrows

Sparrows made as was said for larks, with hot sauce. Place in pastry, just enough, with a little fine spice and salt with hot sauce for folks who are cold.[120]

Ducks

Joint ducks and then parboil them. Place in pastry with fine spice, cloves, salt, salted pork fat cut in small pieces. Put dodine with verjuice inside when they are nearly cooked, or muscadelle wine.

Mutton pie

Break down a leg of mutton and remove the silver skin, and stick with lard, cloves, then place it in a pastry like venison, add fine spice, salt and the crust will be of coarse flour, rather thick and when it is nearly cooked a little good vinegar. Serve warm.

Goslings

Joint goslings, place in a pastry with a little white powder, salt and then take peas or young fava beans in the shell and blanch them then dry them, place on top of the birds with well-chopped salted pork fat. Serve warm.

Put together as above without beans but with peeled oranges and salted pork fat in little pieces, spices on top. Serve hot.

Partridge

Place partridge in pastry, add a little fine spices, salt, whole cloves, some add hot sauce while cooking, or when it is nearly cooked. No sauce is needed when you want to eat them cold.

---

120. This is a rare reference to humoral medicine. This is not intended for those who feel cold due to the weather, but rather those who are humorally phlegmatic, for whom hot spices and relatively heating small birds would serve as a medicinal corrective.

Congnins.

❡ Congnins faictes comme dessus excepte qu'il fault conquasser & despecer lesdictz congnins menues espices sel et du lart en cernes en lieu de groiselles saulce chaulde en yver.

Lievre.

❡ Prenes grant lievre mis par pieces larde de cloudz du long comme patisseries de venaysons c'est assavoir les cuisses le rable mys en troncons mys en paste avec menues espices, sel mettes tremper en vin aigre avec ce le mettre en paste, puis mettes ledict vinaigre dans le paste quant il sera presque cuict soit mys en paste menues espices sel larde en cernes mys dessus avec groiselles ou aigret.

Lievre hache.

❡ Prenes les quartiers de derriere et le rable tires la chair d'avec les os & le haches bien menu, puis assaisonnes de menues espices et du sel acheves de hacher puis pouldroyes le bout d'ung haist avec farine puis prenes de vostre chair ung petit de laquelle estendrez *[fol. 55v]* le plus doulx que pourres de la grandeur que vouldres faire vostre paste, ayes aussi des lardons de lart que arrengeres par dessus et ferez ung aultre lict de vostredict chair et remettes des lardons jusques il sera asses gras le feres aussi puis dresses le. Et le faconnes avec farine en telle sorte que vouldres puis mettes le tremper avec vinaigre menue espice, sel, puis le mettes en paste & cuyre et quant il sera demy cuict mettes le jus que sera demeure la ou aura trempe vostre dit paste dedens & le faictes cuyre a demourant.

Cerf biches, hure de sanglier.

❡ La venayson trempee en vinaigre pouldre Blanche, sel comme pouldre laissez une nuyct en son breuvaige, le lendemain mettes en paste faictes les crostes asses especes d'ung doy, faictes de la farine de seigle ou d'aultre farine si n'en aves et quant il sera demy cuyct mettes

Rabbits

Make rabbits like above except that the said rabbits must be broken down and cut up. Add fine spices, salt and salted pork fat in rounds. In place of gooseberries, hot sauce in winter.

Hare

Take a big hare, cut in pieces, stuck with cloves all over like venison pastries, that is to say, the legs, the saddle cut into slices, added to the pastry with fine spices, salt. Soak in vinegar with everything. Place it in the pastry, then add the said vinegar to the pastry when it is nearly cooked. Add in the pastry fine spices, salt, salted pork fat in rounds and add on top with gooseberries or sour grapes.

Chopped hare

Take the rear quarters and the saddle and pull the flesh from the bones and chop it very fine then season with fine spices and some salt. Having chopped it then dust the end of a board with flour then take a little of your flesh that you spread out as gently as you can, to the size that you would like your pie to be. Add also lardons of pork fat that you arrange on top and make another bed of your said flesh and add more of the lardons until it will be fat enough. Do this also then dress it. And fashion with flour as you like, then add vinegar to moisten, fine spices, salt then place it in the pastry and cook and when it is half cooked add the juice that remains from when you soaked your said pie, and let it cook until solidified.[121]

Stag and hind, boar's head

Soak venison in vinegar, white powder, salt. You can leave it for a night in this marinade. The next day place in pastry, make the crust as thick as a finger, made of rye flour or other flour if you don't have any, and when it is half cooked, add the juice which remains from

---

121. The author is making a kind of large bacon-studded patty of chopped hare, seasoning and moistening it with vinegar, then putting it in the crust. Presumably fat will drip from it, which is replaced through a hole in the top of the pie.

le jus qui en sera demouree dedens dudit breuvaige, ne le fault point blanchir si ne commence d'aller aval, pouldres les lardons avec les lardes de pouldre.

❦ Lamproye.
❦ Escorches et mettes par troncons ou entiers menues espices cynamomon cloux de giroffle assaisonne de sel faictes cuyre en saulce de lemproye ung peu clare *[fol. 56r]* te mesles dedens quant sera cuycte serves chault.
❦ Escorches en troncons pouldre blanche menue espice. Sel saffran. Groiselles este en yver fillet de verjus quant sera presque cuit et du beurre la ou il y a oygnons ne veult estre couvert on le peult servir froit ou il n'y a oygnon.

❦ Carpes bremes.
❦ Escorchez puis couppes ung peu par dessus pouldre sel espice par tout beurre au ventre faictes cuyre a doulx four quant elles seront presque cuyctes peu de verjus vinaigre huylle d'olyve groiselles.
❦ Prenes menues espices pouldre blanche quant sera eschaulde, ostes le ventre, mettes le en paste groiselles beurre ou huylle d'olyve quant sera presque cuict peu de verjus dans serves froict.

❦ Mullet.
❦ Menues espices, sel groiselles, mettes en paste, peu de verjus quant il sera presque cuyct l'on en met deulx ou troys ensemble.

❦ Turbot.
❦ Mettes par pieces quant il est effondre et en paste par troncons comme paste de carpe, sel pouldre blanche. Beurre frays quant il sera presque cuyt ung fillet *[fol. 56v]* de verjus il veult bien cuyre & servir froict a petite paste. Aulcuns la font grosse.

❦ Rouget.
❦ Effondres comme perches par les aureilles mettes en paste deulx

the said marinade. Do not soak it[122] so it doesn't collapse, sprinkle with slivers of bacon.[123]

Lamprey

Skin and cut in segments or keep whole, add fine spices, cinnamon, cloves, season with salt. Cook in a lamprey sauce, a little claret mixed in. When it is cooked, serve hot.

Skin, in segments, white powder, fine spice, salt, saffron. Gooseberries in summer, in winter a dash of verjuice, and when it is nearly cooked, some butter there. When there are onions, it should not be covered. Serve cold when there is no onion.

Carp, bream

Skin then score a bit on top, season with salt, spice, butter all around the interior. Let it cook in a cool oven. When they are nearly cooked, add a little verjuice, vinegar, olive oil, gooseberries.

Take fine spices, white powder. When it is scaled, remove the innards, place it in a pastry with gooseberries, butter or olive oil. When it is nearly cooked, add a little verjuice inside. Serve cold.

Mullet

Fine spices, salt, gooseberries, place in a pastry, add a little verjuice when it is nearly cooked. You can put two or three together.

Turbot

Cut in pieces when it has been gutted, and put in a pastry in slices like the carp pie, with salt and white powder. Add fresh butter when it is nearly cooked and a drizzle of verjuice. It works well to cook and serve cold as a small pie. Some people make it big.

Red mullet

Gut like perch through the gills. Place in a pastry two or three

---

122. You are adding the marinade back into the pie half way through cooking. Blanching doesn't make sense here, but perhaps he means not to get the crust wet.
123. It's not clear why lardons are involved here.

ou troys ensemble menues espices pouldre blanche sel de raisins de corinctes si voules peu de verjus beurre serves froict.

⁋ Grenault*
⁋ Soit faict comme des rougetz sinon que il n'y en fault que ung quant il est Gros mettes des Pruneaulx dedans si voules grosse paste. Il se garde longtemps.

⁋ Soles en paste.
⁋ Prenes solles & les eschardes & les mettes de leur long en paste, menues espices pouldre blanche sel & quant elles seront presque cuyctes peu de verjus & de beurre la paste longue & de grosse paste.

⁋ Coing en paste.
⁋ Prenes coingz & les cures les grains du cueur faictes croste de bonne paste, et le laisses ung peu hasles succre .xxxv. z sz cynamomon coupe menu comme cloudz de giroffle ou en pouldre pour deulx ou .iii. *[fol. 57r]* coingz selon la grosseur qu'ilz auront & picques lesdictz cloux ausdictz coingz et canelle si la voules entiere ou la mettez en pouldre se voulles avec la grosseur d'ung pois de pouldre blanche, mettes le tout ensemble. Aulcuns y mettent beurre ou mouelle de beuf, serves tiedes toutes patisseries de paste fine se veullent menger chauldes. Item si les voules menger froydes n'y mettez point de beurre ny de mouelle.

⁋ Marrons.
⁋ Prenes marrons & les perces & les faictes cuyre peu entre deulx cendres tant que les pourres plumer puis les mettes en paste apres que les aures plumes et les assaisonnes comme les coingz dessusdictz sinon qu'il y fault petit d'ypocras quant ilz seront presque cuictes pour deulx ou troys douzaines. Item fault deulx onces de pouldre de duc. Doulce cloudz de giroffle.

---

* Note our comment regarding the mystery fish *grevot* or possibly *grenot* on p. 158 above. Our suggestion that it is monkfish is tentative.

together, with fine spices, white powder, salt, currants if you like, a little verjuice, butter. Serve cold.

Monkfish

Make like red mullet, except that there should only be one when it is large. Add plums inside if you want a large pie. It will keep for a long time.

Sole pie

Take soles and scale them, and put them lengthwise in a crust with fine spices, white powder, salt. And when they are nearly cooked, add a little verjuice and butter. It should be a thick crust and a large pie.

Quince pie

Take quinces and remove the seeds of the core. Make a crust of good pastry, and let it brown a bit. Add 35 ounces of sugar and half an ounce of cinnamon, cut small into pieces like cloves or in powder for two or three quinces according to their size. Stick the said cloves in the said quinces and cinnamon whole or ground as you like. Add about a pea-sized amount of white powder, and place everything together. Some add butter or beef marrow, serve warm. All pastries with a fine crust should be eaten hot. Note: if you want to eat them cold, don't add butter or marrow.

Chestnuts

Take chestnuts and pierce them and let them cook a little between two coals until you can peel them. Then put them in pastry after they are peeled and season like the quinces mentioned above except that there must be a little hippocras added when they are nearly cooked. Makes two or three dozen. Note: there should be two ounces of Duke's powder. Twelve cloves.

❧ Mesles.
❧ Ostes les queues & aelles quant elle seront bien meures faictes les [crostes de] crostes de paste fine. Et mettes lesdictes mesles dedans avec pouldre de duc. Aulcuns y mettent du beurre quant on les veult menger chauldes ainsi comme coings.

❧ Dariolles pour l'este.
[fol. 57v] ❧ Prenes une quarte de bonne cresme ou de bon laict vieulx gras quant c'est tout faict y fault de beurre & six moyeulx d'oeufz du sel, succre pouldre cynamomon petit de saffran en pouldre puis passes le tout par l'estamine croste de paste bien fine & deslyee & haslee au four puis l'emplisses avec une cuilliere dans ledict four et en remuant ladicte cresme devant que la mettre dans ledict four & la faictes cuyre petit a petit serves la chaulde succre par dessus.
❧ Si voullez en pourres faire flantz en plat & faire cuire comme oeufz au beurre et mettes des myettes de pain que vous passeres par l'estamine avec oeufz & en seront plus fermes.

❧ Brideaulx* a veaulx.
❧ Paste avec farine moyeulx d'oeufz beurre Succre eaue rose Sel assez claire peu de formaige blanc & fault faire ledict paste plus ferme & engresses une feuille de papier de beurre & estendes vostredict paste par dessus de l'espesseur de deulx doigz cuyses au four doulx, et quant il sera cuictz tires le & le coupes par dessus a l'orenge d'un demy doigtz & ayez de beurre fondu que mettrez par dessus mettez succre par dessus.

❧ Blanc menger de chapon.
❧ Prenes le blanc de chapon quant il est boully ou ro*[fol. 58r]*sty hache bien menu broyes amandes pignolac aussi vostredicte chair

---

*   A version of this word also appears in Rabelais as *bride à veaux*. Cotgrave defines it as 'Hollow, round and wreathed cracknels of fine flower, sugar, salt and yoalkes of egs, incorporated together with water, and white wine.' The name seems to derive from a bridle, a strap, which is perhaps what this wreath-shaped biscuit resembles.

Medlars

Remove the stems and seeds when they are very ripe.[124] Make them in a crust of fine pastry. And place the said medlars within with Duke's powder. Some add butter when they want to eat it hot like quinces.

Darioles for the summer[125]

Take a quart of good cream or good old rich milk. When it is all done, add butter and six egg yolks, some salt, sugar, powdered cinnamon, a little ground saffron then pass everything through a sieve. Take fine pastry crust rolled out, brown in an oven, then fill with a spoon in the said oven and stir the said cream before you place it in the said oven and let it cook little by little. Serve hot with sugar on top.

If you want you can make flans on a plate and cook it like eggs in butter and add breadcrumbs that you pass through the sieve with the eggs and it will be firmer.

Calves' bridles

Pastry with flour, egg yolk, butter, sugar, rosewater, salt, thin enough, a little white cheese, and you must make the said pastry firm and grease a sheet of paper with butter and roll out your said pastry on top the thickness of two fingers. Cook in a gentle oven, and when it is cooked remove and cut about a half finger thick. Add orange on top and melted butter along with sugar.

Blancmange of capon

Take the breast of capon, When it is boiled or roasted, chop very finely, grind almonds, sugared pine nuts, also your said flesh. Pass

---

124. Medlars must be eaten extremely ripe, almost to the point of being rotten, a process called bletting, otherwise they are too astringent.
125. This is a dessert made in a small mould lined with a kind of puff pastry.

passes par l'estamine avec cynamomon eaue Rose, puis faictes frire avec bon Beurre frais sel Succre asses lye quant le tout sera frict faictes desfroyer, puis mettes en Croste bien deslye couvert.

☙ Tartes jacopines.
☙ Prenes fin fromaige gras couppes petit de moyeulx d'oeufz eaue rose beurre frays, succre sel mettes en croste & qu'elle soit commotee & quelque orenge e[t] faictes cuyre au four doulx.

☙ Borbonneses.
☙ Soit broye bien fort destrempe de cresme lait de moyeulx d'oeufz & beurre & dresses le plus delye que pourrez d'ung doy de hault & soit remply vostre farine et serves chaulx succre par dessus.

☙ C'est que fault pour fair ung banquet ou nopces apres pasques.
☙ Et premierement.
♣ Bon pain bon vin.
☙ Entree de table.
☙ Petis alloyaulx de venayson.
Sallades d'oranges.
[fol. 58v] Testes de chevreaulx doree
Vinaigrettes.
☙ Potaiges.
✱ Poussins aux herbes ou l'estuvee boully lardez
Poree brayee.
Gigoteau de veau au brouet dore.
☙ Rost.
Oysons a la malvoysie
Lapereaulx de garenne aulx oranges
Poulletz fesandes
Pastes de pigeons.
☙ Second rost.
Levreaulx saulce royalle
Poussins au vinaigre rosat

through a sieve with cinnamon and rosewater, then fry with good fresh butter, salt, sugar. It should be rather thick. When it is all fried, break it up, then place in a crust well rolled out, covered.

Jacobin tarts

Take fine rich cheese cut in small pieces, egg yolks, rosewater, fresh butter, sugar, salt. Place in a crust and mix it together. Add some orange and let it cook in a gentle oven.

Borbonneses [*Tarte bourbonnaise*]

Vigorously beat a batter of cream, milk, egg yolks and butter and prepare it as loosely as you can so that it comes to the height of a finger, and fill your crust and serve hot with sugar on top.

Here's what you need to make a banquet or wedding after Easter

First

Good bread, good wine

First course

Little sirloins of venison
Orange salads
Gilded kids' heads
Vinaigrettes

Pottages

Young chicken with herbs or boiled and larded stew
Puréed leeks
Veal shanks in a golden broth

Roasts

Goslings in malmsey
Young rabbits from the warren with oranges
Hung chicken
Pigeon pies

Second roast

Young hares in royal sauce
Young chicken in rose vinegar

Chevreaulx au verjus d'ozeille
Pigeons en rost.
℘ Tiers service de rost.
℘Venayson de rost saulce realle.
Ung cochon.
Esturgeon
Pastez de venaysons frais.
℘ Issue de table.
✽ Gellee ambree
Papillons de pommes
Fromaiges de cresme
Four* troys pieces au plat.

[fol. 59r] ✽ Ung aultre banquet ou nopces.
℘ Bon pain   Bon vin.

℘ Entree de table.
♣ Abricotz.
Prunes de damas
Petis pastes de venayson chaulx
Talmouses de blanc chapon.
✽ Potaiges.
♣ Boully larde de venaison
poussins a l'estuvee
Bizetz aulx choulx.
✽ Rost.
♣ Perdrix au sel menu
pastez de venayson chaulx
Lappereaulx au sel menu.
℘ Second rost.
℘Heronneaulx
Saulce bastarde

---

* A '*piece de four*' in archaic French means a cake or pastry, so this would seem to mean three pastries: elsewhere it does read *troys pieces de four*.

Kid in sorrel verjuice
Roast pigeons

Third course of roasts

Roast venison in royal sauce
A pig
Sturgeon
Cold venison pies

Dessert

Amber jelly
Apple butterflies
Cream cheeses
Petits fours, three per plate

Another banquet or wedding

Good Bread   Good Wine

First course

Apricots
Damson plums
Little hot pies of venison
Breast of capon cheesecakes

Pottages

Larded broth of venison
Stewed baby chicken
Doves with cabbage

Roast

Partridge with fine salt
Hot venison pies
Young rabbits with fine salt

Second roast

Young heron
Bastard sauce

Levreaulx
Saulce bastarde
Pastes de cailleteaulx.

✱ Tiers service.

♣ Vinaigrette a la saulce cordialle
Poussins au vinaigre rosat
Pastes de haslebran.

℄ Quart service.

[fol. 59v] ℄ Hestoudeau au moust
Oyson a la malvoysie*
poullez fezandes.

℄ Cinquesme service.

℄ Pigeons au succre
Venayson rostye
pastes de venayson frays.

℄ Sixiesme service.

℄ Cochons
pans.
Esturgeon.

♣ Issue de table.

♣ Four troys pieces au plat.
Gellee.
pommes de capendu.

♣ Aultre bancquet.

✱ Bon pain   Bon vin
prunes de damas
Andouilles farcies
Tetine de vache
Touterelles
Langue de beuf
pastes de veau.

---

* *Malvoysie*, now *malvoisie*, was known in English as malmsey (*SOED*). The Duke of Clarence drowned in a butt of malmsey in 1478. Although the malvoisie grape is now grown throughout Europe, it was then most associated with wines from Greece and the Mediterranean and, later, with Madeira.

Young hares
Bastard sauce
Pies of young quail

Third course

Vinaigrette with cordial sauce
Young chicken in rose vinegar
Teal pies

Fourth course

Young capons in grape must
Fowl in malmsey
Hung chicken

Fifth course

Pigeons in sugar
Roast venison
Cold venison pies

Sixth course

Pigs
Peacocks
Sturgeon

Dessert

Petits fours, three per plate
Jelly
Short start apples

Another banquet

Good bread   Good wine
Damson plums
Stuffed andouille sausages
Cow's udder
Turtle doves
Ox tongue
Veal pies

❦ Potaiges.

* Bizetz aulx choulx*
Potaiges de courges
[fol. 60r] Boully larde de venayson
Cocombres farcyes
Cochons houssez
Pastes de venayson chaulx
Perdriaulx
Levreaulx
Poulletz
Oysons farcys
pastes de caille.

❦ Second service.

❦ Lappereaulx
Hestoudeaux
Poussins au vinaigre rosat
Venayson rostye
Cochons
Pastes de moyneaulx
Fesans
Pastes de venayson froide.

❦ Issue de table.

❦ Gellee de troys sortes
Troys pieces de four au plat
Poires nouvelles   pesches
Poyres a l'ypocras
Amandes et cerneaulx
L'eaue rose
Cresme & fourmaige en jonchee.†

---

*   This is a dish referenced in Rabelais's *Gargantua and Pantagruel* Book IV chapter 24, where Panurge speaks of all the mistakes cooks make, like boiling partridges with cabbage, pigeons with leeks, doves with turnips, as if everyone would know that doves go with cabbage. Rabelais may very well have seen a copy of this cookbook.

†   Cotgrave translates *jonchee* as 'green cheese', which was a fresh cheese which was sat on a bed of rushes (*jonc*) to assist in the draining.

Pottages

Doves with cabbage
Gourd pottage
Larded venison broth
Stuffed cucumbers
Pigs *houssez*[126]
Hot venison pies
Young partridges
Young hares
Chicken
Stuffed gosling
Quail pies

Second course

Young rabbits
Young capons
Young chicken in rose vinegar
Roast venison
Pigs
Sparrow pies
Pheasants
Cold venison pies

Dessert

Three kinds of jelly
Three petits fours on a plate
New pears   Peaches
Pears in hippocras
Almonds and walnuts
Rosewater
Cream and junket cheese

---

126. Cotgrave glosses *houssé* as either covered with a cloth, such as a horse blanket, or as clean or swept, as in a chimney. To *housé*, he gives the meaning of 'booted'.

[fol. 60v] ❡ Aultre service

Bon pain   Bon vin.

❡ Entree de table.

❡ Pastes de venayson chaulx
pesches   Raisins
Fricassees.

❡ Potaiges.

❡ Chapons boulluz
Ramiers a la poyvrade
Grave de petit oyseaulx

❡ Rost

❡ Lappereaulx deulx au plat
perdriaux deulx au plat
Cappes.

❡ Second service.

❡ Poullettes fezandees
Heronneaulx saulce realle
Olyves.

❡ Entremetz troussez.
❡ Tiers service de rost.

❡ Becasseaulx.
Hestoudeaulx au saulge
pigeons
Sallades de cytrons.

♣ Quart service de rost.

♣ Venaison rostye.
[fol. 61r] Canards a la dodine
Cocombres confictz
Pastes de venayson frais.

❡ Issue de table.

❡ Gellee clarete en mouelle
Angelotz de gellee blanche
Tartes de pommes
Tarte de cresme
poire a l'ypocras

Another course

Good bread   Good wine

First course

Hot venison pies
Peaches   Grapes
Fricassees

Pottages

Boiled capons
Wood pigeons in pepper sauce
Gravy of little birds

Roast

Young rabbits, two to a plate
Young partridges, two to a plate
Apples

Second course

Hung chicken
Young herons in royal sauce
Olives

Trussed *entremets*
Third roast course

Young woodcocks
Young capons in sage
Pigeons
Citron salads

Fourth roast course

Roast venison
Ducks in dodine sauce
Preserved cucumbers
Cold venison pies

Dessert

Claret jelly with marrow
Little angels of white jelly
Apple tarts
Cream tarts
Pear in hippocras

Papillons de pommes
poires cuittes.

☾ Ung aultre bancquet ou nopces.

♣ Bon pain   Bon vin
Pesches
Raisins
Prunes de damas
Fricassees
pastes de veau.

☾ Potaiges.

✶ Boullon dore
poree broyee.

✶ Rost.

Ung cartier de cochon
Ung oyson
Troys pigeons
[fol. 61v] Ung hestoudeau au mouste.

✶ Second rost.

Deulx lappereaulx
Deulx poullettes fezandees
Ung paste de pigeons.

☾ Issue de table.

Tartes   Poires
Amundes & cerneaulx pelles.

☾ Boucherie pour faire boullon.

✶ Ung flanchet de beuf
Ung car[t]ier de mouton deulx livres de gresse

✶ Pour l'espicerie.

♣ Quatre pointes pour espouser
Quatre onces gingembre batu
Une carrte verjus, pinte vinaigre
Ung sizain saffran batu

Butterflies of apples
Cooked pears

Another banquet or wedding

Good bread   Good wine
Peaches
Grapes
Damson plums
Fricassees
Veal pies

Pottages

Golden broth
Puréed leeks

Roast

A quarter of a pig
A gosling
Three pigeons
A young capon in grape must

Second roast

Two young rabbits
Two hung chicken
Pigeon pie

Dessert

Tarts   Pears
Almonds and shelled walnuts

Butchery to make broth

A flank of beef
A mutton quarter, two pounds of fat

For spices

Four points to espouse
Four ounces of ground ginger
A quart of verjuice, a pint of vinegar
A sixth of an ounce of ground saffron

Trois carterons d'oeufz
Deulx mines de charbon.

♣ Aultre feste ou bancquet d'este.

♣ Bon pain   Bon vin.

* Entree de table.

* Andouilles farcyes
Langues de mouton sallees
Tetines de vache, poree de blanc de poussins
piedz de mouton Servelat milannois
Fricassee de poulletz au verjus de grain
Confiture de frize de poussin
[fol. 62r] Ventree de chevreaulx confitz
Teste de chevreau doree
Foye de veau rosty
Carbonnade a la coulloule*
paste de veau en pot a tout croste
fricassees de menues droitz a la barbe robert
fricassee de poussins a la saulce madame
palays de beuf confitz a force groselles et cy[boulles]
Cailles confictes a la cameline boulles†
Caillette farcye
Burelot de febves nouvelles.

❡ Aultre entree de table pour yver.

❡ Langues de mouton a l'estuvee
Hachis de gigotz
Chauldun de poyvre   Saulcisses
pastes a la saulce chaulde.

❡ Potaiges

❡ Cercelles aulx poreaulx.
Gigoteau de veau au brouet dore
Bizetz aulx choulx.

---

*   *Coulloule* is a mystery. We are grateful to Philip and Mary Hyman for their suggestion that it might be a misprint for 'Toulouse', but the proposal is by no means definitive.

†   In the text, the word *boulles* is detached from *cameline* and most likely belongs to the *cy* of the line above, i.e. *cyboulles* or *ciboules*, 'chives or scallions'

Seventy-five eggs
Two hundred pounds[127] of coal

Another feast or banquet in summer

Good bread   Good wine

First course

Stuffed andouille sausages
Salted sheep's tongues
Cows' udders, pottage of baby chicken breast
Sheep's trotters, Milanese cervelat
Fricassee of chicken with freshly pressed verjuice
Confit of young chicken offal
Stomach of kid in confit
Gilded kid's head
Roasted calf's liver
Carbonade *à la Toulouse*
Veal potted pie with crust intact
Fricassee of fine offal in Robert's beard sauce
Fricassee of baby chickens in sauce madame
Palates of beef confit with a lot of gooseberries and scallions
Quail cooked in cameline sauce
Stuffed young quail
Burelot of new fava beans

Another first course for winter

Stewed sheep's tongues
Hash of legs
Chowder of pepper   Sausages
Pies with hot sauce

Pottages

Teals with leeks
Veal shank in golden broth
Doves with cabbage

---

127. A *mine* is about 110–120 pounds according to Cotgrave. Why eggs and coal are kept with spices is not clear.

ℭ Rost.

perdrix aux oranges Beccasses alesquesal
chapons Congnins
Cochons pastes de canart.

ℭ Issue de table.

Gasteau [fu]eillete poires.
ℭ[G]ellee lozengee.

[fol. 62v] ℭ Cedict jour a soupper.

ℭ Bon pain Bon vin

ℭ Entree de table.

ℭAlloyaulx de venaison a la saulce realle
Talmouses de blanc de chapon
Sallades d'oranges
pastes de venayson chaulx.

ℭ Potaiges.

* Perdrix aulx choulx
Sanglier aulx naveaulx Fromentee.
Hochepot de pigeons.

ℭ Rost.

ℭPerdrix aulx orenges
Venayson saulce realle
pastes d'alouettes Saulce hypocras
Beccasses a lesquesal Herons
Levreaulx paste de touterelles
Venayson de sanglier Connins
pastes de cercelles
pans pour entremetz.

ℭ Aulrte service.

Pigeons Poussins
Cochons paste frais piedz a la saulce d'enfer.

Roasts

Partridges with oranges   Woodcock *alesquesal* [128]
Capons   Rabbits
Pigs   Duck pies

Dessert

Flaky layer cake   Pears
Jelly diamonds

This said day for supper

Good Bread   Good wine

First course

Sirloin of venison in royal sauce
Breast of capon cheesecakes
Orange salads
Hot venison pies

Pottages

Partridge in cabbage
Boar with turnips   Frumenty
Hodge-podge of pigeons

Roast

Partridges with oranges
Venison in royal sauce
Lark pies   Hippocras sauce
Woodcock *à lesquesal*   Herons
Young hares   Turtle dove pie
Boar venison   Rabbits
Teal pies
Peacocks for *entremets*

Another course

Pigeons   Young chicken
Cold pork pies   Trotters in hell sauce

---

128. As with many of these menu items, there is no corresponding recipe in the book. J.-L. Flandrin also despaired of figuring out exactly what this dish might mean in his discussion of the menus in his book *Arranging the Meal*, p. 65 (see Bibliography).

♣ Issuye de table.

♣ Gellee blanche clarette & ambree
[fol. 63r] Trois pieces de four au plat
pastes de congnins
ypocras
La dragee espices de chambre

Neffles frittes
Eaue rose a laver

♣ Pour une aultre feste ou bancquet.

♣ Bon pain
Bon vin

♣ Assiette de table.

♣ Andouilles et saulcisses
Pastes a la saulce chaulde.

♣ Potaiges.

Cive de liepvre
Brouet dore.

♣ Rost.

♣ Demy cochon
Deulx chapons
Deulx poullettes fezandees
Ung paste de canart.

Deulx connins

♣ Issue de table.

Tarte d'angleterre
poire cuycte
Marrans

♣ Entree de table pour le soupper.

✷ Sallades de cicoree
Bizetz aulx choulx
Sallades de pestanades

♣ Rost.

Venayson rostye
Beccaces
pastes d'alouettes
Chapon

perdrix
Connins
Cochons de laict
Olives.

[fol. 63v] ♣ Issue de table.

Poyres a l'ypocras.
Tartes de pommes chiquettees.
Ung gasteau mollet.
Une talamouse.

Dessert

Jelly, clear and amber
Three petits fours on a plate
Rabbit pies   Fried medlars
Hippocras   Rosewater to wash
Candied spices

Another feast or banquet

Good bread   Good wine

First table

Andouilles and sausages
Pies with hot sauce

Pottages

Civet of hare   Golden broth

Roast

Half pig
Two capons   Two rabbits
Two hung chicken
A duck pie

Dessert

English tart
Cooked pears   Chestnuts

First course for supper

Salads of chicory   Salads of parsnips
Doves with cabbage

Roast

Roast venison   Partridge
Woodcock   Rabbits
Lark pies   Sucking pigs
Capon   Olives

Dessert

Pears in hippocras
Chopped apple tarts.
A soft cake   A cheesecake

❦ Pour confire des amandes nouvelles qui n'ont encore la peau dure.

✱ Vous les Plumeres comme pesches & les bouteres tremper en belle eaue fresche, puis les ostes de l'eaue & les boutes dedans ung pot de vin blanc canelle entiere cloudz de giroffle, & succre. Et les la laisses consumer fort qu'il n'y demeure point comme de boullon & servez a yssue de table.

♣ Abricotz.

❦ Pareillement en peulx faire de nouveaulx abricotz & de noix nouvelles. Mais les noix se doibvent tremper une nuict.

♣ Tartes rouges.

♣ Pour faire tartes rouges de pommes plumes voz pommes & faictes tremper en vin rouge, & succre & canelle batue avec ung petit de beurre frais et passez tout par l'estamine & faictes voz tartes.

✱ Papillons de pommes de capendu.

[fol. 64r] ❦ Il fault faire boullir du vin, du succre & canelle Avec ung petit de cloud de giroffle, puis quant aura boully quelque espace jectera les pommes par quartiers dedans & les fera boullir jusques a ce que il soit tout consume puis les laissez froidir & servez en tasses.

❦ Saulce realle.

❦ Prenez vin vermeil, vinaigre, & autant de l'ung comme de l'aultre. Canelle entiere, cloudz de giroffle succre & boutes tout bouillir en ung beau pot jusques qu'il soit diminue quasi de la moytie & servez sur vostre venaison.

♣ Oeufz perdus.

❦ Prenes moyeulx d'oeufz crus pain gratuize destrempe en eaue rose & fine fleur de farine sans passer par l'estamine, puis les feras frire en la poelle en bon beurre aussi n'oublye a les saller, & quant seront cuictz succres les.

To preserve green almonds that don't yet have a hard shell
You peel them like peaches and place to soak in fresh water, then take them out of the water and place them in a pot of white wine with whole cinnamon, cloves and sugar. And let them absorb all of the broth and serve as a dessert.

Apricots
Likewise, you can make green apricots or green walnuts. But the walnuts must be soaked for a night.

Red tarts
To make red apple tarts, peel your apples and soak them in red wine, with sugar and cinnamon beaten, with a little fresh butter, then pass everything through a sieve and make your tarts.

Butterflies of short start apples
It is necessary to boil wine, sugar and cinnamon with a little bit of clove. Then when it has boiled a while, throw in the apples in quarters, and let it boil just until they are finished then let them chill and serve in cups.

Royal sauce
Take red wine, vinegar, as much of one as the other. Whole cinnamon, cloves, sugar, put all on to boil in a nice pot just until it is reduced by about half, and serve with your venison.

Lost eggs
Take raw egg yolks, breadcrumbs soaked in rosewater and finest flour without passing through a sieve, then you let it fry in a pan in good butter. Also you do not forget to salt it, and when it is cooked, sugar them.

✻ Dodine blanche.

✻ Pour faire dodine blanche prenes lait de vache moyeulx d'oeufz durs pouldre blanche des oygnons bien frit par roelle. Et passes le tout par l'estamine et le faictes cuyre en une poelle, & n'oublyez a y bouter succre et goustez de sel. Ensemble la gresse de ton carnart.

☙ Dodine rouge.

☙ Prenes du pain blanc & le faictes Rostyr bien roux sur le gril. Et le mettes tremper en vin fort vermeil *[fol. 64v]* puis faictes frire des Oygnons par les ou par rouelles en sain de lard et passes vostre pain par l'estamine puis pour espices canelle, muscades cloux de giroffle succre, & goustes de sel & faictes tout boullir ensemble avec la gresse de vostre canart, & quant il sera cuict jectes sur vostre canart ou oyseau de riviere.

✻ Gigot de mouton a l'estuvee.

☙ Prenes ung gigot de mouton & l'escorches & lardez de bon lard, & cloux de giroffle & de bastons de canelle, prenes de bon boullon, & le mettes dedans une terrasse ou ung pot qui soit asses aysement, & pour espices muscades et menue espice, & le remues & le laisses bien boullir par l'espace de deulx bonnes heures, aulcuns y boutent des dates. Les autres des raisins de corinthe les aultres des pruneaulx.

♣ Chapon au brouet d'alemaigne.

♣ Faictes rostir ung bon chapon, puis prenes amandes & les faictes fricasser en une poelle comme chastaignes & les broyez en ung mortier avec vin vermeil, verjus, petit vinaigre une tostee de pain rostie trempee de bon boullon, & boutes tout en vostre pot, avec vostre chappon, pour espices, muscade, Gingembre cloux, & succre, & goustes de sel.

♣ Beurre d'amandes en Karesme.

♣ Prenes des amandes plumees & les faictes bien fort broyer en ung mortier avec ung petit eaue Rose ung *[fol. 65r]* petit de boullon de carpe ou trche boullue en eaue sans sel a court boullon puis quant

White dodine sauce

To make a white dodine take cow's milk, hard-boiled egg yolks, white powder, well fried onion rounds. Pass everything through a sieve and let it cook in a pan and don't forget to add sugar and salt to taste. Add to the fat of your duck.

Red dodine sauce

Take white bread and toast it until well browned on the grill. And place it to soak in strong red wine, then fry the onions [chopped] or in rounds in melted lard and pass your bread through the sieve then your spices, cinnamon, nutmeg, cloves, sugar and salt to taste and let everything boil with the fat from your duck and when it is cooked throw it on your duck or river fowl.

Stewed mutton leg

Take a leg of mutton and skin it and lard with good salted pork fat and cloves and little sticks of cinnamon. Take good broth and place in a clay vessel or a pot that is large enough. And for spices, nutmeg and fine spices, and stir and let it boil well for the space of two good hours. Some add dates. Others add currants or prunes.

German capon broth

Roast a good capon, then take almonds and fry them in a pan like chestnuts and pound them in a mortar with good red wine, verjuice, a little vinegar, toasted bread soaked in good broth, and place everything in your pot with your capon. For spices, nutmeg, ginger, cloves, sugar and salt to taste.

Almond butter for Lent

Take shelled almonds and crush them forcefully in a mortar with a little rosewater, a little broth of carp or tench boiled in water without salt in a court bouillon then, when it is well pounded until it can't be

seront bien fort broyez tant que l'on ne scauroit plus fort passez par l'estamine. Et bouttes ung petit de succre dedans: puis ayes ung beau linge blanc. Et l'enveloppe dedans, & qu'il soit bien serre, & le laisses esgouster, puis le coupperez par lesches & boutteres en moulle.

ℭ Brochet larde.
ℭ Prenes ledict brochet & le nettoye fort avec une serviette blanche et le mettes tremper en vinaigre et regardes la quantite des platz que vous en vouldres faire, prenes une chauldiere & y bouttes vin blanc verjus, vinaigre, petit d'eaue & sel & quelque peu de bonnes herbes & le faictes boullir a petit feu, puis jecteres vostre brochet dedans, quant il sera cuyct tires le & jectez ung petit de verjus et de vin aigre par dessus pour le faire froidir puis quant sera froit boutes dessus une serviette et le plumes et faictes des lardons de pain blanc comme si voules larder ung poussin, puis mettes du beurre en ung plat sur le feu ung petit de canelle pouldre blanche ensemble les lardons, & quant ilz seront froitz lardez vostre brochet puis quant sera larde prenez du jus d'orenges avec du verjus et canelle si jectes dedans vostre poelle avec ledict beurre & du sucre dedans. Et mettes vostre saulce sur vostre brochet, *[fol. 65v]* quis [puis] le boutes sur les charbons couvert jusques a ce que vueilles servir a table. Et se sert volentiers au premier service de poisson.

ℭ Potaige lavatif.
ℭ Pour faire ung potaige lavatif.
ℭ Prenes une poulle noire avec ung Trumeau de beuf & mettes ensemble en ung petit pot de terre sans sel, puis quant il sera escume boutes ung baston de canelle, & ung petit de sel et quant il aura boully et qu'il sera diminue de la moytie & prenes vostre trumerau et vostre poulle & les rompes l'ung avec l'aultre dedans ledict pet [pot], puis prenes du pain de seigle ou aultre et le boutes en eaue de fontaine ou de riviere apres que ledict pain sera trempe boutes en une estamine et le esguichez fort ladicte eaue qu'il n'y en demeure goute a celle fin qu'il soit sec, puis prendres ung aultre petit pot de terre, & boutes ledict pain dedans l'estamine, puis prendres le boullon de

pounded any more, pass through a sieve. And add a little sugar, then take a nice white cloth. And envelop it within, so that it is very tight and let it drain. Then cut into slices and place in a mould.

Larded pike

Take said pike and clean it well with a white napkin and place it to soak in vinegar and take note of the number of dishes you would like to make. Take a cauldron and add white wine, verjuice, vinegar, a little water and salt, and some good herbs and let it boil over a gentle fire, then throw your pike inside. When it's cooked, remove it and throw a little verjuice and vinegar on top to let it cool. Then when it is cold, place on top of a napkin and skin and make lardons of white bread as if you wanted to lard a young chicken, then place butter on a plate over a small flame, a little cinnamon, white powder together with the lardons, and when they are fried, lard your pike. Then when it is larded take some orange juice with verjuice and cinnamon and throw it in your pan with the said butter and sugar in it. And place your sauce on your pike, then place it over the coals covered just until you want to serve it at the table. And it works well as a first fish course.

Cleansing pottage
To make a cleansing pottage

Take a black hen with a shin of beef and put together in a little earthenware pot without salt, then when it is skimmed add a cinnamon stick, a little bit of salt and when it comes to the boil and it has reduced by half, take your shin and your hen and break them both up in the pot, then take rye bread or some other kind and put it in fountain or river water. After said bread is well soaked, place in a sieve and squeeze out forcefully the said water so that no drop remains and it is dry. Then take another earthenware pot and place the said bread in the sieve then take the broth from the hen and shin

la poulle & du Trumeau et mettes dedans ledict pot. Et fault qu'il boulle avec ledict pain. Et prenes ung petit eaue rose avecques canelle en pouldre & mettes dedans ledict boullon. Et le bailles au patient sans bouillir & toutes heures qu'il en vouldra humer & gardez qu'il ne sente la fumee.

> *[fol. 66r]* ℭ Potaige digestif.
> ℭ Pour faire ung potaige digestif.

ℭ Prenes ung chapon, ung gigot de veau et ung demy collet de mouton & boutes tout bouillir ensemble avec ung petit de sel. Et le faictes fort bouillir et qu'il soit bien cuyct, prenes le boullon & le passes par l'estamine & mettes dedans ung pot de terre, puis prenes cloudz de giroffle canelle entiere dedans ung drap blanc & le boutes dedans ledict pot & ung petit de eaue rose ainsi que verres qu'il lui en fault par raison, puis prenes mye de pain blanc, & le esgrenes, moyeulx d'oeuf ung petit de saffran, & verjus, pouldre blanche Succre, & vin blanc, & canelle, & gettes tout ensemble avec ledict boullon & le remues qu'il ne sente la fumee et le bailles quant mestier en sera.

> ℭ Neige de gellee.
> ℭ Pour faire neige de gellee.

ℭ Prenes piedz de veau selon la quantite que vouldres, et les boutes bouillir en belle eaue claire: Et les laissez bouillir jusques au tiers quant verres que le boullon sera despesse prendres demy voirre d'eaue ce qui vous semblera estre bon & le jecteres dedans ledict boullon avec amandes plumees & broyes destrempes dudict boullon, puis les passes par l'estamine comme laict D'a*[fol. 66v]*mandes avec succre fin & le jecteres dedans. Ce faict boutes le en la ca[v]e et le battes avec ung aulbin d'oeuf bien fort en sorte qu'il soit chault & quant en vouldres servir en prendres avec une Cuillier & le boutes en rochet.

and place in the said pot. And let it boil with said bread. And take a little rosewater with ground cinnamon and add to the said broth. And give it to the patient without boiling and at all hours that he would like to take it and make sure it doesn't smell of smoke.

Digestive pottage
To make a digestive pottage

Take a capon, a leg of veal and a half neck of mutton and place everything to boil together with a little salt. Let it boil vigorously and when it is well cooked, take the broth and pass it through a sieve and place in an earthenware pot, then take cloves, whole cinnamon in a white cloth and place in the said pot with a little rosewater such as you might judge reasonable, then take the crumb of white bread and pick apart, and egg yolk, a little saffron, and verjuice, white powder, sugar and white wine, and cinnamon, and throw everything together with your said broth and stir it so it doesn't smell of smoke and serve when needed.

Snow from jelly
To make snow from jelly

Take calves' feet according to the quantity you want, and place them to boil in nice clear water: And let them boil a third of the way. When you see that the broth is thick, take half a glass of water that seems to you to be good and throw it in the said broth with shelled ground almonds, soaked in the said broth, then pass it through a sieve as you do almond milk with fine sugar and throw it in. When done, put it in the cellar and beat it with an egg white very forcefully so that it will rise high, and when you want to serve it take some with a spoon and mound it as if on a rock.[129]

---

129. This is akin to a recipe for snow in the *Proper Newe Boke of Cokery* that features an apple with rosemary twig, onto which the snow is passed through a sieve. Here perhaps a similar scene is made to resemble a rock, replicating a snowy mountain.

⁂ Cresme houssue.
✱ Pour faire cresme houssue.
⁂ Prenes du beurre bien clarifie et battes des moyeulx d'oeuf avec eaue rose succre et pain gratuize. Et le tout jectes en ung pot et le remues fort, puis jectes ung demy voirre de eaue dedans, puis le laisses rassayer pres du feu, & le servir quant vouldrez.

✱ Cresme de poys nouveaulx.
♣ Pour faire cresme de poys nouveaulx.
⁂ Vous les feres avec moytie Vin Blanc, et eaue, puis quant ilz seront cuictz prendres mye de pain blanc Et le tout cuyres ensemble & le laisseres refroidir: puis passes par l'estamine avec beurre clarifie & n'oublies a succrer se vous voulez, aulcuns ne le succrent point.

⁂ Pour faire andouilles de foye de veau.
⁂ Prenes ledict foye de veau gresse de Beuf et lart & le tout faire cuire ensemble, puis le haches bien menu, puis prenes des raisins de corinthe, cloux de giroffle & menues espices & force de fines herbes & moyeulx *[fol. 67r]* d'oeuf, puis prenes taye de veau ou de mouton et les enveloppes en facon de andouilles et les rotisses sur le gril & les serves a l'entree de table.

⁂ Pour faire crespes faictes en poelle.
⁂ Prenes beurre bien clarifie et pour faire vostre paste prenes fleur farine & vin blanc & le blanc d'oeuf et le tout passes par l'estamine asses espes, puis prenes ledit beurre bien clarifie fort chault vous prendrez ung antonnouer et l'esmouveres parmy vostre paste puis le cuises.

⁂ Pour faire lymatz d'alemaigne.
⁂ Pour faire limatz d'allemaigne en fuelle de saulge, prenes de l'eaue & la faictes bouillir et jectes vostre farine dedans comme si voules faire de la boullie & le tout boullez ensemble & le remues fort puis aures moyeulx d'oeufz & vin blanc dedans lesquelz les fault destremper & faictes paste forte asses, puis aurez de beurre affine qui soit chault

Fuzzy cream
To make fuzzy[130] cream

Take well clarified butter and beat egg yolks with rosewater, sugar and breadcrumbs. And put everything in a pot and stir it well, then put in half a glass of water, then let it sit near the fire and serve it when you like.

Cream of fresh peas
To make cream of fresh peas

You make it with half white wine and water, then when it is cooked take white breadcrumbs and cook it all together and let it cool. Then pass it through a sieve with clarified butter and don't forget to add sugar if you like, some don't add any sugar at all.

To make andouille of calf's liver

Take the said calf's liver, beef fat and lard and cook it all together, then chop it finely, then take currants, cloves and fine spices and a lot of fine herbs and egg yolks, then take a veal or mutton casing and stuff it like andouilles and roast them on a grill and serve as a first course.

To make crepes in a pan

Take well-clarified butter and to make your batter fine flour and white wine and the white of an egg, pass everything through a sieve so it's thick enough, then take the well-clarified butter, very hot, take a funnel and pour your batter through it, then cook it.

To make German snails

To make German snails, in sage leaf, take water and boil it and throw in your flour as if you want to make a porridge, and boil everything together and stir it vigorously. Then, take egg yolks, white wine in with which you steep them and make a very thick batter. Then take

---

130. Cotgrave glosses this word as hairy, though how one can describe cream with either of these terms remains confusing.

& boutes voz limatz dedans & les remuez avec la poincte d'ung cousteau & ne les faictes jusques les vouldres servir, puis jectes du succre dessus.

⁋ Pour faire cresme d'amandes nouvelles.
[fol. 67v] ⁋ Les fault plumer & les bouter en belle eaue fresche & le broyer avec eaue rose Succre fin & pain gratuise & le faire cuyre en bon beurre frais qui soit blanc sans luy donner couleur. Et le tout bien broye ensemble et ne passes point & la faictes cuyre en bon beurre frais si en voules faire tarte faire le povez.

⁋ Cresme de noix nouvelles.
⁋ Prenes persil nouveau, du baselicque du tin bien espluche & le tout broye avec lesdictes noix nouvelles ung petit d'eaue Rose & de mye de pain blanc gratuise & demy douzaine d'oeufz & de l'eaue Rose & le tout passeres par l'estamine, puis le frises en bon Beurre frais et de bon succre, & au servir semes de la pouldre de duc.

⁋ Entree de table d'yver.

⁋Ipocras blanc	
Marchepains	Fleurons
⁋Brocheletz de paste royalle	
Chemine*	Gasteau sec.

⁋ Entree de cuysine.

⁋Pompons	Gouges blanches
Saulcisses millannoys	
Langues de mouton a la trimollette	

---

* This may have some connection to the *pastes de cheminee au sucre* listed in the *Viandier* as a possible first dish in a *'bancquet pour madamoyselle'*.

fine butter that is hot and add in your snails and stir them with the point of a knife and do not make them until just when you want to serve them, then sprinkle sugar on top.

To make a cream of new almonds

You must shell them and place in nice fresh water[131] and grind with rosewater, fine sugar and breadcrumbs and let them cook in good fresh butter that is white so as not to give it colour. And grind everything together and don't pass at all [through a sieve] and let it cook in good fresh butter. If you want to make a tart of it, you can do it.

Cream of new walnuts

Take fresh parsley, basil, thyme well picked and grind it all with the said new nuts with a little rosewater, toasted white breadcrumbs and half a dozen eggs and rosewater, and pass it all through a sieve, then fry in good fresh butter and some good sugar, and to serve sprinkle with Duke's powder.

First course for the winter

White hippocras
Marzipan   Fried pastry shapes
Little skewers of royal [choux] pastry
Chimneys   Dry cake

First course from the kitchen

Melons[132]   White gourds
Milanese sausages
Sheep's tongues *à la trimollette*

---

131. The logic here is to remove the brown skin. This is often called blanching, but does not involve cooking, merely soaking overnight and then slipping off the skins. From it pure white almond milk can be made once the almonds are pounded and mixed with hot water, then strained. The recipe for almond milk above specifies this and the author did not think it necessary to repeat it here.

132. *Pompons* usually at this date refer to melons, although Cotgrave will later translate them as 'winter pumpkins'. The New World species is most unlikely to be intended here.

Ramiers a la grenade
[fol. 68r] Chevreaulx aulx oranges
Moygneaulx farcis pastez de hallebran.
⁋ Potaiges.
* Chapons revestus a court boullon
Laictues en pommes conficte
poussins aulx poys
Rouleau de venayson aulx fines herbellettes*
Oysons aulx cappes.
* Issue de table.

⁋ Artichaulx	Marsouin
Laiches clavees	Courge conficte
Froumaige de cresme	Cerises
pommes de capendu	Fromentee. &

* Dixiesme mectz.

* Ung gasteau flamen
Tartes a deulx visaiges. Ung flajol
Une rose d'angletteere Fraizes
Gellee blanche Gobeletz d'amandes.

⁋ Fromentee de venayson.
⁋ Fromentee de venayson prenes ung chevreau ou aigneau c'est tout ung rotisses le et haches fort menu Ayes de la cresme & froment cuyct apres que vostredict boullon sera froict vous jecteres vostre venayson dedans avec oeufz pouldre blanche marjolaine & le tout jectes dedans ladicte fromentee.

---

*   The word, and dish, *herbellettes* derives from the MF *arbolastre* and indicates a dish, often but not always an omelette or custard, containing many chopped herbs. It is common in medieval French, English and Italian sources and may be expressed as *arbolettys, erbolat, erbolato, herbulata, arboulastre* or *herbetella*.

Wood pigeons with pomegranate
Kid with oranges
Stuffed sparrows   Teal pies

Pottages

Capons in their feathers in court bouillon
Confit of cabbage lettuce
Young chicken with peas
Roulade of venison with herb custards
Gosling with apples

Dessert

Artichokes   Porpoise
Cloven slices   Candied gourd [133]
Cream cheese   Cherries
Short start apples [134]   Frumenty

Tenth course

A Flemish cake
Two-faced tarts   A flute
An English rose   Strawberries
White jelly   Goblets of almonds

Frumenty of venison

Frumenty of venison take a kid or lamb, either one, roast it and chop it up very finely. Add cream and cooked wheat.[135] After your said broth is cold, add your venison to the eggs, with white powder, marjoram and add everything into the said frumenty.

---

133. *Courge* is later applied to New World squash species, as in the familiar word *courgette*. It is very unlikely that a cookbook would call for any New World species, as they were only just beginning to gain notice among botanists in the mid-sixteenth century.

134. Cotgrave defines *Carpendu/Capendu* as a 'shorte-start' apple (also mentioned by Tradescant), whereas we now describe it as 'short stalk'. Today, the court pendu is a recognized variety among English and European orchardists.

135. This is a standard medieval dish with venison. Use whole-wheat berries, gently cooked in milk, which comes out something like a risotto in texture. It is not clear why chopped kid or lamb is used, unless the author omitted a line about making a bouillon with it, their inclusion here might be a mistake entirely.

ℭ Fromentee de chevreau.
[fol. 68v] ℭ Vous prendres ledict chevreau & le bouteres par morceaulx, puis le feres cuyre en bonnes herbes & bon boullon, puis ayes vostre froment cuict en laict comme se faisies une fromentee avec ung petit de pouldre blanche canelle & succre.

ℭ Raymolles de blanc chapon.*
ℭ Pour faire raymolles de blanc chapon & de moelle de beuf et raysins de corinthe fault prendre ung bon chapon fort cuyt & le desserner† & le hacher bien avec ladicte mouelle & raisins de corinthe puis feres de petites obbesses de paste comme tartelletes et les mettes chascun a par soy et les frises dedans la poelle en saing de lart et les serves a l'yssue de table. Et les succres puis jecteres vostre cresme dedans si en voules faire des tartes en pourres faire ou servir en platz ou a vostre discretion.

ℭ Pour faire tartes d'espinars.
Tartes d'espinars nouveaulx faictes leur ung boullon puis les broyez au mortier avec mye de pain blanc des moyeulx d'oeufz & deux doigtz d'eaue rose Le tout passeres par l'estamine, feres cuyre en bon beurre puis les feres en dariolles ou ainsi que vous vouldres.

♣ Pour faire ung potaige.
[fol. 69r] ℭ Prenes poulles et les plumes mais qu'ilz ne soyent point refaictz puis les farces bien avecques les foyes du lard & fines herbes pouldre blanche & cloux de giroffle, puis les boutes en ung pot a court boullon, et qu'ilz soient de bon sel.

ℭ Poree broyee.
ℭ Il ne fault prendre que la fueille et la faictes parbouillir et haches menu & broyer au mortier avec du persil puis boutteres en ung pot avec bon boullon et gresse de Beuf et de belles Riblettes de lart et gouttes de sel.

---

*   Cotgrave describes *raymolles* as, 'the brawne of a capon, Raisins of the Sunne, and marrow shred all together, then made into little cakes or loaves'.
†   Probably a misspelling for *dessevrer*.

Frumenty of kid

You take the said kid and cut it into morsels, then let it cook in good herbs and good broth, then have your wheat cooked in milk as you make a frumenty with a little white powder, cinnamon, and sugar.

Raymolles of capon breast

To make *raymolles* of capon breast and beef marrow and currants, you must take a good well-cooked capon, pull apart and chop it well with the said marrow and currants. Then you make little abbesses of pastry like little tarts and place in each one individually and fry them in a pan of lard and serve as a last course. And sugar them then add your cream inside if you want to make tarts and you can make or serve on a plate at your discretion.

To make spinach tarts

Tarts of young spinach, give them a boil, then beat in a mortar with white breadcrumb, egg yolks and two fingers of rosewater. Pass everything through a sieve, let it cook in good butter then make into darioles [136] or whatever you like.

To make a pottage

Take hens and pluck them but they should not be parboiled, then stuff them well with livers, some salted pork fat and fine herbs, white powder, and cloves. Then place them in a pot with court bouillon, and they should be well salted.

Puréed leeks

You must take only the leaves and parboil them and chop very fine and pound in a mortar with parsley, then place in a pot with good broth and beef fat and pretty strips of streaky bacon and salt to taste.

---

136. A *dariole* is a pastry made in a small cylindrical mold.

❡ Pour faire de langues.
❡ Prenes boyaulx de mouton & les nectoyes beaux & netz prenes de la fraise de veau & de la gresse de veau Beuf ou de pourceau autant comme de fraize. Et les haches ensemble tout creus, prenes pouldre blanche & poyvre a l'equipollent de vostre chair & emplisses lesditz boyaulx. Et quant vous le vouldrez servir boutes boullir au boullon de vostre pot quant seront cuictz Bouttes sur le gril puis serves a entree de table.

❡ Pour faire saulcisses de blanc chapon.
❡ Prenes boyaulx de pourceau & faictes bouillir ung chapon avec gresse de beuf. Et ung morceau de lar*[fol. 69v]*gras & le tout haches ensemble, puis ayez de la pouldre blanche et marjolaine aussi du laict de vache et demye douzaine de moyeulx d'oeufz. Bouttes tout ensemble les dictes denrees et le battes bien fort et emplisses voz boyaulx de ceste confection. Et n'oublyes aussi a les saller se tu veux en lieu de Marjolaine tu peulx mettre de l'ongnon hache fort menu puis leur faictes ung boullon. Et gardez que ne soit trop plain que il ne creve, puis quant tu vouldras menger boute les rostir dessus le gril.

❡ Pour chapons a la canelle.
❡ Prenes canelle dattes moelle de beuf raisins de corinthe. Et le tout bouteres en ung bon boullon. Rostisses vostre chapon & quant il sera rosty jectes ledire [ledict] Chapon dedans vostre Boullon et le laisses fort consummer [c]*

❡ Cervelat.
❡ Pour faire cervelat prenes deux livres de chair de pourceau maigre une livre de gresse & haches le tout bien menu, puis prenes poivre Muscades et sallez a point puis emplisses voz boyaulx et les lyez par les boutz & les faictes boullir ung boullon et se garde longtemps.

---

*   'c' is a misprint.

To make [sausages] [137]

Take mutton intestines and wash them nice and clean. Take veal caul and as much veal, beef or pork fat as caul. And chop everything together raw. Take white powder and pepper according to the amount of your meat, and fill the said intestines. And when you want to serve it, put it to boil in broth from your pot. When it is well cooked, place on the grill then serve as a first course.

To make capon breast sausages

Take the intestines of piglets and boil a capon with beef fat. Add a piece of salted pork fat and chop everything together, then add white powder and marjoram. Add also some cow's milk and half a dozen egg yolks. Place all of these foodstuffs together and beat well and fill your intestines with this mixture. And don't forget also to salt them. If you want to replace the marjoram, you can add very finely chopped onions, then boil them. And be careful that they aren't too full so they don't burst, and when you want to eat place them to roast on the grill.

For capons with cinnamon

Take cinnamon, dates, beef marrow, currants. And place everything in a good broth. Roast your capon and when it is well roasted add the said capon to your broth and let it finish cooking.

Cervelat sausages

To make cervelat take two pounds of lean flesh of young pig, a pound of fat and chop all very finely, then take pepper, nutmeg and salt just right, fill your casings and tie at the ends, and let them boil in a good broth and they keep a long time.

---

137. Clearly this recipe has nothing to do with tongue, and it seems difficult to imagine how these sausages could be construed as a metaphorical tongue. This word in French is likely a misspelling of *luganes,* which appears in the table of contents. Here, the caul is the lining of the gut, usually used as a wrapping for meatballs and sausages in its own right, since it is studded with fat and in effect bastes the meat wrapped within.

[fol. 70r] ℭ 'C'est qui fault pour ung souper:
♣ Entree de table.

♣ Sallades d'herbes	Alloyaulx de venaison
prunes de damas	Sallades de pasquenades
Soleil de blanc de chapon	
pasquenades de gellee.	

ℭ Potaiges.

Fromentee	Navee de sanglier
Boully larde de venayson	
pigeons a la canelle	
paste de venayson tiede	
Une poulle en faisant	

premier rost.*

Levreaulx	perdriaulx
Poulletz au vigaigre [vinaigre] rosat.	Venayson rostye
pastes de moygneaulx	Gellee maullee

ℭ Second rost.*

	Poulletes fezandees
Estoudeaulx aulx moust	
Lappereaulx	Cochons
pignonneaulx	
pastes de venayson frais	
Gellee ambree a poincte de dyamant.	

ℭ Issue de [t]able.

ℭPoire a l'ypocras	
Amandes & cerneaulx pelles	
poyres a deulx testes	
Bauldrier de pommes	Rozee d'angletterre
[fol. 70v] Tartes de verjus	Gasteau feullete
Gelee blanche picquee d'amandes.	

* In the text, the sub-title heading 'premier rost.' was misplaced by the printer to a second column in the line above and was not given a pilcrow or paragraph mark. The sub-title heading 'ℭ *Second rost.*' was not centred as were other sub-titles, but was aligned to the left-hand margin, with '*Poulletes fezandees*' on the same line, in a second column. These two sub-titles have been re-arranged for ease of comprehension.

THE MOST EXCELLENT BOOK OF COOKERY

What is necessary for a supper
First course

Herb salads	Sirloin of venison
Damson plums	Salads of parsnips
Sunbursts of capon breast	
Parsnips in jelly	

Pottages

Frumenty	*Navee*[138] of boar
Larded broth of venison	
Pigeons in cinnamon	
Warm venison pie	
A hen prepared like pheasant	

First roast

Young hares	Partridge
Chicken in rose vinegar	Roast venison
Sparrow pies	Moulded jelly

Second roast

	Hung chicken
Pigeons in grape must	
Young rabbits	Pigs
Squabs	
Cold venison pies	
Ambered jelly in diamond points	

Dessert

Pears in hippocras	
Peeled almonds and walnuts	
Pears with two heads	
Turnover[139] of apples	English rose
Verjuice tarts	Flaky cake
White jelly stuck with almonds	

---

138. The meaning of this term remains obscure.
139. Julie E. Johnson with Sylvie and Antonio Roder, the translators of Jean-Louis Flandrin's *Arranging the Meal*, p. 69, rendered the *bauldrier* as a turnover. The word today means a baldric, or belt to hold up a sword. So it could be a long thin pastry.

LIVRE FORT EXCELLENT DE CUYSINE

❡ Espices de chambre.

❡ Espices de chambre   Dragee
Eaue de damas a laver les mains.

❡ Memoire quant tu vouldras faire ung bancquet regarde en ce chapitre tu trouveras des memoires pour faire ton escripteau.
❡ Et premierement.

❡ Chapons pelerin*	Cercelles confictes
Lyons de blanc chapon.	Andouilles de gelee
Venayson de sanglier aulx marrons	
Cresme fromentee.	Perdrix a la tonnelette
pastes a la tonnellette	
pastes de venayson chaulx.	
Sallades vertes	Sallades d'entremetz
Aultrement trouveras faisans	Levreaulx
Butors. Venaison de chevreau.	pluviers
pastes d'allouettes	
Gelee en poincte de dyament	
pans revestus	pigonneaulx
Chevreaulx farcis.	Oysons a la malvoysie
piedz a la saulce d'enfer	plus esturgeon
perdrix Congnins	Cercelles
❡ Poussins au vinaigre rosat	
[fol. 71r] pastes de pigeons	pastes de venaison frais
Chevreaulx ou fromaige de millan†	
Gellee ambree	Gellee moullee
Gellee blanche picques	Lanches lombardes §
Taillis d'angleterre	Marsouin contrefaict
Jaspe Olive	perce pierre
pourpier confict	Cocombre confictz.

*   *Chapons pelerin* is a medieval dish, found in the *Ménagier de Paris* as well as Chiquart, of spit-roasted capons wrapped in either lamprey or eel.
†   *Fromaige de millan*, i.e. cheese from Milan, refers most likely to Parmesan.
§   *Lanches lombardes* is a misspelling of *lesches lombardes* and was called in England 'Leach Lombard', a sweetmeat of various ingredients, fruit, flesh or fish, that was cooked to a stiff texture that could be sliced.

Candied spices

Candied spices Candies
Sweet water to wash the hands

MEMORANDUM: WHEN YOU WANT TO THROW A BANQUET, LOOK AT THIS CHAPTER AND YOU WILL FIND REMINDERS TO MAKE YOUR MENU

First

Pilgrim capons	Teal confit
Lions of capon breast	Andouille of jelly
Boar venison with chestnuts	
Cream of frumenty	Partridge *à la tonnelette*
Pies *à la tonnelette*	
Hot venison pies	
Green salads	Salads of *entremets*
Otherwise you will find pheasants	Young hares
Bustard Venison of kid	Plovers
Lark pies	
Jelly in diamond points	
Peacocks in their feathers	Squabs
Stuffed kid	Goslings in malmsey
Trotters in hell sauce	Plus sturgeon
Partridge Rabbits	Teals
Young chicken in rose-flavoured vinegar	
Pigeon pies	Cold venison pies
Kid or cheese from Milan	
Amber jelly	Moulded jelly
White spiked jelly	Lombard slices
English slices	Counterfeit porpoise
Jasper Olive	Samphire[140]
Preserved purslane	Preserved cucumbers

---

140. *Crithmum maritimum* is often picked and served much like olives and capers, more typical of English cuisine.

❡ Patisserie.

❡ Pastes de coings	Escussons de gellee
Tartes sanaydes	Blanc menger
Fleur de lys de gelle	
Gasteaulx feulletez	Tartes d'angleterre
Bauldrier de pommes	Flajotz
pastes de marrons	
Tartes de cresme	Angelotz de gellee
Sallades de poires de bon chrestien	
poires a l'ypocras	poires de bon chrestien entiers
Gauffres coulisses	
Estriers* de pruneaulx	Biscuict
Bignetz	Neffles a l'ipocras
ypocras	Marchepin
pommes au castelin	Donfitures
fromaige de millan	
Aultrement	Sallades de lectues
Faisans	Cailles au lorier
Fromentee a venayson sallee	
[fol. 71v] perdrix aulx cappes	
Soleil de blanc chapon	
Venayson aulx navetz.	Gellee undee
Pastes de chapon	Gasteaulx yta[l]iens
Sauscisses de veau	Andouilles de gellee
Aultrement	Sallades blanches
Oysons farsis	Levreaulx
pigeons de boys	
Chapon gras de lodun†	pluviers
Chevreaulx	herons
Venayson de sanglier	

* *Estriers* or *estrées* were a sort of *oublie* or wafer. They were most famous in Lyon. Cotgrave describes *estrié* as a 'kind of bread, or paste, of fine flower kneaded with water, white wine, the yolkes of eggs, salt, and sugar.'

† *Chapon gras de lodun* refers to the famed black capons of Loudun in Poitou. Rabelais records that Grandgousier celebrated the return of his son Gargantua with a feast that included, along with much else, four hundred capons from Loudun.

Pastry

Quince pies	Escutcheons in jelly
Tarts *sanaydes*	Blancmange
Fleur de lys in jelly	
Flaky cake	English tarts
Apple turnover	Flutes
Chestnut pies	
Cream tarts	Angels of jelly
Salads of Bon Chrétien pears	
Pears in hippocras	Whole Bon Chrétien pears
Portcullis wafers	
Pastries of prunes	Biscuits
Doughnuts	Medlars in hippocras
Hippocras	Marzipan
Apples *au castelin*	Confections
Cheese from Milan	
Otherwise	Lettuce salads
Pheasants	Quail with bay leaves
Frumenty of salted venison	
Partridge with apples	
Sunburst of chicken breast	
Venison with turnips	Wavy jelly
Capon pies	Italian cakes
Veal sausages	Andouilles of jelly
Otherwise	White salads
Stuffed goslings	Young hares
Wood pigeons	
Fat capon of Loudun	Plovers
Kid	Herons
Boar venison	

pastes de cercelles
Sallades de hobelon
pastes de artichaulx
Artichaulx a la poyvrade
Jambon de maiance
Sallades vertes
Connins a la grenade
poulletz
Langues de beuf
pasquenades
Cresme de merles
Marrons
Escus de gellee
plus cervelatz
Cive de cerf aulx naveaulx
[fol. 72r] Langues de mouton a la vinaigrette
pastes de becasse au bec dore
pastes de piedz de beuf
pastes de langue sain beuf
Tartes de vin blanc
Testes de chevreax
Sarcelles
pigeons
Cytrons
pastes de piedz de mouton
Tarte ytalienne
faisans   pluviers   poulletz
Lappereaulx
pastes de pigeons
Ramiers en poyvrade.
Tartes de pommes
Beccasses a lequesal
Tartes de mouelle de beuf

Cercelles
friteaulx

gellee chiquetee
Esperges

Blanc menger
Sallades blanches

hure de sanglier
Bignetz
Lymons confictz
papillons
Gasteau joly.
Lesches lombardes
perdrix a l'orange

pains revestus

Chapons rostys
Butors.
Cappes
pastes d'allouettes

plus saulce de veau
Oysons
Olyves
fontaine de gellee

Herons
Allouettes
pastes de poulletz

Teal pies			Chopped jelly
Hop shoot salads			Asparagus
Artichoke pies			
Artichokes in pepper sauce			
Mainz [Mayence] ham			Blancmange
Green salads			White salads
Rabbits with pomegranate			
Chicken		Teals	Boar's head
Ox tongues		Fritters	Doughnuts
Parsnips			Preserved lemon
Cream of blackbirds			Butterflies
Chestnuts			Pretty cake
Jelly coins			Lombard slices
More *cervelats*			Partridge in orange
Civet of venison with turnips			
Sheep's tongues in vinaigrette			
Pies of woodcock with gilded beak			
Cowheel pies			
Pies of tongue, lard, beef			Peacocks in their feathers
White wine tarts			
Kids' heads			Roast capons
Teals			Bustards
Pigeons			Apples
Citrons			Lark pies
Sheep's trotter pies			
Italian tart			Plus veal sauce
Pheasants	Plovers	Chicken	Goslings
Hares			Olives
Pigeon pies			Jelly fountain
Wood pigeons in pepper sauce			
Apple tarts			Herons
Woodcocks *à lequesal*			Larks
Tarts of beef marrow			Chicken pies

Ouflans* de gellee Moust
Tartes de pruneaulx
pesches Beccassines
Levreaulx Cailles
Signes Albanoys
Coffres de gellee plain d'escus
pastes de pommes
Tartes angoulousees
[fol. 72v] Tartes de pommes hachees Bien en broc †
Venayson de chevreau.
Hure de sanglier Gelle commune
Neige en rommarin pastes de coingz
Tartes de cresme tartes d'angleterre
Gasteaulx fuelletes Gasteau joyeulx
Fromaige plaisantin Butoris
petis poussins.

❡ Plus rissollees.

❡ Petis choulx tous chaulx
Gasteletz baveulx Rastons de formaige
poires a l'ypocras
poires en sallades Marrons
pommes de capendu
Sallades de citrons
Sallades de grenades
Escuz de gelee

❡ Finis.

❡ Cy finist le livre de Cuysine nouvellement Imprime a Lyon par Olivier Arnoullet le .ix. jour de Mars. Mil. CCCCC.lv.

---

* *Ouflans* is printed as *oriflans* in the *Grand cuisinier* and may thus be deemed a misprint. *Oriflant* is translated by Cotgrave as 'elephant'.

† The word *broc* refers to a flagon and the phrase seems to suggest something you down quickly.

Jelly elephants
Prune tarts
Peaches
Young hares
Swans
Coffers of jelly filled with coins
Apple pies
Tarts from Angoulême
Tarts of chopped apples
Kid venison
Boar's head
Snow on rosemary
Cream tarts
Flaky cakes
Piacenza[141] cheese
Little baby chicken

Must

Snipe
Quails
[?Albanian birds]

Bien en broc

Common jelly
Quince pies
English tarts
Joyous cake
Butter

THEN CROQUETTES

Little round hot buns
Little filled cakes
Pears in hippocras
Pears in salads
Short start apples
Citron salads
Pomegranate salads
Jelly coins

Cheese *rastons*[142]

Chestnuts

END

Here endeth the Book of Cookery newly printed at Lyon by Olivier Arnoullet the 9th day of March 1555.

---

141. In the sixteenth century, this was considered the best hard Italian cheese, superior to Parmesan.
142. *Rastons* are a medieval dish, mentioned for example in the English Harleian manuscript 279. They are basically a loaf hollowed out, with the crumb mixed with other ingredients, stuffed back in and rebaked. In this case it is with cheese.

FRENCH INDEX

This is an index of recipe titles (and implied recipe titles where no heading exists), and other headings in the French text. It also includes those dishes listed in the menus in the text, but not the table of contents. It is a literal index, accepting the spellings of the text itself, save for the conventions of transcription already touched upon.

abremont de laict, 104
abricotz, 212, 228
aesles, de poulletz chapons chevreaulx oyes cochon, 134
aigneaulx (chapitre de rost), 174
albanoys, 254
alebran, *see* hallebran
alemaigne [Allemagne]
    chapon au brouet d', 230
    lymatz d', 236
alesquesal, beccasses, 224
allouettes (alouettes), 156, 252
    (paste d'), 198
    pastes d', 224, 226, 248, 252
alloyaulx de venaison, 246
    a la saulce realle, 224
    petis, 210
aloze, alozes, 158, 190
    ou carpes a la castille [Castile], 184
amandes, 216, 220, 246
    beurre d', en Karesme, 230
    cresmes d', 84
    en escusson, 184
    gelee blanche picquee d', 246
    gobeletz d', 240
    laict d', 84
amandes nouvelles
    cresme d', 238
    pour confire, 228
andouilles, 226
    farcies (farcyes), 214, 222
    de foye de veau, 236
    de gellee, 250
    d'oeufz, 158
andouillette verte, 160

angelotz
    de gellee, 250
    de gellee blanche, 218
angleterre
    rose (rozee) d', 240, 246
    saulce d', becquet a, 74
    taillis d', 66, 248
    tarte(s) d', 226, 250, 254
angoulousees, tartes, 254
anguille(s)
    boullies, 96
    estuvee, 166
    en paste, 96
    pastez de carpes & d'anguilles, 74
    en potaige, 96
    rosties, 96
    viande exquise et qui est fort bonne, 168
artichaulx, 240
    pastes de, 252
    a la poyvrade, 252
aulx
    blans, 190
    soupe aux, 78
bancquet (banquet), 210, 212, 214, 220, 226, 248
    d'este, 222
barbe robert, saulce, 162, 222
bastarde, saulce, 212, 214
bauldrier de pommes, 246, 250
becasseaulx, 218
beccasse(s) (becasse, beccaces), 194, 226
    au bec dore, pastes de, 252
    a lequesal (alesquesal, a lesquesal), 224, 252

beccassines, 254
becquet
    en aultre maniere, 76
    brochet pour ung, 76
    carpes & plye pour ung becquet, 74
    a saulce d'angleterre, 74
beuf
    costes de, 136
    flanchet de, 220
    foyes de cerf, chevreaulx ou de beuf, 134
    langue(s) de, 136, 214, 252
    langue de, paste en pot de, 114
    mouelle de, tartes de, 252
    palays de, confitz a force groselles et cy[namomon], 222
    pastes de langue sain beuf, 252
    piedz de, pastes de, 252
    rosty, saulce pour le, 188
    tartre a moelle de, 64
beurre, 152, 180
    d'amandes en Karesme, 230
    aultre, 118
    frays frit, 116
bien en broc, 254
bignetz, 250, 252
    carpes aulx, 90
biscuict, 250
bizetz aulx choulx, 212, 216, 222, 226
blanc menger, 194, 250, 252
    de chapon, 208
blettes, coste de, paste de, 104
borbonneses, 210
boucherie pour fair boullon, 220
bouldin(s) (boudins), 136, 138
    blanc, 138
boullon dore, 220
boully larde de venayson (venaison), 212, 216, 246
boulongne [Bologna], saulcisses de, 140
bresme (bremes), 94
    (paste de), 204
brideaulx a veaulx, 208

brocheletz de paste royalle, 238
brochet, 106, 158
    boully, 92
    & carpes, 180
    a l'estuvee, 92
    frit, 92
    larde, 232
    pour ung becquet, 76
brocheton(s)
    estuvee, 166
    estuvee noire, 166
    rosty, 90
brouet (broet), 126
    d'alemaigne [Allemagne], chapon au, 230
    dore, 128
    dore, gigoteau de veau au (ou), 210, 222
    georget, 126
butoris, 254
butors, 174, 248, 252
caille(s), 254
    confictes a la cameline boulles, 222
    au lorier, 250
    pastes de, 216
cailleteaulx, pastes de, 214
caillette farcye, 222
cameline, 192
    cailles confictes a la, 222
canard(s) (canart, canardz)
    a la dodine, 174, 218
    (paste de), 200
    paste(s) de, 224, 226
canelle
    chapons a la, 244
    pigeons a la, 246
capilorde, souppes a la, 110
capilotaste, 82
cappes, 218, 252
    oysons aulx, 240
    perdrix aulx, 250
carbonnade(s)
    a la coulloule, 222
    pour souppe, 138
carpe(s)

FRENCH INDEX

alozes ou carpes a la castille
    [Castile], 184
  aulx bignetz, 90
  boullies, 90
  & brochet, 180
  a l'estuvee, 88
  estuvee noire, 166
  oeufz de, ou layctance, 152
  (paste de), 204
  paste en pot de, 90
  pastez de carpes & d'anguilles, 74
  & plye pour ung becquet, 74
  rostyes, 88
castelin, pommes au, 250
castille [Castile], alozes ou carpes a la, 184
cercelles (sarcelles), 248, 252
  confictes, 248
  pastes de, 224, 252
  aulx poreaulx, 222
cerf, 124
  cive de, aulx naveaulx, 252
  foyes de cerf, chevreaulx ou de beuf, 134
cerf biches (paste de), 202
cerises, 240
  confittes, 154
cerneaulx (cerneaux), 216
cerneaulx pelles, 220, 246
cervelat(z) (servelat), 244, 252
  milannois, 222
chair, lamproye de, 64
champignons, 150
chapon(s) (chappons), 174, 182, 196, 224, 226
  aesles de poulletz chapons chevreaulx oyes cochon, 134
  barbe, 176
  blanc menger de, 208
  boullus, 218
  boully, 54
  au brouet d'alemaigne, 230
  a la canelle, 244
  [cougnins], 186
  gras de lodun [Loudun], 250
  lyons de blanc, 248
  oysons poulles, poulletz fricasses, 162
  pans et chapons bardez a porc espic, 178
  pastes de, 250
  pelerin, 248
  potaige blanc de, ou de poulles, 118
  poulletz vollailles rostyes oyseaulx de riviere, 190
  raymolles de blanc, 242
  revestus a court boullon, 240
  rosty(s), 60, 252
  saulcisses de blanc, 244
  soleil de blanc, 246, 250
  talmouses de blanc (de), 212, 224
charbon, 222
chaulde, saulce, pastes a la, 222, 226
chauldeau, 156
chauldume (chauldun), 172
  pour le cervau, 168
  de poyvre, 222
chemine, 238
chevreau(lx), 174, 248, 250
  aesles de poulletz chapons chevreaulx oyes cochon, 134
  farcir foye de veau de mouton & chevreaulx, 134
  foye de veau rosty de mouton & de chevreaulx, 130
  foyes de cerf, chevreaulx ou de beuf, 134
  fromentee de, 242
  farcis, 248
  aulx oranges, 240
  (paste de), 198
  pommes de veaulx ou de chevreaulx de ventre, 120
  potaige de ventre de veaulx ou chevreaulx, 122
  testes de, 252
  testes de, doree, 210
  teste de chevreau doree, 222
  testes de chevreaulx frictes dorees, 136

venayson de, 248, 254
ventree de chevreaulx confitz, 222
au verjus d'ozeille, 212
choulx, 110, 170
 bizetz au, 216, 212, 222, 226
 cabutz, 170
 perdrix aulx, 82, 224
 pommes de, 112
choulx, petis, toux chaulx, 254
cicoree, sallades de, 226
cines (signes), 174, 254
cive (cyve)
 de cerf aulx naveaulx, 252
 de liepvre (lyevres), 124, 226
clarete
 gellee clarete en mouelle, 218
cochon(s), 146, 212, 214, 216, 224
 aesles de poulletz chapons chevreaulx oyes cochon, 134
 ung cartier de, 220
 demy, 226
 houssez, 216
 de laict, 226
 paste frais, 224
cocombre(s), 108, 172
 confictz, 218, 248
 contrefaict, saulcisse, 142
 farcyes, 216
coffres de gellee plain d'escus, 254
coing(s)
 en paste, 206
 pastes de, 250, 254
 pomme de, 60
confiture de frize de poussin, 222
congnins (cognins, cougnins, connins), 186, 224, 226, 248
 a la grenade, 252
 pastes de, 202, 226
cordialle, saulce, vinaigrette a la, 214
coste de blettes, paste de, 104
couldres, 108
coulloule, carbonnade a la, 222
courge(s)
 conficte, 240
 potaige(s) de, 66, 216

court boullon, chapons revestus a, 240
cresme(s), 216
 d'amandes, 84
 d'amandes nouvelles, 238
 bastarde, 80
 fritte, 80
 de fromentee, 248
 froumaige de, 240
 houssue, 236
 de merles, 252
 de noix nouvelles, 238
 de poys nouveaulx, 236
 tarte(s) de, 218, 250, 254
 tartelettes de, 64
crespes faictes en poelle, 236
cresson, & jeunes herbes, 152
cretonne(e)
 laict, 124
 potaige, 122
 de poys nouveaulx ou febves, 122
croste de paste de papier, 180
cygoignes (chapitre de rost), 174
cynamomon, palays de beuf confitz a force groselles et cy[namomon], 222
cytrons (citrons), 252
 sallades de, 218, 254
dariolles pour l'este, 208
dodine
 blanche, 190, 230
 canards a la, 218
 rouge, 230
donfitures [confitures], 250
dragee, 248
 espices de chambre, 226
eaue
 de damas a laver les mains, 248
 fontaine d', 52
 rose, 216
 rose a laver, 226
enfer, saulce d', 144
 piedz a la, 224, 248
entree de cuysine, 238
entree de table, 134, 136, 210, 212, 218, 222, 224, 246

a jours gras, 130
    pour le soupper, 226
    d'yver, 222, 238
entremetz troussez, 218
escrevisses, 98, 164
escus (escuz)
    coffres de gellee plain d', 254
    de gellee (gelee), 250, 252
escussons de gellee, 250
esperges, 252
espicerie, 220
espices, menues, 128
espices de chambre, 226, 248
espinars, 168, 170
    tartes d', 242
estoudeaulx, *see* hestoudeau
estriers de pruneaulx, 250
esturgeon, 212, 214, 248
    boully, 102
    hastellees d', 72
    en paste, 72
    rosty, 70
estuvee, 166
    boully lardez (de poussins aux herbes), 210
    brochet a l', 92
    carpes a l', 88
    gigot de mouton a l', 230
    langues de mouton a l', 222
    poussins au, 212
faisans (fesans), 174, 216, 248, 250, 252
farcir foye de veau de mouton & chevreaulx, 134
febves, 164
    cretonnee de poys nouveaulx ou febves, 122
feste, 226
    d'este, 222
flajol, 240
flajotz, 250
flaman [Flamand], gasteau, 240
fleur de lys de gelle, 250
fleur de sux, friteaulx de, 116
fleurons, 238
fontaine d'eaue, 52

fontaine de gellee, 252
formaige, *see* fromaige
four troys pieces au plat, 212, 214; *see also* pieces de four
foye(s), 114, 144
    de cerf, chevreaulx ou de beuf, 134
    de poulletz chapons chevreaulx oyes cochon, 134
    de veau, andouilles de, 236
    de veau, de mouton & chevreaulx, farcir, 134
    de veau, rosty, 222
    de veau, rosty de mouton & de chevreaulx, 130
    de veaulx, haricot de, 154
    de veaulx ou d'aultres, saulce de, 132
    de veaulx, hastereaulx de, 132
fraizes, 240
fricassee(s), 140, 218, 220
    de menues droitz a la barbe robert, 222
    de poulletz au verjus de grain, 222
    de poussins a la saulce madame, 222
frictures de mer, 182
friteaulx, 154, 252
    de fleur de sux, 116
    maigres, 148
froide saulce, 86
fromaige(s) (formaige, fourmaige, froumaige)
    de cresme, 212, 240
    en jonchee, 216
    de millan [Milan], 248, 250
    plaisantin [Piacenza], 254
    rastons de, 254
fromentee, 78, 224, 240, 246
    de chevreau, 242
    cresme de, 248
    de venayson, 240
    a venayson sallee, 250
galimaffree, 144
gallentine, 88
gardons, 98

gasteau(lx/x)
    feullete(z/s), 246, 250, 254
    flaman [Flamand], 240
    joly, 252
    joyeulx, 254
    mollet, 226
    saeillete, 224
    sec, 238
    ytaliens [Italiens], 250
gasteletz baveulx, 254
gauffres coulisses, 250
gave de petit oyseaulx, 218
gellee(s) (gelee, gelle), 214
    ambree, 212, 248
    ambree a poincte de dyamant, 246
    andouilles de, 250
    angelotz de, 250
    blanche, 240
    blanche, angelotz de, 218
    blanche clarette & ambree, 226
    blanche picquee d'amandes, 246
    blanche picques, 248
    chiquetee, 252
    clarete en mouelle, 218
    coffres de, plain d'escus, 254
    commune, 254
    escus (escuz) de, 252, 254
    escussons de, 250
    fleur de lys de, 250
    fontaine de, 252
    lozengee, 224
    maullee (moullee), 246, 248
    noire, 66
    de poires, 60
    neige de, 234
    ouflans de, 254
    en poincte de dyament, 248
    de troys sortes, 216
    undee, 250
    a l'ypocras, 62
gibiers rostyes, 176
gigot de mouton a l'estuvee, 230
gigoteau de veau ou brouet dore, 210, 222
gigotz, hachis de, 222

gingembre, 220
gobeletz d'amandes, 240
gouges blanches, 238
goujons, 96
gousier, piedz de mouton pour le, 138
grenade(s)
    connins a la, 252
    ramiers a la, 240
    sallades de, 254
grenault (paste de), 206
grevot [grenot], 158
groselles
    palays de beuf confitz a force groselles et cy[namomon], 222
grues (chapitre de rost), 174
hachis de gigotz, 222
hallebran (alebran, haslebran), paste(s/z) de, 196, 214, 240
haricot de foyes de veaulx, 154
hastellees
    d'esturgeon, 72
    de plyes, 74
hastereaulx, 140
    de foyes de veaulx, 132
herbelettes, rouleau de venayson aulx fines, 240
herbes
    jeunes, & cresson, 152
    [menues herbes], 130
    poussins aux herbes ou l'estuvee boully lardez, 210
    sallades d', 246
heronneaulx, 212
    saulce realle, 218
herons, 224, 250, 252
hestoudeau(lx/x), 216
    au moust(e), 214, 220, 246
    au saulge, 218
hobelon, sallades de, 252
hochepot
    de pigeons, 86, 224
    de poussins, 86
hure de sanglier, 136, 202, 252, 254
huytres (huyctres)
    au cyve, 164

en escailles, 104
a l'estuvee, 102
frittes, 102
hypocras, ipocras, see ypocras
issue (issuye) de table, 212, 214, 216, 218, 220, 224, 226, 240, 246
[Italie], see ytalienne, ytaliens
jacopine
souppe, 56
tartes, 210
jambon, 140
de maiance [Mayence, Mainz], 252
jaspe, 248
de laict, 118
laiches clavees, 240
laict
abremont de, 104
d'amandes, 84
cretonne, 114
gras larde, 146
jaspe de, 118
saulce doulx au, 188
laictues (lectues)
en pommes conficte, 240
sallades de, 250
lamproye, 186, 204
de chair, 64
lanches lombardes, 248
langue(s), 244
de beuf, 214, 252
de beuf, paste en pot de, 114
de mouton a l'estuvee, 222
de mouton sallees, 222
de mouton a la trimollette, 238
de mouton a la vinaigrette, 252
pastes de langue sain beuf, 252
lappereaulx (lapereaulx), 216, 220, 246, 252
deulx au plat, 218
de garenne aulx oranges, 210
au sel menu, 212
lardeaulx de venaison, 68
layctance de carpe, 152
lequesal (lesquesal), beccasses a, 224, 252

lesches lombardes, 252
levreaulx, 214, 216, 224, 246, 248, 250, 254
saulce royalle, 210
lievre(s) (liepvre, lyevres)
cive (cyve) de, 124, 226
(paste de), 202
hache (paste de), 202
limandes, frictures de mer, 182
loches, 96
lodun [Loudun], chapon gras de, 250
lombardes [Lombard]
lanches, 248
lesches, 252
lombardie [Lombardy]
saulcisses de, 142
tortue de, 62
tortue de, en aultre maniere, 70
lorier, cailles au, 250
lymatz d'alemaigne [Allemagne], 236
lymons confictz, 252
lyons de blanc chapon, 248
madame, saulce, 188
fricassee de poussins a la, 222
maiance [Mayence, Mainz], jambon de, 252
maigres friteaulx, 148
malvoysie, oyson(s) a la, 210, 214, 248
marchepain (marchpin), 238, 250
marles, see merles
marrons (marrans), 172, 226, 252, 254
(en paste), 206
pastes de, 250
venayson de sanglier aulx, 248
marsouin, 100, 240
contrefaicte, 248
en potaige, 100
menger, 194; see also blanc menger
menues espices, 128
[menues herbes], 130
merlans, frictures de mer, 182
merles (marles)
cresme de, 252
(paste de), 198
mesles (mefles), 152, 168

(paste de), 208
mettre les mains en eaue boullante,
    pour, 178
milannois (millanoys) [Milanese]
    saulcisses, 238
    servelat, 222
millan [Milan]
    fromaige de, 248, 250
moelle (mouelle)
    de beuf, tartre a, 64
    de beuf, tartes de, 252
    gellee clarete en mouelle, 218
moust (mouste, moulx), 188, 254
    hestoudeau (estoudeaulx) au(lx),
        214, 220, 246
mouton, 176
    cartier de, 220
    farcir foye de veau de mouton &
        chevreaulx, 134
    foye de veau rosty de mouton &
        de chevreaulx, 130
    gigot de, a l'estuvee, 230
    langues de, a l'estuvee, 222
    langues de, sallees, 222
    langues de, a la trimollette, 238
    langues de, a la vinaigrette, 252
    en paste, 200
    paste de, 198
    paste de gigot de, 178
    paste de veau ou de mouton, 136
    paste en pot de, 108
    paste en pot de gigot de mouton
        rosty ou longe de veau rostye
        froide, 110
    piedz de, 68, 222
    piedz de, pastes de, 252
    piedz de, potaige de, 68
    potaige de, 158
    saulcisses de gigot de, 134
moygneaulx (moyneaulx)
    farcis, 240
    pastes de, 216, 246
mullet (paste de), 204
muscade, 186
naveaulx (navetz), 108

cive de cerf aulx, 252
sanglier aulx, 224
venayson aulx, 250
navee de sanglier, 246
neffles
    frittes, 226
    a l'ipocras, 250
neige (naige)
    contrefaicte, 180
    de gellee, 234
    en rommarin, 254
noces (nopces), 210, 212, 220
noire, saulce, 186
noire gelee, 66
noix nouvelles, cresme de, 238
oeufz, 222
    andouilles d', 158
    cuictz sans feu, 160
    cuytz en eaue, 160
    en paste en pot, 166
    perdus, 228
    poches au beurre en plat, 160
    de plusieurs couleurs, 160
oeufz de carpe, 152
olive(s) (olyves), 218, 226, 248, 252
orange(s)
    chevreaulx aulx, 240
    lapereaulx de garenne aulx, 210
    perdrix a l' (aulx), 224, 252
    sallades d', 210, 224
orge munde, 84
oublyes farcees, 64
ouflans de gellee, 254
oyes, 112, 136, 174
    aesles de poulletz chapons
        chevreaulx oyes cochon, 134
oygnons, 152
oyseaulx, petit, grave de, 218
oyseau(lx) de riviere (chapitre de rost),
    174
    chapons poulletz vollailles rostyes
        oyseaulx de riviere, 190
    en potaige, 68
oyson(s), 174, 220, 252
    aulx cappes, 240

[264]

chappons oysons poulles, poulletz
  fricasses, 162
farcys (farsis), 216
a la malvoysie, 210, 214, 248
(paste de), 200
ozeille, verjus d', chevreaulx au, 212
paillettes, frictures de mer, 182
pain, bon, 210, 212, 214, 218, 220, 222,
  224, 226
palays de beuf confitz a force groselles
  et cy[namomon], 222
pan(s) (pains), 214
  pans et chapons bardez a porc
    espic, 178
  pour entremetz, 224
  revestu(s), 176, 248, 252
papillons, 252
papillon(s) de pommes, 212, 220
pasquenades (pestanades), 252
  sallades de, 226, 246
passereaulx (paste de), 200
paste(s/z)
  d'allouettes (alouettes), 198, 224,
    226, 248, 252
  anguille en, 96
  de artichaulx, 252
  de becasse au bec dore, 252
  (de) bremes, 204
  de caille, 216
  de cailleteaulx, 214
  (de) canardz (canart), 200, 224,
    226
  (de) carpes, 204
  de carpes & d'anguilles, 74
  de cercelles, 224, 252
  (de) cerf biches, 202
  de chapon, 250
  (de) chevreaulx, 198
  coing en, 206
  de coings(z), 250, 254
  (de) congnins, 202, 226
  de coste de blettes, 104
  frais, cochons, 224
  de gigot de mouton, 178
  (de) grenault, 206
  de hallebran (alebran, haslebran),
    196, 214, 240
  de langue sain beuf, 252
  (de) lievre, 202
  (de) lievre hache, 202
  (de) marles, 198
  marrons en, 206
  de marrons, 250
  (de) mesles, 208
  de mouton, 198
  mouton en, 200
  de moygneaulx (moyneaulx), 216,
    246
  (de) mullet, 204
  nourris, 62
  (d') oysons, 200
  (de) passereaulx, 200
  perche en, 94
  (de) perdrix, 200
  de piedz de beuf, 252
  de piedz de mouton, 252
  de pigeons, 210, 220, 248, 252
  (de) pigeons ramiers, 198
  (de) pinsons, 198
  de pommes, 254
  de poulletz, 252
  (de) rouget, 204
  a la saulce chaulde, 194, 222, 226
  saulmon en, 100
  soles en, 206
  de touterelles, 224
  a troys, 180
  (de) turbot, 204
  de veau(lx), 116, 196, 214, 220
  de veau en pot a tout croste, 222
  de veau ou de mouton, 136
  de venayson chaulx, 212, 216, 218,
    224, 248
  de venayson chaulx, petis, 212
  de venayson(s) frais (frays), 212,
    214, 218, 246, 248
  de venayson froide, 216
  de venayson tiede, 246
paste de papier, croste de, 180
paste en pot, 80, 112

de carpes, 90
de gigot de mouton rosty ou longe
    de veau rostye froide, 110
de langue de beuf, 114
de mouton, 108
oeufz en, 166
de trippes, 156
de veau, 80
paste royalle, brocheletz, 238
patisserie, 250
perce pierre, 248
perche, 158
    boullie, 92
    fritte, 94
    en paste, 94
perdrix (perdriaulx), 176, 216, 226,
    246, 248
    aulx cappes, 250
    aulx choulx, 82, 224
    deulx au plat, 218
    motee, 56
    a l'orange/aulx oranges, 252
    (paste de), 200
    au sel menu, 212
    a la tonnolette (tonnelette,
        tonolette, tonnollete), 82, 248
pesches, 216, 218, 220, 254
pestanades, see pasquenades
petis alloyaulx de venayson, 210
petis choulx tous chaulx, 254
petis pastes de venayson chaulx, 212
petis poussins, 254
pieces de four au plat, trois (pieces de
    four, troys, au plat), 212, 214, 216,
    226
piedz, de poulletz chapons chevreaulx
    oyes cochon, 134
piedz de beuf, pastes de, 252
piedz de mouton, 222
    pour le gousier, 138
    pastes de, 252
    potaige de, 68
piedz a la saulce d'enfer, 224, 248
pigeonneaulx (pig(n)onneaulx), 246, 248
pigeons, 174, 218, 220, 224, 252

a la canelle, 246
confitz, 86
hochepot de, 86, 224
paste(s) de, 210, 220, 248, 252
en rost, 212
au succre, 214
pigeons de boys, 250
pigeons ramiers (paste de), 198
pinsons (paste de), 198
plaisantin [Piacenza], fromaige, 254
pluviers, 248, 250, 252
plye, 102
    carpes & plye pour ung becquet,
        74
    hastellees de, 74
poire(s) (poyres), 220, 224
    de bon chrestien entiers, 250
    de bon chrestien, sallades de, 250
    contrefaict, saulcisse, 142
    cuycte (cuites), 220, 226
    a deulx testes, 246
    gelees de, 60
    nouvelles, 216
    en sallades, 254
    a l'ypocras, 216, 218, 226, 246, 250,
        254
poissons en sauce sallemine, 170
pomme(s), 114
    au castelin, 250
    chiquettees, tartes de, 226
    de capendu, 214, 240, 254
    hachees, tartes de, 254
    bauldrier de, 246, 250
    papillons de, 212, 220
    pastes de, 254
    tartes de, 218, 252
    tartes rouges de, 228
pomme de coing, 60
pomme contrefaict, saulcisse, 142
pommes de choulx, 112
pommes de veaulx ou de chevreaulx de
    ventre, 120
pomons, 144
pompons, 238
poreaulx, 106, 170

cercelles aulx, 222
poree, 106
    de blanc de poussins, 222
    brayee (broyee), 210, 220, 242
potaige(s), 210, 212, 216, 218, 220, 222, 224, 226, 240, 242, 246
    anguilles en, 96
    blanc de chappon ou de poulles, 118
    de courge, 66, 216
    cretonne, 122
    digestif, 234
    lavatif, 232
    marsouin en, 100
    [de mouton], 158
    oyseau de riviere en, 68
    de piedz de mouton, 68
    rouge, 120
    [de trippes], 156
    venaison contrefaicte en, 126
    de ventre de veaulx ou chevreaulx, 122
    vert, 118
    violet, 120
pouldre blanche, 128
pouldre de duc, 128
poullailles a la saulce robert, 196
poulle(s), 174
    en faisant, 246
    (en potaige), 242
    chappons oysons poulles, poulletz fricasses, 162
poulles, potaige blanc de chappon ou de, 118
poulletz (poullettes, poulletes), 174, 216, 252
    aesles de poulletz chapons chevreaulx oyes cochon, 134
    chappons oysons poulles, poulletz fricasses, 162
    chapons poulletz vollailles rostyes oyseaulx de riviere, 190
    fezandees (fesandes, fezandes), 210, 214, 218, 220, 226, 246
    fricassee de, au verjus de grain, 222

pastes de, 252
    au vi[n]aigre rosat, 246
pourpier confict, 248
poussin(s), 224
    confiture de frize de, 222
    a l'estuvee, 212
    aux herbes ou l'estuvee boully lardez, 210
    hochepot de, 86
    poree de blanc de, 222
    aulx poys, 240
    au vinaigre rosat, 210, 214, 216, 248
poys
    de lundy, 108
    poussins aulx, 240
    saulgrenee de, 164
poys nouveaulx, 162
    cresme de, 236
    cretonnee de poys nouveaulx ou febves, 122
poyvrade
    artichaulx a la, 252
    chauldun de, 222
    ramiers a la, 218
    ramiers en, 252
pruneaulx
    estriers de, 250
    tartes de, 254
prunes de damas, 212, 214, 220, 246
raisin, moulx de, 188
raisins, 218, 220
ramiers
    a la grenade, 240
    a la (en) poyvrade, 218, 252
rappe, 162
rastons de formaige, 254
raymolles de blanc chapon, 242
realle (royalle), saulce, 228
    alloyaulx de venaison a la, 224
    heronneaulx, 218
    levreaulx, 210
    venayson, 224
    venayson de rost, 212
ris, 84, 108, 150
rissollees, 254

robert, saulce, poullailles a la, 196
rommarin, neige en, 254
rose (rozee) d'angleterre [Angleterre], 240, 246
rost, 210, 212, 218, 220, 224, 226, 226
    chapitre de, 174
    premier, 246
    quart service de, 218
    second, 210, 212, 220, 246
    tiers service de (en), 212, 218
rosty sanglant, 176
rouget, 158
    (paste de), 204
rouleau de venayson aulx fines herbelettes, 240
royalle, paste, brocheletz de, 238
royalle, *see also* realle
saffran, 220
sain, pastes de langue sain beuf, 252
sallades
    blanches, 250, 252
    de cicoree, 226
    de citrons (cytrons), 218, 254
    d'entremetz, 248
    de grenades, 254
    d'herbes, 246
    de hobelon, 252
    de lectues, 250
    d'oranges, 210 224
    de pasquenades (pestanades), 226, 246
    de poires de bon chrestien, 250
    vertes, 248, 252
sallemine, saulce, poissons en, 170
sanaydes, tartes, 250
sanglier, 124
    aulx naveaulx, 224
    hure de, 136, 202, 252, 254
    navee de, 246
    venayson de, 80, 224, 250
    venayson de, aulx marrons, 248
sarcelles, *see* cercelles
saulce
    d'angleterre, becquet a, 74
    barbe robert, 162, 222

bastarde, 212, 214
chaulde, paste(s) a la, 194, 222, 226
doulx au laict, 188
d'enfer, 144
d'enfer, piedz a la, 224, 248
de foyes de veaulx ou d'aultres, 132
froide, 86
hypocras, 224
madame, 188
madame, fricassee de poussins a la, 222
noire, 186
pour le beuf rosty, 188
realle, 228
realle, alloyaulx de venaison a la, 224
realle, heronneaulx, 218
realle, venayson, 224
realle, venayson de rost, 212
robert, poullailles a la, 196
royalle, levreaulx, 210
sallemine, poissons en, 170
de trahyson, 58
de veau, 252
de venayson, 192
vert, 188, 192
saulcisse(s) (sauscisses), 222, 226, 244
    de blanc chapon, 244
    de boulongne [Bologna], 140
    cocombre contrefaict saulcisse, pomme, poire, 142
    de gigot de mouton, 134
    de lombardie [Lombardy], 142
    millannoys [Milanese], 238
    de veau, 250
saulcyrion en may, 150
saulge, hestoudeaulx au, 218
saulgrenee de poys, 164
saulmon, 158
    boully, 98
    frais rosty, 98
    en paste, 100
seiches
    frictures de mer, 182
    frittes, 104

sel menu
    lappereaulx au, 212
    perdrix au, 212
servelat, see cervelat
signes, see cines
soleil de blanc (de) chapon, 246, 250
soles (solles)
    frictures de mer, 182
    en paste, 206
souppe (soupe)
    aux aulx, 78
    carbonnades pour, 138
    jacopine, 56
    vermeil, 78
soupper (souper), 224, 226, 246
souppes a la capilorde, 110
soustree, 58
    vermeil, 58
succre, pigeons au, 214
taillis d'angleterre [Angleterre], 66, 248
talmouses (talamouse), 226
    de blanc chapon, 212, 224
tarte(s) (tartre), 220
    d'angleterre [Angleterre], 226, 250, 254
    angoulousees [Angoumoisines, i.e. from Angoulême], 254
    de cresme, 218, 250, 254
    a deulx visaiges, 240
    d'espinars, 242
    jacopines, 210
    a moelle de beuf, 64
    de mouelle de beuf, 252
    de pommes, 218, 252
    de pommes chiquettees, 226
    de pommes hachees, 254
    de pruneaulx, 254
    rouges de pommes, 228
    sanaydes, 250
    de vin blanc, 252
    ytalienne [Italienne], 252
tartelettes de cresme, 64
tenches, 184
teste(s)
    de chevreax, 252
    de chevreau(lx) doree, 210, 222
    de chevreaulx frictes dorees, 136
tetine de vache, 214, 222
tonnolette (tonnelette, tonolette, tonnollete)
    perdrix a la, 82, 248
tortue
    de lombardie, 62, 70
    en poille d'une aultre sorte, 70
tortues, 148
touterelles, 214
    paste de, 224
trahyson, saulce de, 58
trimollete, langues de mouton a la, 238
trippes, 136, 174
    paste en pot de, 156
    potaige de, 156
truicte
    boullye, 98
    fritte, 76
turbot, 102, 158
    (paste de), 204
vache, tetine de, 214, 222
veau(lx), 174
    brideaulx a, 208
    farcir foye de veau de mouton & chevreaulx, 134
    foye de veau rosty de mouton & de chevreaulx, 130
    foye de, rosty, 222
    gigoteau de, au (ou) brouet dore, 210, 222
    haricot de foyes de veaulx, 154
    hastereaulx de foyes de, 132
    paste(s/z) de, 116, 196, 214, 220
    paste de veau a tout croste, 222
    paste de veau ou de mouton, 136
    paste en pot de, 80
    paste en pot de gigot de mouton
    rosty ou longe de veau rostye froide, 110
    pommes de veaulx ou de chevreaulx de ventre, 120
    potaige de ventre de veaulx ou chevreaulx, 122

saulce de, 252
saulce de foyes de, 132
sauscisses de, 250
venayson (venaison)
    alloyaulx de, 246
    boully larde de, 212, 216, 246
    de chevreau, 248, 254
    contrefaicte en potaige, 126
    froide, 136
    froide, pastes de, 216
    fromentee de, 240
    lardeaulx de, 68
    aulx navetz, 250
    pastes/z chaulx de, 212, 216, 218, 224, 248
    pastes/z frais (frays) de, 212, 214, 218, 246, 248
    paste tiede de, 246
    petis alloyaulx de, 210
    petis pastes chaulx de, 212
    de rost saulce realle, 212
    rostye, 214, 216, 218, 226, 246
    sallee, fromentee a, 250
    de sanglier, 80, 224, 250
    de sanglier aulx marrons, 248
    saulce de, 192
    saulce realle, 224
vendoyses, 98
ventre(e)
    de chevreaulx confitz, 222
    pommes de veaulx ou de chevreaulx de ventre, 120
    potaige de ventre de veaulx ou chevreaulx, 122

verjus, 220
    de grain, fricassee de poulletz au, 222
    d'ozeille, chevreaulx au, 212
vert, saulce, 188, 192
vin, bon, 210, 212, 214, 218, 220, 222, 224, 226
vin blanc, tartes de, 252
vinaigre, 220
vinaigre rosat
    poussins au, 210, 214, 216, 248
    poulletz au, 246
vinaigrette(s), 210
    a la saulce cordialle, 214
    langues de mouton a la, 252
vive, 100
vollailles
    chapons poulletz vollailles rostyes oyseaulx de riviere, 190
    saulvaiges, 136
vollatilles saulvaiges (chapitre de rost), 174
ypocras (hipocras, ipocras), 226, 250
    blanc, 238
    gelee a l', 62
    neffles a l', 250
    poire(s) (poyres) a l', 216, 218, 226, 246, 250
    saulce, 224
ytalienne [Italienne], tarte, 252
ytaliens [Italiens], gasteau, 250

ENGLISH INDEX

As with the French, this is an index of recipe titles (and implied recipe titles where no heading exists), and other headings in the French text, although not including the table of contents at the front. It is not an index of ingredients, save where they have been drawn upon to provide a dish name where no recipe title exists. In the text, some types of recipe are grouped together, as are some types of dish within the menus towards the end of the book. The dish names or recipe titles do not reflect this, but the index does. Thus recipes from the pie section that begins after p. 195 are indexed under 'pie(s)' as well as by their printed title.

Albanian birds, 255
almond(s), 217, 221; cream, 85; cream of new, 239; goblets of, 241; green, to preserve, 229; milk, 85, 131; peeled, 247; white jelly stuck with, 247
amber jelly, 213, 227, 249; in diamond points, 247
andouille(s), 227; of calf's liver, 235; of jelly, 249, 251; little green, 161; sausages of egg, 159; sausages, stuffed, 223; stuffed, 215
angels, of jelly, 251; little, of white jelly, 219
Angoulême, tarts from, 255
apple(s), 219, 253; *au castelin*, 251; butterflies, 213, 221; butterflies of short start, 229; court pendu, *see* short start; gosling with, 241; partridge with, 251; pies, 255; short start, 215, 241, 255; tarts, 219, 253; tarts of chopped, 255; turnover, 247, 251
'apples' made from calves' or kids' stomachs, 121
apricots, 213, 229
artichoke(s), 241; in pepper sauce, 253; pies, 253
asparagus, 253

banquet, 213, 215, 221, 227, 249; after Easter, 211; in summer, 223
barbed capon, 177
bastard sauce, 213, 215
beans, fava, 165; *burelot* of new, 223; cretonnée of new peas or fava beans, 123
beef, flank of, 221; marrow tart(s), 65, 253; palates of beef confit with a lot of gooseberries and scallions, 223; pies, 253; ribs, 137; sauce for roast, 189; *see also* cow, cowheel, ox
bien en broc, 255
birds, little, gravy of , 219
biscuits, 251
black jelly, 67
black sauce, 187
black stew, 167
blackbird(s), cream of, 253; pie, 159
blancmange, 195, 251, 253; of capon, 209
bloody roast, 177
boar, 125; navee of, 247; with turnips, 225; venison of, 81, 225, 251; venison of, with chestnuts, 249
boar's head, 137, 203, 253, 255
boiled, capon(s), 55, 219; carp, 91; eel, 97; and larded stew, 211; perch, 93; pike, 93; salmon, 99; sturgeon, 103;

[271]

trout, 99
Bologna sausages, 141
Bon Chrétien pears, 251
borbonnese [Bourbonnaise], 211
brain, chowder for the, 169
bread, good, 211, 213, 215, 219, 221, 223, 225, 227
bream, 95; pie, 205
breast of capon cheesecakes, 213, 225
bridles, calves', 209
broad beans, *see* beans, fava
broth, butchery to make, 221; golden, 221, 227; golden, veal shank(s) in, 211, 223; larded venison, 213, 217, 247
brouet, another; *georget,* 127
buns, little round hot, 255
burelot of new fava beans, 223
bustard, 249, 253; roast, 175
butchery to make broth, 221
butter, 119, 153, 181, 255; eggs poached in butter on a plate, 161; fried fresh, 117
butterflies, 253; of apples, 213, 221; of short start apples, 229
button mushrooms in May, 151
cabbage, 111, 113; cabbage heads, 171; doves with, 213, 217, 223, 227; partridge(s) in, 83, 225
cabbage lettuce, confit of, 241
cake(s), dry, 239; flaky, 247, 251, 255; flaky layer, 225; Flemish, 241; Italian, 251; joyous, 255; little filled, 255; pretty, 253; soft, 227
calf's liver, andouille of, 235; 'apples' of mutton or kid and calf's liver, 115; blanched roast liver of calf, mutton or kid, 131; haricot of, 155; *hastereaux*, 133; roasted, 223; sauce with, 133; stuffed calf's, mutton, or kid's, 135
calves' bridles, 209
calves' stomachs, 'apples' made from calves' or kids' stomachs, 121; calves' or kids' stomach pottage, 123

cameline sauce, 193; quail cooked in in, 223
candied gourd, 241
candied spices, 227, 249
candies, 249
capirotada, 83; sops *à la,* 111
capon(s), 183; barbed, 177; blancmange of, 209; boiled, 55, 219; breast of capon cheesecakes, 213, 225; breast, lions of, 249; chicken, capon, kid, goose and pig liver vinaigrette, 135; with cinnamon, 245; fat, of Loudun, 251; in their feathers in court bouillon, 241; fried capons, goslings, hens, chickens, 163; *à l'orange*, red roasted, 61; peacock and capons barded like porcupines, 179; pie(s), 197, 251; pilgrim, 249; *raymolles* of white, 243; roast, 61, 175, 177, 187, 191, 225, 227, 253; sunbursts of white, 247; white pottage of capon or chicken, 119; young, in grape must, 215, 221; young (roast), 217; young, in sage (roast), 219
carbonade *à la Toulouse*, 223
carbonades for sops, 139
carp, 181; black stew, 167; boiled, 91; and eel pies, 75; eggs and milt, 153; fritters, 91; pie, 205; and plaice in place of pike, 75; potted pie of, 91; roast, 89; shad or carp *à la castille*, 185; stewed, 89
castelin, apples *au,* 251
Castile, shad or carp *à la castille*, 185
caudle, 157, 173
cervelat(s), 245, 253; Milanese, 223
chaffinch pie, 199
chard pie, 105
cheese(s), cream, 213, 241; green, 217; from Milan, 249, 251; Piacenza, 255; rastons, 255
cheesecake, 227
cheesecakes, breast of capon, 213, 225
cherries, 241; preserved, 155

ENGLISH INDEX

chestnuts, 173, 227, 253, 255; pie(s), 207, 251; venison of boar with, 249

chicken(s), 217, 253; and capon, kid, goose and pig liver vinaigrette, 135; fricassee of, in sauce madame, 223; fricassee of, with freshly pressed verjuice, 223; fried capons, goslings, hens, chickens, 163; hash, 137; with herbs, 211; hodge-podge, 87; hung (roast), 211, 215, 219, 221, 227, 247; little, 255; offal, confit of, 223; with peas, 241; pies, 253; pottage of chicken breast, 223; prepared like pheasant, 247; roast, 175, 187, 191; in rose vinegar, 211, 215, 217, 247, 249; sausages of breast of, 245; stewed, 213; sunburst of breast, 251; white pottage of capon or chicken, 119

chicory, salads of, 227

chimneys, 239

chives, *see* scallions

chopped apple tarts, 227, 255

chopped hare pie, 203

chopped jelly, 253

chowder, for the brain, 169; of pepper, 223

cinnamon, capons with, 245; palates of beef confit with a lot of gooseberries and, 223; pigeons in, 247

citron(s), 253; salads, 219, 255

civet, of deer with turnips, 253; of hare, 125, 227

claret jelly with marrow, 219

cleansing pottage, 231

clear jelly, 227

cloven slices, 241

coal, 223

coat of arms jelly, 185

coffers of jelly filled with coins, 255

coins, jelly, 253, 255; coffers of jelly filled with, 255

cold pork pies, 225

cold sauce, 87

cold venison pies, 213, 215, 217, 219, 247, 249

common jelly, 255

confit, of cabbage lettuce, 241; of chicken offal, 223; of cucumbers, 219, 249; palates of beef with a lot of gooseberries and cinnamon, 223; pigeon, 87; stomach of kid in, 223; teal, 249

cordial sauce, vinaigrette with, 215

counterfeit cream, 81

counterfeit cucumber (apple, pear) sausage, 143

counterfeit porpoise, 249

counterfeit snow, 181

counterfeit venison pottage, 127

court bouillon, capons in their feathers in, 241

cow's udder, 215, 223

cowheel pies, 253

crane, roast, 175

crayfish, 99, 165

cream, 217; of blackbirds, 253; cheese, 213, 241; counterfeit, 81; of fresh peas, 235; fried, 81; of frumenty, 249; fuzzy, 235; of new almonds, 239; of new walnuts, 239; tarts, 219, 251, 255

cress, and young herbs, 153

cretonné(e), milk, 125; of new peas or fava beans, 123; pottage, 123

croquettes, 255

crust for pastry made of paper, 181

cucumbers, 109, 173; preserved, 219, 249; stuffed, 217

custard(s), herb, roulade of venison with, 241; tartlets, 65

cuttlefish, fried, 105

cygnet, roast, 175

dace, 99

damson plums, 213, 215, 221, 247

darioles, 209

deer, civet of, with turnips, 253

dessert, 213, 215, 217, 219, 221, 225, 227, 241, 247

[273]

digestive pottage, 233
dodine sauce, ducks in (roast), 219; white, 191
doughnuts, 251, 253
dove(s) with cabbage, 213, 217, 223, 227; *see also* pigeon(s); turtle dove(s); wood pigeon(s)
dry cake, 239
duck(s) in dodine sauce, roast, 175, 219; pie(s), 201, 225, 227
Duke's powder, 129
eel, 169; boiled, 97; carp and eel pies, 75; pie, 97; pike or eel stew, 167; pottage, 97; roast, 97
egg(s), 223; andouille sausages of, 159; cooked in water, 161; cooked without fire, 161; lost, 229; of many colours, 161; poached in butter on a plate, 161; potted pie of, 167
eggs, carp, 153
elderflower fritters, 117
elephants, jelly, 255
English rose(s), 241, 247
English sauce, pike in, 75
English slices, 67, 249
English tart(s), 227, 251, 255
entremets, peacocks for (roast), 225; salads of, 249; trussed, 219
escutcheons in jelly, 251
fat, 221; rendered, 59
fat capon of Loudun, 251
fat larded milk, 147
fava beans, 165; *burelot* of new, 223; cretonnée of new peas or fava beans, 123
feast, 227; in summer, 223
fifth course, 215
fine spices, 129
first course, 135, 211, 213, 219, 223, 225, 227, 247, 249; from the kitchen, 239; on meat days, 131; for supper, 227; for winter, 223; for the winter table, 239
fish in *sallemine* sauce, 171
flaky (layer) cake(s), 225, 247, 251, 255

Flemish cake, 241
fleur de lys jelly, 251
flute(s), 241, 251
fountain, jelly, 253; water, 53
fourth course, 215
fourth roast course, 219
fowl in malmsey, 215
French barley, 85
fresh roasted salmon, 99
fricassee(s), 141, 219, 221; of chickens in sauce madame, 223; of chicken with freshly pressed verjuice, 223; of fine offal with Robert's beard sauce, 223
fried, capons, goslings, hens, chickens, 163; cream, 81; cuttlefish, 105; fresh butter, 117; medlars, 227; oysters, 103; pastry shapes, 239; perch, 95; pike, 93; trout, 77
fritters, 155, 253; carp, 91; elderflower, 117; lean, 149; seafood, 183
frumenty, 79, 225, 241, 247; cream of, 249; of kid, 243; of salted venison, 251; of venison, 241
fuzzy cream, 235
galantine, 89
gallimaufry, 145
garlic, soup, 79; white, 191
German snails, 237
gilded kid's head, 211, 223
ginger, ground, 221
gnocchi, 151
goblets of almonds, 241
golden broth, 221, 227; veal shank(s) in, 211, 223
goose, chicken, capon, kid, goose and pig liver vinaigrette, 135; cold roast, 137; roast, 113, 175
gooseberries, palates of beef confit with a lot of gooseberries and cinnamon, 223
gosling(s), 253; with apples, 241; fried capons, goslings, hens, chickens, 163; in malmsey, 211, 249; pie, 201; roast, 175, 221; stuffed, 217, 251

gourd(s), 109; candied, 241; pottage, 217; soup, 67; white, 239
grape(s) 219, 221; must, pigeons in, 247; must, young capon(s) in, 215, 221; sauce, 189
gravy of little birds, 219
green almonds, to preserve, 229
green pottage, 119
green salads, 249, 253
green sauce, 189, 193
grenot, 159
gudgeon, 97
ham, 141; Mainz (Mayence), 253
hare(s) 247, 249, 251, 253 , 255; chopped, pie, 203; civet, 125, 227; pie, 203
hare(s), young (roast), 215, 217, 225; in royal sauce, 211
haricot of calf's liver, 155
hash of legs, 223
hastereau(l)x, 133, 141
head(s), boar's, 137, 253, 255; kids', 253; kid's, fried and gilded, 137; kid's gilded, 211, 223
hell sauce, 145; trotters in, 225, 249
hen(s), fried capons, goslings, hens, chickens, 163; pottage, 243; roast, 175; with sauce Robert, 197
herb(s), chickens with, 211; custards, roulade of venison with, 241; pottage, 107; salads, 247; young, and cress, 153
herbes, menues, 131
heron(s), 225, 251, 253; young (roast), 213; young, in royal sauce, 219
hippocras, 227, 251; medlars in, 251; pears in, 217, 219, 227, 247, 251, 255; sauce, 225; white, 239
hodge-podge, chicken, 87; of pigeons, 87, 225
hop shoot salads, 253
hot sauce, pie(s) with, 195, 223, 227; veal or mutton pie in, 137
hot venison pies, 213, 217, 219, 225, 249
hung chicken (roast), 211, 215, 219, 247, 221
Italian cakes, 251
Italian tart, 253
jacobin soup, 57
jacobin tarts, 211
jasper, 249; milk, 119
jelly, 215; amber, 213, 249; ambered, in diamond points, 247; andouille of, 249, 251; angels of, 251; black, 67; chopped, 253; claret, with marrow, 219; clear and amber 227; coat of arms, 185; coffers of, filled with coins, 255; coins, 253, 255; common, 255; in diamond points, 249; diamonds, 225; elephants, 255; escutcheons in, 251; fleur de lys, 251; fountain, 253; moulded, 247, 249; mulled wine, 63; parsnips in, 247; pear, 61; from snow, 233; three kinds of, 217; wavy, 251; white, 241; white, little angels of, 219; white, stuck with almonds, 247; white spiked, 249
joyous cake, 255
kebabs of plaice, 75; of sturgeon, 73
kid(s), 249, 251; 'apples' of mutton or kid and calf's liver, 115; blanched roast liver of calf, mutton or kid, 131; chicken, capon, kid, goose and pig liver vinaigrette, 135; frumenty of, 243; with oranges, 241; pie, 199; roast, 175; in sorrel verjuice, 213; stag, kid or ox liver, 135; stuffed, 249; stuffed calf's, mutton, or kid's liver, 135; venison of, 249, 255
kids' head(s), 253; head(s), gilded, 211, 223; heads fried and gilded, 137
kids' stomach(s)s, 'apples' made from calves' or kids', 121; calves' or kids' stomach pottage, 123; in confit, 223
lamb, roast, 175
lamprey, 187; meat, 65; pie, 205
lard pies, 253
larded broth of venison, 213, 217, 247
larded pike, 231

lark(s), 157, 253; pie(s), 199, 225, 227, 249, 253
lean fritters, 149
leeks, 107, 171; puréed, 211, 221, 243; teals with, 223
legs, hash of, 223
lemon, preserved, 253
lequesal (à lesquesal/alesquesal), woodcocks à, 225, 253
lettuce salads, 251
lettuce, cabbage, confit of, 241
leveret, *see* hare(s), young
lions of capon breast, 249
little angels of white jelly, 219
little birds, gravy of, 219
little green andouille, 161
little hot pies of venison, 213
little sirloins of venison, 211
little skewers of royal pastry, 239
liver, blanched roast liver of calf, mutton or kid, 131; calf's, and other kinds, sauce with, 133; calf's, andouille of, 235; calf's, haricot of, 155; calf's, *hastereaux* of, 133; calf's, roasted, 223; chicken, capon, kid, goose and pig, vinaigrette, 135; mutton or kid and calf's, 'apples' of, 115; stag, kid, or ox, 135; stuffed calf's, mutton, or kid's liver, 135
livers and lungs, 145
loach, 97
Lombard sausages, 143
Lombard slices, 249, 253
Lombard tart, 63, 71
lost eggs, 229
Loudun, fat capon of, 251
lungs, and livers, 145
madame, sauce, 189; fricassee of chickens in, 223
Mainz (Mayence) ham, 253
malmsey, fowl in, 215; gosling(s) in, 211, 249
marrow, beef, claret jelly with, 219; tart, 65, 253
marzipan, 239, 251

meat lamprey, 65
medlar(s), 153, 169; fried, 227; in hippocras, 251; pie, 209
melons, 239
menues herbes, 131
Milan, cheese from, 249, 251
Milanese *cervelat*, 223
Milanese sausages, 239
milk, *cretonné*, 125; fat larded, 147; jasper, 119; sweet sauce with, 189; white sauce of, 105
milt, carp, 153
Monday peas, 109
monkfish pie, 207
moulded jelly, 247, 249
mulled wine jelly, 63
mullet, 101, 159' pie, 205
mushrooms, 151
must, 255; grape, pigeons in, 247; grape, young capon in, 215, 221
mutton, 'apples' of mutton or kid and calf's liver, 115; blanched roast liver of calf, mutton or kid, 131; leg pâté, 179; leg sausages, 135; pie, 199, 201; pottage of, 159; potted pie, 109; potted pie of roast leg of mutton or cold roast loin of veal, 111; quarter of, 221; roast, 177; stuffed calf's, mutton, or kid's liver, 135; veal or mutton pie in hot sauce, 137
navee of boar, 247
new almonds, cream of, 239
new peas, 163
new walnuts, cream of, 239
nourishing pies, 63
nutmeg sauce, 187
offal, chicken, confit of, 223; fine, fricassee of, with Robert's beard sauce, 223
olives, 219, 227, 249, 253
onions, 153; *see also* scallions
orange(s), kid with, 241; partridge with, 225, 253; red roasted capon *à l'orange*, 61; salads, 211, 225; young

rabbits from the warren with, 211
ox, to cook stag, kid or ox liver, 135
ox tongue, 137, 215, 253; potted pie of, 115
oysters, fried, 103; in the shell, 105; stewed, 103, 165
palates of beef confit with a lot of gooseberries and scallions, 223
pancakes, 236
paper, crust for pastry made of, 181
parsnips, 253; in jelly, 247; salads of, 227, 247
partridge(s), 249; in cabbage, 83, 225; with fine salt (roast), 213; on a hill, 57; with orange, 225, 253; pie, 201; roast, 177, 227; *à la tonnelette* (*tonnelette*), 83, 177, 249; young, 217, 219, 247
pastries of prunes, 251
pastry, 251; crust of pastry made of paper, 181; fried shapes, 239; little skewers of royal, 239
pâté, mutton leg, 179
peaches, 217, 219, 221, 255
peacock(s), and capons barded like porcupines, 179; for *entremets* (roast), 225; in the feathers, 249, 253; redressed, 177; roast, 175, 215
pear(s), 221, 225; Bon Chrétien, 251; cooked, 221, 227; in hippocras, 217, 219, 227, 247, 251, 255; jelly, 61; new, 217; in salads, 255; salads of Bon Chrétien, 251
peas, chicken with, 241; cream of fresh, 235; Monday, 109; new, 163; new, *cretonnée* of new peas or fava beans, 123
pease pottage, 165
pepper, chowder of, 223
pepper sauce, artichokes in, 253; wood pigeons in, 219, 253
perch, 159; boiled, 93; fried, 95; pie, 95
petits fours, 213, 215, 217, 227
pheasant(s), 249, 251, 253; roast, 175, 217

Piacenza cheese, 255
pickerel, roast, 91
pie(s), apple, 255; artichoke, 253; beef, 253; blackbird, 199; borbonnese, 211; capon, 197, 251; carp, 205; carp and eel, 75; chaffinch, 199; chard, 105; chestnut, 207, 251; chicken, 253; chopped hare, 203; cold pork, 225; cold venison, 213, 215, 217, 219, 247, 249; cowheel, 253; duck, 201, 225, 227; eel, 97; gosling, 201; hare, 203; hens with sauce Robert, 197; with hot sauce, 195, 223, 227; hot venison, 213, 217, 219, 225, 249; kid, 199; lamprey, 205; lard, 253; lark, 199, 225, 227, 249, 253; little hot, of venison, 213; medlar, 209; monkfish, 207; mullet, 205; mutton, 199, 201; nourishing, 63; partridge, 201; perch, 95; pigeon, 211, 221, 249, 253; quail, 215, 217; quince, 207, 251, 255; rabbit, 203, 227; red mullet, 205; roebuck, 203; salmon, 101; sheep's trotter, 253; sole, 207; sparrow, 201, 217, 247; sturgeon in a, 73; teal, 197, 215, 225, 253; tongue, 253; *à la tonnelette*, 249; triple, 181; turbot, 205; turtle dove, 225; veal, 117, 197, 215, 221; warm venison, 247; wood pigeon, 199; of woodcock with gilded beak, 253; *see also* potted pie
pig(s), 147; chicken, capon, kid, goose and pig liver vinaigrette, 135; half (roast), 227; *houssez*, 217; a quarter of (roast), 221; (roast), 213, 215, 217, 225, 247; sucking (roast), 227
pigeon(s), 219, 221, 225, 253; in cinnamon, 247; confit, 87; in grape must, 247; hodge-podge of, 87, 225; pie(s), 211, 221, 249, 253; roast, 175, 177; in sugar, 215; young, 247, 249; *see also* dove(s); turtle dove(s); wood pigeon(s)
pike, 107, 159, 181; in another way, 77;

black stew, 167; boiled, 93; carp and plaice in place of, 75; or eel stew, 167; in English sauce, 75; fried, 93; larded, 231; a large pike for a small pike, 77; stewed, 93
pilgrim capons, 249
plaice, 103; carp and plaice in place of pike, 75; kebabs of, 75
plover(s), roast, 177, 249, 251, 253
plums, *see* damson plums
pomegranate, rabbits with, 253; salads, 255; wood pigeons with, 241
pork, *see* pig
pork pies, cold, 225
porpoise, 101, 241; counterfeit, 249; pottage, 101
portcullis wafers, 251
pottage(s), 211, 213, 217, 219, 221, 223, 225, 227, 241, 247; calves' or kids' stomach, 123; of chicken breast, 223; cleansing, 231; counterfeit venison, 127; *cretonné*, 123; digestive, 233; eel, 97; gourd, 217; green, 119; hen, 243; herb, 107; of mutton, 159; pease, 165; porpoise, 101; quinces in a, 61; red, 121; sheep's trotter, 69; of tripe, 157; violet, 121; waterfowl, 69; white, of capon or chicken, 119
potted pie, 81, 113; of carp, 91; of eggs, 167; mutton, 109; of ox tongue, 115; of roast leg of mutton or cold roast loin of veal, 111; of tripe, 157; veal, 81; veal, with crust intact, 223
poultry, roast, 191
powder, Duke's, 129; white, 129
preserved cherries, 155
preserved lemon, 253
preserved purslane, 249
pretty cake, 253
prune(s), pastries of, 251; tarts, 255
pudding(s), 133, 139; white, 139
puréed leeks, 211, 221, 243
purslane, preserved, 249
quail, 255; with bay leaves, 251; pies, 217; pies of young, 215; quail, young, stuffed, 223; cooked in cameline sauce, 223
quince, pie(s), 207, 251, 255; in a pottage, 61
rabbits, 187, 225, 227, 249; pie(s), 203, 227; with pomegranate, 253; young, with fine salt, 213; young (roast), 217, 219, 221, 247; young, from the warren with oranges, 211
rastons, cheese, 255
raymolles of white capon, 243
red mullet pie, 205
red pottage, 121
red soup, 79
red tarts, 229
redressed peacock, 177
rendered fat, 59
ribs, beef, 137
rice, 85; rice, 109; rice, 151
river fowl, roast, 175, 191
roach, 99
roast(s), 175, 211, 213, 219, 221, 225, 227; blanched roast liver of calf, mutton or kid, 131; bloody, 177; bustard, 175; capon(s), 61, 175, 177, 187, 191, 253; calf's liver, 223; carp, 89; chicken, 175, 187, 191; crane, 175; cygnet, 175; duck in dodine, 175; eel, 97; first, 247; fourth course, 219; fresh roasted salmon, 99; goose, 113, 175; goose, cold, 137; gosling, 175; hen, 175; kid, 175; lamb, 175; mutton, 177; partridge, 177; partridge *à la tonnelette*, 177; peacock, 175; pheasant, 175; pickerel, 91; pigeon, 175, 177; plover, 177; poultry, 191; red roasted capon *à l'orange*, 61; river fowl, 175, 191; second, 211, 213, 221, 247; sturgeon, 71; swan, 175; third, 213, 219; veal, 175; venison, 215, 217, 219, 227, 247; venison in royal sauce, 213; waterfowl, 175; wildfowl, cold, 137; wood pigeon,

177; woodcock, 195
Robert, sauce, hens with, 197
Robert's beard sauce, 163; fricassee of fine offal with, 223
roebuck pie, 203
rose(s), English, 241, 247
rose vinegar, chicken(s) in, 211, 215, 247, 249
rosemary, snow on, 255
rosewater, 217, 227
roulade of venison with herb custards, 241
royal pastry, little skewers of, 239
royal sauce, 229; young hares in, 211; roast venison in, 213; sirloin of venison in, 225; venison in (roast), 225; young herons in, 219
saffron, ground, 221
sage, young capons in (roast), 219
salads, of Bon Chrétien pears, 251; of chicory, 227; citron, 219, 255; of *entremets*, 249; green, 249, 253; herb, 247; hop shoot, 253; lettuce, 251; orange, 211, 225; of parsnips, 227, 247; pears in, 255; pomegranate, 255; white, 251
sallemine sauce, fish in, 171
salmon, 159; boiled, 99; fresh roasted, 99; pie, 101
salt, partridge with fine (roast), 213; young rabbits with fine (roast), 213
salted sheep's tongues, 223
salted venison, frumenty of, 251
samphire, 249
sanaydes, tarts, 251
sauce, bastard, 213, 215; black, 187; with calf's or other kinds of liver, 133; cameline, 193, 223; cold, 87; cordial, vinaigrette with, 215; dodine, ducks in (roast), 219; English, pike in, 75; grape, 189; green, 189, 193; hell, 145; hell, trotters in, 225, 249; hippocras, 225; hot, pie(s) with, 195, 223, 227; hot, veal or mutton pie in, 137;

madame, 189; madame, fricassee of chickens in, 223; nutmeg, 187; pepper, artichokes in, 253; pepper, wood pigeons in, 219, 253; for roast beef, 189; Robert, hens with, 197; Robert's beard, 163; royal, 229; royal, young hares in, 211; royal, roast venison in, 213; royal, sirloin of venison in, 225; royal, venison in (roast), 225; royal, young herons in, 219; *sallemine*, fish in , 171; sweet, with milk, 189; treason, 59; veal, 253; venison, 193; verjuice, 163; white dodine, 191; white milk, 105
sausage(s), 137, 139, 223, 227, 245; Bologna, 141; *cervelat(s)*, 245, 253; chicken breast, 245; counterfeit cucumber (apple, pear), 143; Lombard, 143; Milanese, 239; Milanese *cervelat*, 223; mutton leg, 135; stuffed *andouille*, 215, 223; veal, 251; white, 139; *see also* pudding
scallions, palates of beef confit with a lot of gooseberries and scallions, 223
seafood fritters, 183
second roast, 211, 213, 221, 247
shad, 159, 183, 191; or carp *à la castille*, 185
shapes, fried pastry, 239
sheep's tongues, salted, 223; stewed, 223; *à la trimollette*, 239; in vinaigrette, 253
sheep's trotters, 69, 139, 223; pies, 253; pottage, 69
short start apples, 215, 241, 255; butterflies of, 229
sirloin of venison, 247; little, 211; in royal sauce, 225
sixth course, 215
skewers of royal pastry, little, 239
slices, cloven, 241; English, 67, 249; Lombard, 249, 253; venison, 69
snack, 139

snails, German, 237
snipe, 255
snow, counterfeit, 181; from jelly, 233; on rosemary, 255
soft cake, 227
sole pie, 207
sops *à la capirotada*, 111; carbonades for, 139
sorrel verjuice, kid in, 213
soup, garlic, 79; gourd, 67; jacobin, 57; red, 79
sparrow pie(s), 201, 217, 247; stuffed, 241
spices, 221; candied, 227, 249; fine, 129
spinach, 169, 171; tarts, 243
stag, 125; to cook stag, kid or ox liver, 135
stew or stewed, black, 167; boiled and larded, 211; carp, 89; chickens, 213; oyster, 103, 165; pike, 93; pike or eel, 167; sheep's tongues, 223
stomach(s), 'apples' made from calves' or kids', 121; calves' or kids', pottage, 123; of kid in confit, 223
strawberries, 241
stuffed andouille sausages, 215, 223
stuffed calf's, mutton, or kid's liver, 135
stuffed, cucumbers, 217; gosling(s), 217, 251; kid, 249; sparrows, 241; wafers, 65; young quail, 223
sturgeon, boiled, 103; kebabs of, 73; in a pie, 73; roast, 71, 213, 215
sucking pig(s), 227
sugar, chickens in, 215
sunburst of chicken breast, 251; of white capon meat, 247
supper, 225, 227, 247
swans, 255; roast, 175
sweet sauce with milk, 189
sweet water to wash the hands, 249
tart(s), 221; from Angoulême, 255; apple, 219, 253; beef marrow, 65, 253; borbonneses [Bourbonnaise], 217; chopped apple, 227, 255; cream, 219, 251, 255; English, 227, 251, 255; Italian, 253; jacobin, 211; Lombard, 63, 71; in a pan, another way, 71; prune, 255; *raymolles* of white capon, 243; red, 229; *sanaydes*, 251; spinach, 243; two-faced, 241; verjuice, 247; white wine, 253
tartlets, custard, 65
teal, 249, 253; confit, 249; with leeks, 223; pie, 197, 215, 225, 253
tench, 183
tenth course, 241
third roast course, 213, 219
third course, 213, 215
to place your hands in boiling water, 179
tongue, ox, 137, 215, 253; potted pie of, 115
tongues, sheep's, salted, 223; stewed, 223; *à la trimollette*, 239; in vinaigrette, 253
tongue pies, 253
tonnelette / tonnolette, partridge *à la*, 83, 249; pies *à la*, 249
tortoise, 149
treason sauce, 59
trimollette, sheep's tongues *à la*, 239
tripe, 175; as a first course, 137; pottage of, 157; potted pie of, 157
triple pie, 181
trotters in hell sauce, 225, 249
trotter(s), sheep's, 69, 139, 223; pottage, 69
trout, boiled, 99; fried, 77
trussed *entremets*, 219
turbot, 103, 159; pie, 205
turnips, 109; boar with, 225; civet of deer with, 253; venison with, 251
turnover of apples, 247, 251
turtle dove(s), 215; pie, 225
two-faced tarts, 241
udder, cow's, 215, 223
veal, or mutton pie in hot sauce, 137; pie(s), 117, 197, 215, 221; potted pie, 81; potted pie with crust intact,

223; potted pie of roast leg of mutton or cold roast loin of veal, 111; roast, 175; sauce, 253; sausages, 251; shank(s) in golden broth, 211, 223

venison, of boar, 81, 225, 251; of boar with chestnuts, 249; cold, 137; cold pies, 213, 215, 217, 219, 247, 249; counterfeit, pottage, 127; frumenty of, 241; frumenty of salted, 251; hot pies, 213, 217, 219, 225, 249; of kid, 249, 255; larded broth, 213, 217, 247; little hot pies of, 213; little sirloins of, 211; roast, 215, 217, 219, 227, 247; roast, in royal sauce, 213, 225; roulade of venison with herb custards, 241; sauce, 193; sirloin of, 247; sirloin in royal sauce, 225; slices, 69; with turnips, 251; warm pie, 247; *see also* deer, roebuck, stag

verjuice, 221; freshly pressed, fricassee of chicken with, 223; sauce, 163; sorrel verjuice, kid in, 213; tarts, 247

vinaigrette(s), 211; with cordial sauce, 215; sheep's tongues in, 253

vinegar, 221; rose, chicken in, 211, 215, 217, 247, 249

violet pottage, 121

wafers, portcullis, 251; stuffed, 65

walnuts, 217; cream of new, 239; peeled, 247; shelled, 221

warm venison pie, 247

water fountain, 53

waterfowl, pottage, 69; roast, 175

wavy jelly, 251

wedding, 213, 221; after Easter, 211

weever, 101

white dodine sauce, 191
white garlic, 191
white gourds, 239
white hippocras, 239
white jelly, 241; little angels of, 219; stuck with almonds, 247
white milk sauce, 105
white pottage of capon or chicken, 119
white powder, 129
white salads, 251
white sausages, 139
white spiked jelly, 249
white wine tarts, 253
wild boar, *see* boar
wildfowl, cold roast, 137
wine, good, 211, 213, 215, 219, 221, 223, 225, 227
wine jelly, mulled, 63
wood pigeon(s), 251; in pepper sauce, 219, 253; pie, 199; with pomegranate, 241; roast, 177, 227
woodcock, *alesquesal (à lequesal)*, 253, 225; with gilded beak, pies of, 253; roast, 195; young (roast), 219
young capons (roast), 217; in grape must, 215; in sage (roast), 219
young hare (roast), 215, 217, 225; in royal sauce, 211
young heron (roast), 213; in royal sauce, 219
young partridges (roast), 217, 219
young pigeons (roast), 247, 249
young quail, stuffed, 223
young rabbits (roast), 217, 219, 221, 247; from the warren with oranges, 211; with fine salt (roast), 213
young woodcocks (roast), 219